CRUST and CRUMB

CRUST

MASTER

FORMULAS

FOR

SERIOUS

BREAD

BAKERS

PETER REINHART

AND CRUMB

TEN SPEED PRESS
Berkeley | Toronto

Ten Speed Press
PO Box 7123
Berkeley, California 94707

Distributed in Canada by Ten Speed Canada, in New Zealand by Tandem Press, in Australia
by Simon and Schuster Australia, in South Africa by Real Books, in Singapore and Malaysia
by Berkeley Books, and in the United Kingdom and Europe by Publishers Group UK.

Cover and text design by Nancy Austin
Illustrations by Ellen Sasaki

Library of Congress Cataloging-in-Publication Data
Reinhart, Peter.
    Crust & Crumb: master formulas for serious bread bakers / by
    Peter Reinhart.
        p. cm.
    Includes bibliographical references and index.
    ISBN 1-58008-003-0
    1. Bread. I. Title.
    TX769.R415 1998   98-18538
    641.8'15—dc21   CIP

ISBN-13 (ppr): 978-1-58008-802-2
ISBN-10 (ppr): 1-58008-802-3

First paperback printing, 2006
Printed in China

1 2 3 4 5 6 7 8 9 10 – 10 09 08 07 06

CONTENTS

While I was writing my first two books, the editors continually reminded me to view my books first and foremost as cookbooks and only secondarily as vehicles for philosophizing. Thankfully, I was able to achieve a balance that was acceptable to me, the publisher, and the many readers who sent me favorable comments. So I thought it pleasantly ironic when one of the editors I worked with on this book said, "Don't forget the philosophy. We don't want this to be just a recipe book." With that in mind, I have delved into my experience for more insights into the relationship, both metaphorical and physical, between bread and life.

Life goes on from moment to moment, experience to experience, and never seems to stop offering lessons for growth. What many people lack, though, is a way to tie these experiences into a meaningful whole, a context in which to experience the connectedness of all creation. Many of these potential life lessons slip past us because we do not have an adequate gathering net. For me, bread is one of those nets.

There is a form of writing called object poetry. The idea, when writing object poetry, is to describe something not with similes and metaphors, but in very concrete terms. Like peeling layers of an onion (a simile that, ironically, would not meet the criteria), the more deeply you explore the actuality of an object the more it seems to transcend itself and become universal, archetypal, and ideal. This book was written to capture that spirit. Rather than try to build metaphorical bridges between the real and ideal, as I did in my previous books, I have focused on the actuality of bread. I want this book to be an object poem that takes you deeper into the subject as it broadens your experience.

I was quoted once in a food magazine discussing the mystical qualities of bread making and how I thought bread bakers were spiritual even if they might not view themselves as particularly religious. One baker wrote an angry response saying she did not make bread for a religious experience and did not think that making bread was particularly spiritual. She was not looking for deeper meaning from bread; she wanted to make something that tasted good and looked beautiful. Period.

She would probably be surprised to find me agreeing with her. I do, however, also happen to think that dedicating oneself to making things that taste good and look beautiful is a very spiritual act indeed; it sounds to me as though she had come close to tapping into one of the mysteries of the meaning of life, and I deeply respect her achievement, by whatever name she calls it.

The word religion derives from a Latin root word, *religio*, meaning "to be connected to." I find that many bread bakers have an intuitive sense of connectedness, whether or not they consider themselves spiritual or religious. The quest for beauty and goodness, in any endeavor, is the basis for many metaphorical and mystical, as well as practical, excursions.

In this book, I will explain much about building, rather than making, a loaf of bread, because I have discovered that the best bread is built in stages and thus has many levels. We will explore the value of slow-rise fermentation techniques, not because slow rise is a metaphor but because it is an effective method. I will not be rhapsodizing about beauty and truth, much as I might like to. Instead, I will be teaching you how to make a loaf of bread that is rhapsodically beautiful and exceptionally delicious.

Along the way I will share some of the things I have learned about bread during my culinary journey. The life part, for you and for me, will just have to happen as part of the process, nourished by the hoped-for objects of goodness and beauty that we will make together.

Peter Reinhart
Summer 1998
Santa Rosa, California

ACKNOWLEDGMENTS

As always, my chief collaborator is my wife, Susan, who supported me through the daily grind and served as my pre-editor on all levels. Her palate and patience are big parts of our success.

My students at the California Culinary Academy (CCA), too numerous to mention by name, were also among the first to test the formulas developed for this book, pointing out where instructions were unclear or measurements slightly off and oftentimes making improvements. They were beneficiaries of my knowledge, guinea pigs for my experiments, and always joyful co-conspirators in furthering the bread revolution. I must also thank Keith Keough, president of the CCA; Greg Tompkins, director of faculty (now at the National Baking Center in Minneapolis); and Robert Parks, my department head in the Baking and Pastry Program for their continual support and encouragement. I have been privileged to work with outstanding colleagues at the CCA and thank them all for accepting me as their peer. A special thanks to Chef Tony Marano for his help with the instructional graphics.

This book was given its original life by Meesha Halm, who recruited me for a publisher other than Ten Speed Press. Fortunately for all of us, after a publishing adventure worthy of Tolkien, we were then encouraged to place my manuscript into the nurturing hands of Ten Speed, under the direction of publisher Kirsty Melville; my editor, Chelsea Vaughn; and the superb Ten Speed team, especially art director Nancy Austin. I owe all of them my gratitude for their enthusiastic belief in the importance of this book and their role in shaping it. I also must give a hearty thank-you to Kathy Martin, who did a superb job of editing the original manuscript into shape for submission, and to Susan Derecskey for her fine-tuning and editorial expertise.

I was thrilled beyond belief when Ten Speed offered to bring in Teri Sandison as the photographer. I have long been a fan of her work, especially in her collaborations with her husband, Hugh Carpenter, on their many books. I could not have asked for a better Christmas gift than to find her pictures in my stocking. A special thank you to Kathleen Kennedy for her help with the food styling. And thanks also to R.S. Basso in St. Helena, California, for loaning us props and accessories for the photos; and to Food for Thought Bakery in Santa Rosa, California, for allowing us to use their beautiful loaves for our cover shot.

As always, thanks to my superb agent, Pam Bernstein, and her wonderful assistant Donna Downing, for protecting me and freeing me to focus on my writing.

Finally, to the many bread revolutionaries who have fanned the flames that make a book like this possible: to Tom McMahon and Greg Mistell of the Bread Bakers Guild of America for creating, fostering, and training a network of committed bread fanatics and devotees; to Craig Ponsford and Didier Rosada for developing their world championship formulas and allowing me to modify them for home use; to Flo Braker, Marion Cunningham, Fran Gage, and other members of the Bakers Dozen in San Francisco for their ongoing support; to Christ the Saviour Brotherhood for my spiritual formation, the real genesis of this book; to Phyllis Reinhart and Connie Thayer for their undying love and support; to Ron and Lorene Colvin of Brother Juniper's Bakery in Santa Rosa for liberating me to move on to the next stage of my career; and to all the bold and adventurous bakers who have opened neighborhood bread bakeries and committed themselves to this noble craft, the grueling hours, and the awakening of the American public to the realm of the possible. This book is dedicated to each of you.

CRUST and CRUMB

Left: Building wild yeast breads begins with a mother starter, like this spongy barm (lower right). It is then elaborated into an intermediate, or firm, starter (upper right) and finally into the finished dough (left), where salt and other ingredients are added (pages 68–74).

Below left: A properly shaped and risen hearth bread, like this sourdough boule (pages 75–78), should have an irregular crumb, with holes of different sizes. The open holes allow the grain to bake more deeply, bringing forth more complex, nutty qualities.

Below right: The rich golden crust and blistery aspect of this wild yeast (sourdough) boule (pages 75–78) results from long, slow fermentation and a three-step building process that produces an unmatched, complex flavor.

THE BREAD REVOLUTION

Many people are intimidated by the process of making bread, especially sourdough, or as I prefer to call it, wild yeast bread. The thought of nurturing a container of living, bubbling dough, feeding it every few hours lest it die, is just too daunting for some. I know many fine cooks who are convinced that they simply do not have a feel for bread, as if it were a separate and mysterious category of the culinary arts. What this probably means is that they have tried to bake bread a few times but have never made a winning loaf.

This book is intended to remedy any such sense of limitation. You really can make world-class, conversation-stopping bread at home without feverishly waking up in the middle of the night to feed your starter. Having won a national bread championship against other professional bakers with a loaf I developed at home, I can guarantee this.

Bread, like so many of life's formulas, relies on the 80/20 principle, in this instance, 80 percent technique and 20 percent equipment. (I might also add 80 percent perspiration for every 20 percent inspiration.) Most home bakers are concerned about their lack of the proper equipment, but the equipment problem is easy to solve, as you will see. Most of what you will learn in this book is technique, dough technique: how to build, rather than simply make, a loaf of bread. This is easier than you might think. I will arm you with the knowledge, formulas, and confidence necessary to make world-class bread at home, and I am confident in return that you will become a passionate bread maker if you are not one already.

When I wrote *Brother Juniper's Bread*

Book in 1991, I actually knew very little about how bread works. I was self-taught and had some talent for the process, but was driven forward more by my spiritual and religious vocation than by knowledge. That I succeeded as well as I did was serendipitous. As my success opened doors into the greater bread world, I became acutely aware of how lucky I had been and how much growth awaited me.

My niche in the bread world was built largely on the success of a number of neo-traditional breads I developed at Brother Juniper's Bakery. The most notable is Struan, a bread I still consider my greatest contribution to the bread lexicon. More than half of my early recipes were variations of that basic multigrain formula. From it I derived what I feel is the perfect proportion, a golden mean of bread flour in relation to other ingredients, which allows for a seemingly infinite number of spin-offs. Since then I have developed a strong interest in traditional hearth-baked breads, especially the naturally leavened, or wild yeast, kind. In North America we categorize these as sourdoughs. In Europe they are called *levains, desums,* or barm breads and are made in much the same way as sourdough, but with less of the sour flavor typically found in American sourdoughs.

In his wonderful newsletter, *Simple Cooking,* food writer John Thorne observed that the greatest challenge for an artisanal baker is to work without a net, using wild yeast starters under conditions that allow for the possibility of bread that is good beyond belief, while posing the greatest risk of failure. I countered this argument in my first book with the contention that an equal challenge is to consistently produce good-beyond-belief bread under controlled conditions, whether with wild yeast or the faster-working and more consistent commercial yeast, which is the economic necessity all commercial bakers face. It was, in retrospect, an apples and oranges argument. The commercial wild-yeast baker needs consistency, just as the artisanal hobbyist must be free to fail superbly in the quest for the perfect loaf.

My challenge was to bridge these paradoxes by developing master formulas that could yield both consistency and good-beyond-belief flavor and texture. I have tried to consolidate all the bread makers' secrets I could unearth and put them in your kneady hands. I think I have succeeded, though along the way I have realized what a never-ending quest it is. I learn new things about bread every day, but the formulas in this book should keep you busy and satisfied for a long time to come.

In addition to commercially yeasted and wild-yeast methods, this book explores such alternative techniques as carbon dioxide-leavened quick breads and flat-out unleavened breads. In each case I offer basic principles and formulas from which countless variations can spring. I am not out to impress you with the number of recipes, but with their quality. I want you to be convinced when you taste these breads that they are the best you have ever had, or at the very least, the best you have ever made. My goal is to empower you not only to produce phenomenal bread but to understand how you did so. I want to feed your bread pilgrimage much as others have fed mine.

A NEW PARADIGM

Paradigm was a buzzword in the 1980s. New paradigms were hailed in religion, politics, science, and business as if they were the Newest Testament. This trend grew out of the human potential movement, which was itself based on an astute interpretation of another conceptual buzzword, *Zeitgeist,* German for "the spirit of the times." It refers to forces that are at work independently yet simultaneously, such as the discovery of a vaccine in the United States and France at the same time. "An idea whose time has come" is another way of putting it. Paradigms are patterns, models, examples, standards. I think of paradigms not as content, but as context. For many years in the United States the paradigm for bread, for example, has been assembly-line white bread, Wonder Bread, which is both a trademarked brand name and a generic image, like Jell-O and Kleenex, that transcends the category.

Since that time a new paradigm, what I call the "bread revolution," has been gradually manifesting itself in many forms. While the culinary world in general has experienced its own revolution and renaissance, as illustrated by the ascent of celebrity chefs and media stars, bakers—both professionals and hobbyists—quietly went about making their own significant contribution to the paradigm shift in food consciousness. It is really a revisioning of the possibilities of crust and crumb, the heart and soul of bread. I have been calling it a revolution because exposure to higher and higher standards of quality brought about an irreversible change in consumer attitudes toward bread. There have been three waves of this revolution of crust and crumb, each contributing an important energy.

The first wave began in the late 1960s, picked up steam in the 1970s, and hit full stride in the mid-1980s—the whole-grain or health movement that originated in the hippie and counterculture restaurants and bakeries and drew support from nutritionists and health professionals. Many names are associated with this movement: Rodale, Pritikin, Adele Davis, and the illustrious English grande dame, Elizabeth David—all of whom made contributions to the revival of whole-grain baking. The early breads were somewhat heavy and were burdened by the health-food onus, but when Oroweat and other large bakeries began producing enjoyable loaves, whole grains entered the mainstream. In the 1980s, independent bakeries such as Sonoma County's Alvarado Street Bakery and national franchises like Great Harvest Bread Company and Big Sky Bread Company gave bread consumers fresh, high-quality alternatives.

Concurrent with the whole-grain and health boom, young bakers on their own culinary pilgrimages were exposed to traditional European breads. Restaurants like Berkeley's Chez Panisse offered these classics, including slow-rising *levains* and *biga*-style, starter-based breads. Eventually, as in the case of Berkeley's famed Acme Bread Company, which spun off from Chez Panisse, restaurants began supporting these new independent bakeries by contracting with them for table breads. While

Berkeley, San Francisco, Oakland, Sonoma County, and the Bay Area in general became focal points for this bread renaissance, the idea was not lost on other regions. The Pacific Northwest, a harbinger of new trends as usual, now has dozens of world-class bakeries to complement their hundreds of coffeehouses and espresso bars. Los Angeles, Chicago, New York, Atlanta, Austin, Philadelphia, and many small, less-cosmopolitan communities boast fabulous bakeries and breads. The culmination of this activity was the formation of the Bread Bakers Guild of America, which fielded the teams in the "International Bread Olympics" (the Coupe du Monde) that put American bread makers on the world map.

The third wave in this revolution is what I call the "neotraditional movement." The Tassajara Bakery of San Francisco is one of the better-known examples, thanks to its success and longevity, as well as the success of Ed Espe Brown's *Tassajara Bread Book*. Neotraditional breads combine elements of the whole grain–health movement and the traditional bread movement, following classic slow-rise methods while striking out with creative grain blends, esoteric ingredients, and new flavor explorations. The bakery I founded, Brother Juniper's, falls into this category.

Together, these three waves have exposed consumers across the country to alternatives to white bread not available ten or twenty years ago. Given the growing interest in both health and culinary quality, and the advent of exceptional restaurants that feature it, bread has become an important, even vital, part of the dining experience.

Adding strength to this movement is the proliferation of excellent bread books, many of which are designed to help people use their bread machines. (Whether or not the bread machine endures and becomes indispensable, like a VCR or food processor, as some predict, it arrived as a hot consumer item at the same time as the explosion of interest in bread.) These books indicate that the bread revolution has hit critical mass, allowing us all to enjoy the crumbs. Among the especially good books that have contributed to this swelling tide of interest are Bernard Clayton and James Beard's high-profile books, Judith and Evan Jones's *Book of Bread*, the aforementioned *Tassajara Bread Book*, Elizabeth David's classic *English Bread and Yeast Cookery*, Beth Hensberger's many books, Lora Brody's bread machine books, *The Laurel's Kitchen Bread Book*, Carol Field's *The Italian Baker*, and more recently, my own *Brother Juniper's Bread Book: Slow Rise as Method and Metaphor*. Many of these books focus on simple straight-dough breads, with whole-grain recipes and neotraditional ingredient variations. None of these books, however, teaches the home baker how to make traditional or artisanal breads as good as the European, and now, the new American bakeries.

Then, in 1993, Joe Ortiz recounted his bread journey in *The Village Baker*. He tells of visiting many humble, unknown bakers of France and Italy, each employing techniques learned in the classic master-apprentice manner. Though it seemed unrealistic to think that we could reproduce breads of such exquisite quality without paying similar dues, Joe revealed the necessary methods. In his equally thorough and beautiful book, *Bread Alone,* Daniel Leader covered similar ground later that same year. Since then, Nancy Silverton of Los Angeles's famed LaBrea Bakery and Amy Scherber and Toy Kim Dupree of Manhattan's wonderful Amy's Bread have contributed excellent books to the genre.

The impact of culinary academies and television cooking shows, the publication of exceptional cookbooks, and the convergence of economic prosperity and ecological, earth-to-table awareness have ushered in a major paradigm shift on the American culinary scene. At the same time—and out of the same *Zeitgeist*—a crust and crumb revolution occurred that has forever changed the way people in this country view bread. Thanks to this revolution, it can be said that the United States now produces some of the finest bread in the world (while still producing massive quantities of mediocre bread). A large and growing number of consumers support bakeries that produce traditional, neotraditional, and even the once-dreaded "health" breads. A new standard has been established in the bread world.

The bread revolution was fought and won on all three fronts: whole-grain awareness, traditional methodology, and neotraditional creativity. This book is an instruction manual for the home baker who wants to heed the call to arms. Evidence of the revolution is springing up like loaves in a hot oven as new bakeries appear daily throughout the country. For this reason, there are undoubtedly gaps in my reference list of pivotal bakeries and bakers, and I apologize for these unavoidable omissions. I am confident, however, that the stories,

recipes, and techniques in this book will bring you fully into the new paradigm and give you the tools you need to make bread that truly is good beyond belief.

A NOTE ON FORMAT

I use the term *formula* rather than *recipe* because I want you to understand not just the *how* but the *why.* Each master formula is accompanied by parallel commentaries that amplify the instructions, provide background information, or suggest alternatives.

HOW TO GET THE MOST OUT OF THIS BOOK

❏ Do not try to make any of the formulas until you have read chapters 1 and 2. They include important technique, ingredient, and equipment information. Almost every formula refers to this information and assumes you have read it. In addition, many of the breads require one of the pre-ferments explained in the initial master formulas.

❏ Some of these pre-ferments can be made a day in advance, but others, especially the wild yeast starters, need to be started well in advance (up to five days, in some instances). Once they are made, you can keep them primed and ready in the refrigerator.

❏ Think about your bread-making strategy a few days ahead. Many, though not all, of these breads take two or three days to build. They are neither complicated nor time consuming but they *do* require advance planning. My goal is to give you the means to make bread at home that is every bit as good as what you will find at your favorite bakery. These techniques allow you to make your dough and still have a life (unlike many professional bakers I know), but if you want world-class results, you cannot get them from simplified recipes—you must apply the proper techniques.

❏ Remain focused while preparing the formulas. These master formulas are not like recipes you will find elsewhere. They require you to get some inexpensive but important tools for your kitchen and become committed to the process. These are not bread-machine recipes that you can throw together and have waiting for you when you get home from work, though bread machines can be used to make some of them, as explained on page 12. These recipes demand a degree of focus. The methods described in this book assume that you feel passionate about bread or want to nurture the same passion that drives me and the thousands of other bread revolutionaries around the country.

❏ You will need to set up your *mise en place,* your work station. This means you must do the following *before you start:* Get the tools you need (see page 16), begin making your starters and pre-

ferments, read the chapter introductions, and go over the formulas carefully.

❏ Read the formulas from start to finish before beginning your breads. You would be amazed at how many times I repeat that sentence in my classes! It will make a tremendous difference if you adhere to that policy.

❏ Read the commentaries attached to each formula. Many of the so-called tricks of the trade are discussed in these sections. The commentaries are my attempt to be in the kitchen with you as you make these breads, giving you hints along the way and trying to expand your understanding of what is taking place. They are, in essence, my tutorial for you—the fruits of my own bread explorations.

This is not a conventional cookbook, as you will see. It is a book of formulas, not just a collection of recipes. I hope that the difference will become evident as you proceed.

May your bread always rise!

1

WHAT IS WORLD-CLASS BREAD?

On one particular occasion, and I remember it as if it just occurred though it happened more than ten years ago, we took our customary sample bites and heard the crust crackle in what I now think of as The Moment. *I said to my assistant, "That's it! That's the sound! It's as important as the taste. It's the sound of perfection and it is so deeply satisfying!" Then I stopped my exclamation because my eyes were watering and I was beginning, in this perfect bread moment, to cry.*

"The Sound of Crust,"
Brother Juniper's Bread Book

I use the term *world-class bread* rather freely throughout this book. It is an arbitrary term—more poetic than actual—an image to differentiate between everyday, run-of-the-mill bread and bread that is good beyond belief. Where the line falls is both subjective and objective.

The subjective aspect depends upon your experience: the extent to which you have known the depth and breadth of bread possibilities. There was a time when tasting a wide variety of breads and encountering exceptional examples was only possible in Europe. In recent years, artisan-style bakeries have appeared in this country, exposing us to better bread and expanding our expectations and imaginations. We may not always know why or how, but we can sense when a bread has moved up to the next rung of wonderfulness.

My bread epiphany occurred a few years before the bread revolution hit full force. I was cooking for the seminary of a Christian order in San Francisco (I am still a lay brother in that order, the Christ the Saviour Brotherhood). One of my friends, a very talented cook named Brother Philip Goodrich, took on the then-practically-unheard-of challenge of following all eight pages of Julia Child's instructions, in *From Julia's Kitchen,* for making French bread. The results were so spectacular that I followed his example, forcing myself to carry out every little step and consulting with him when I stumbled. The bread was so much better than anything we could buy, even the fabled sourdough of San Francisco, that I began making bread every day. Sometimes the results were disastrous, especially when I strayed too far from what I now know to be common bread sense. However, when the bread came out right—even accidentally—when the crust crackled and then dissolved into sweet, roasted wheatiness and the interior felt cool and buttery even without butter, I was hooked. This was my subjective initiation.

Objective criteria also cause this passionate reaction. These criteria are especially important as we attempt to bake world-class bread at home because they give us guideposts to assure us we are on the right track. Permit me an analogy: There is a school of thought that says the best way to learn tennis is to identify the sound of the "sweet spot"—the spot that delivers the most power from your swing when the ball hits your racquet—and then keep aiming for that sound. It is difficult, of course, to hit that spot without good fundamentals, repetition, a smooth stroke, and proper hand-eye coordination. But once you know the sound and lock into it, your game will never be the same. Likewise, the objective and subjective characteristics of world-class bread help us lock into the sound of the sweet spot, or more appropriately, the sweet sound of crust.

In general, hearth breads (also called *lean breads* because they are made without fat or other oils) depend upon great crust. Conditioned, flavored, or enriched breads—that is, breads made with more than the basic flour, water, salt, and leaven—are less dependent on crust and instead should have an exceptional crumb (the inside of the bread), as well as great flavor throughout. In either case the feel of the bread in our mouths is crucial; we want a cool and creamy mouthfeel. Lean breads should have a pleasant burst of flavor, a particular kind of crackle in the crust (again, the sound of crust), and a long, pleasant finish in which the complex, fermented grain flavor lingers on the palate after swallowing. (This brings to mind the old story of the butler who tells a visitor that his master, a famous gourmand, cannot come to the door because he is still enjoying dinner. When the man protests that it is far too late to still be eating, the houseman replies, "I didn't say he was still eating dinner; I said he was still enjoying dinner.")

These qualities are all functions of careful fermentation, proper pH balance, judicious use of steam and high heat, and high-quality ingredients mixed in the right proportion.

A properly baked crust has a sweetness that comes forth the more one chews. The natural sugars inside the wheat grains caramelize from the intense oven heat, a process that makes them turn golden brown and retain their crisp crackle even after the bread cools. (In contrast, mass-produced hearth-style breads are often purposely underbaked so they will stay moist longer, since shelf life is the key to profitability.) Because Europeans prefer a more intense flavor, European village bakeries make their loaves so dark they seem almost burned in comparison to American versions.

When a dough is fermented correctly—slowly, over a long period of time—the starchy interior of the loaf develops a gelatinized sheen, a nutty flavor that is a result of the large, open-holed structure exposing the gluten strands of the dough to the fullest heat, and a creamy, melt-in-your-mouth texture. The bread should taste almost buttery; adding butter, in fact, hides the true flavor.

In flavored and enriched breads much of the taste is provided by enrichment ingredients such as sugar, milk, eggs, oil, and butter, and supplemental ingredients like spices, cheese, and seeds. The most critical components are the flavor burst and the mouthfeel. A moist, light crumb (interior webbing) is also crucial, a result not of extra liquid or fat but of a full final rise that exposes the gluten/protein strands to more heat and the starches to a deeper gelatinization.

Fermentation is trickier when sugars are added to the dough to make flavored breads, because overproofing yields a beery, yeasty aftertaste. When these doughs are mixed properly, however, the protein strands bond and the gluten develops fully, just as in lean breads. After the dough is given its two full rises, flavored breads can be every bit as satisfying as classic French bread, developing not only a long flavor-finish but also a beautifully rich, golden, caramelized crust.

THE BASIC TYPES OF BREAD

Now let's take a closer look at some of the better-known and more distinctive breads of the world, many of which you will learn to make in the subsequent chapters.

French baguette and pain ordinaire, *or* pain français: Though only about 150 years old, the baguette loaf has become the universal symbol of bread. It is characterized by a thin, crackly crust, diagonal cuts across the top that "bloom" open into crusty flaps called *ears,* a length of 18 to 36 inches (or longer!), and color varying from light gold to deep gold with tones of reddish brown. The coloring is caused both by caramelization and by the Maillard reaction, two types of sugar—heat reactions that affect all yeasted breads. (The Maillard reaction, which also causes the browning of roasted coffee and cocoa beans, nuts, and meats, occurs when carbohydrates and certain types of amino acids are exposed together to high heat.)

The interior crumb of French bread has irregular holes, some very large and barely connected by strands of gluten and others tighter and smaller. If this webbing is composed of uniform-sized holes, it means the loaves have been shaped too roughly or by mechanical equipment rather than gently by hand, and the flavor of the grain will be less complex.

Baguettes and French breads of other shapes, or *pain ordinaire,* are leavened by commercial yeast, as are the similar Italian-style breads. This dough can easily be made by the "direct," or single-mixing method, but the best loaves are made using pre-fermented dough techniques, or the "indirect method."

Levain: A *levain* is a naturally leavened bread made with a pre-fermented starter developed from wild yeast. There are many versions of this bread and numerous ways to build such a loaf. Country *levains* are made with a small percentage of whole-grain flour, usually wheat or rye, to add complexity and texture. The crust is thicker and chewier than *pain ordinaire* or other yeasted breads. The flavor usually includes acidic sour tones, though Europeans like their *levain* minimally sour.

The crumb should have the same irregular hole structure as a baguette. Because *levain* is often baked in round *(boule)* or oblong *(bâtard)* shapes, it has more interior crumb than a baguette. This allows for even larger, more open holes than in a baguette. The mouthfeel should be cool and creamy, not dry. The crumb webbing should have a slightly shiny, almost translucent quality.

Ciabatta *and rustic breads:* Loaves made from wetter doughs are called *rustic breads,* of which the best known is the Italian *ciabatta.* Other Italian versions include *pugliese, francese, stirato, pane rustico,* and stretch bread. These breads may be made with as much as 80 percent hydration. (Most breads are made with 55 to 66 percent hydration, based on the baker's percentage system in which the flour equals 100 percent and everything else is a percentage of the flour weight. For example, in baguette dough, 100 pounds of flour can be hydrated by 60 pounds of water, for 60 percent hydration.) Rustic bread doughs are sticky and difficult to handle, so it is often necessary to sprinkle additional flour on the dough when shaping it and transferring it to the oven. This accounts for the floury crusts and stretch marks many of these loaves exhibit.

The crumb is extremely open, barely holding the loaf together and sometimes tearing to reveal large holes or tunnels. The gluten is stretched to the maximum, exposing it fully to the heat. This gives the bread a pleasant toasty flavor and a gelatinized, shiny interior. The crust is sweet and nutty from the natural caramelization of the sugars. Rustic breads are often yeasted but may also be naturally leavened.

Pumpernickel and other ryes: There are many versions of rye bread. Pumpernickel is a German/Russian-style bread made with coarse, whole-grain rye flour. Other rye breads use finer, more refined rye flours in various configurations with wheat and other grains.

Rye bread usually has a tighter crumb than wheat bread because, as with all grains other than wheat, there is very little gluten in rye. However, it is possible to make open-crumbed rye breads by following slow-rise techniques and using a high percentage of wheat flour. Rye breads have a distinctive earthy quality and a sweetness from the natural sugars in the rye berry. Some versions are yeasted, but rye bread tastes better when made with natural sourdough starters and is assimilated more easily by the body when fermented with the lactobacillus organisms found in these starters. The use of seeds and flavorings such as caraway, onion, anise, flax, and orange is traditional in various cultures, but it is in no way necessary for a good rye.

White bread (pain de mie): Yeasted white bread—for sandwiches, toast, or as an accompaniment to meals—is as much a European tradition as it is an American one. Dough conditioners such as butter, milk, potato starch (from either cooked or dried potatoes), and sugar are added to soften the crumb and crust.

White breads are baked in loaf pans at a lower heat than hearth breads to prevent early caramelization and a crispy crust. The crumb is uniform in appearance with medium-size holes and a tenderness not found in lean hearth breads. Despite its softness, the mouthfeel is drier than that of hearth breads.

Brioche and enriched breads: The generous addition of butter and eggs pushes some breads into a category called *rich* or *enriched* breads. Brioche is the most famous but other yeasted rich breads include kugelhopf (sometimes spelled *gugelhopf*), savarin, baba, *la mouna* (a crescent-shaped brioche variation with an orange flavor), and fruited holiday breads like stollen, kulich, and panettone. (Croissants, which are made by a "laminating" method in which the fat is rolled into the dough and folded over many times to create hundreds of layers, are also enriched breads but they belong in their own category because of the special handling required.)

Brioche has a beautiful golden color and a soft-as-satin feel. It practically dissolves in the mouth, filling the palate with rich, buttery flavor. The crumb can range from fairly open to tight, but the crust is always thin and tender. Many enriched breads, such as kugelhopf, function more as coffee cakes or tea breads, because of the richness that comes from the additional ingredients.

Flatbreads and focaccia: International flatbreads, especially focaccia, have become very popular in the recent years. Loosely translated, *focaccia* means "everything that's left in the oven"—in other words, a good way to use up leftovers. There are both savory and sweet versions of this pizza-like, Genoese flatbread. The finest focaccia is made from a soft, wet dough. A long fermentation with a small amount of yeast and the addition of olive oil gives the crumb a spongy, shiny aspect similar to but softer than that of the rustic breads. Sometimes the extra ingredients, such as olives, herbs, and cheeses, are incorporated into the dough and sometimes they are placed on top. The dough, baked in sheet pans, is often poked all over just before baking, giving it a dimpled appearance. Pizza is simply another type of focaccia that originated in southern Italy, probably Naples (though New Haven, Connecticut, claims to be the place where pizza, as we currently know it, was invented!). The Tuscan version of focaccia is called *schiacciata.*

Flatbreads like tortillas, naan, crackerbread, matzoh, and chapati are international and universal. They may be either leavened, as in the case of the dozens of versions of naan, or like matzoh and chapati, unleavened. However, the master formulas in this book can be used to make many of these breads, as they are all variations on a simple theme.

Flavored specialty breads: Flavored breads, such as Cajun-style spice breads or cheese-and-herb-filled dinner rolls capture the tastes associated with particular regions and cultures. Their flavor is determined more by added ingredients than by long fermentation, so they are perfectly suited for the direct mixing method and bread machines. They are often, but not always, yeasted rather than naturally leavened, risen once in bulk and then once in the pan. They can be made in four or five hours. The dough texture is determined by the proportion of wheat to nonwheat flours, and by the use of supplementary ingredients such as garlic, raisins, nuts, peppers, and cheese.

Quick breads: Banana bread, corn bread, and other quick breads are not made from fermented doughs, except in rare instances, so their chemistry is very different from that of most breads. Leavening is usually done chemically by neutralizing acid with alkaline ingredients, such as buttermilk with baking soda (sodium bicarbonate), which creates carbon dioxide. The crumb of quick breads is much tighter than that of yeast-leavened breads, and is always very tender due to the inclusion of high levels of oil or butter. Quick breads are so popular in American folk culture that I have included a chapter of master formulas just for these breads.

CRUCIAL CONCEPTS

Finally, here are a few concepts to keep in mind as you prepare to make world-class bread:

There is a difference between "yeasted" and "leavened" breads. All risen breads are leavened, and whether made with commercial yeast or a wild yeast starter, all leavened breads are leavened by yeast. In this book, however, the term *yeasted* refers to commercial yeast *(Saccharomyces cerevisiae),* whether instant (fine and powdery), active dry (coarse and gritty), or fresh (compressed, moist cakes culled from beer vats). The term *leavened* refers to breads such as sourdough and *levain,* raised with starters made from a strain of wild yeast *(Saccharomyces exiguus)* that grows on fruit and grain.

Nearly everything that a professional bakery does can be replicated, to some degree, at home. Great bread is primarily a result of dough technique and only secondarily of oven technique. This means you can make bakery-quality bread at home if you understand proper dough technique and adapt your home oven to replicate a professional oven.

Bread machines are tools that simulate in one device steps done by many machines in professional bakeries. When their use is appropriate, do not hesitate to use them. Bread machines are especially good for making and raising wet doughs because of the containment provided. You can then finish these breads by hand, baking them in your oven, or simply leave them in the bread machine.

There are many ways to make world-class bread. Where one baker uses a *poolish* starter, another uses a *biga* pre-ferment, and yet another uses neither. Some bakers use 20 percent pre-ferment in their doughs, others 50 percent. Only a few guiding principles exist for making world-class bread, and there are many ways to apply them. Choosing from among these options is the art and the craft of baking.

MASTER TECHNIQUES FOR MAKING WORLD-CLASS BREAD

The ingredient and technique information that follows pertains to all the master formulas in this book and will often be referred to in the text. Please read it carefully before beginning your doughs, and mark it for easy reference.

INGREDIENTS

Flour: Most of the formulas in this book call for unbleached bread flour. Bread flour (11.5 percent or more gluten, a particular protein that gives the bread its structure and elasticity) is stronger than all-purpose flour (9 to 11 percent gluten and best for soft rolls, quick breads, and some pastries). High-gluten flour, which contains up to 14.5 percent gluten, is not preferred for basic all-white hearth breads (with the exception of rustic breads) because it makes the dough tough and chewy. It can, however, be used to good effect in combination with weaker flours such as whole wheat or rye. High-gluten flour should not be confused with vital wheat gluten, a pure gluten powder that is sometimes used in small amounts to strengthen weak flours. Vital wheat gluten is much more expensive than flour and is usually found in small bags at specialty and natural food stores.

When baking whole-wheat bread, whole-wheat bread flour, made from either hard winter or spring wheat and available from natural-foods and mail-order sources, is the best choice. Hard flour usually indicates a higher gluten/protein percentage. Spring wheat (i.e., planted in the spring) is often harder than winter wheat.

Unbleached flour retains its natural beta-carotene pigments, which contribute a pleasant though very subtle flavor to the bread. In bleached flour this pigment is chemically removed to make the flour as white as possible. While this may be useful in certain cakes and pastries, bleaching serves no useful purpose in bread and actually diminishes its flavor and aroma.

Some brands of flour, such as King Arthur, Giusto's, White Lily, and locally milled flours, are better than others, but these formulas will work with almost any commercial unbleached bread flour, and when designated, unbleached all-purpose flour or whole-wheat flour. If you have access to locally milled ingredients with a good track record, by all means use them. (See page 199 for more information.) I have an ecological preference for certified-organic flours, but I have not specified them in the formulas because they have not proven to make better bread and can cost as much as 50 percent more than nonorganic flours.

Salt: All salts work in bread baking, though some are ground finer and thus measure differently. The measurements in the master formulas are for regular-grind table or sea salt, though many bakers prefer the clean, rounded flavor of kosher salt. If you are using weight measures, all salt is interchangeable. If measuring by spoons, use 1 1/2 to 2 times the amount of kosher or coarse salt as regular grind to equal the same weight. You will have to experiment by weighing out equivalent amounts and seeing how they relate and taste, depending on the brand.

Milk and eggs: I love to use buttermilk because it is low in fat and has wonderful flavor and acidity, but with the exception of the quick breads, the formulas will work with equal amounts of skim, low-fat, or even regular milk with very little flavor difference. (The buttermilk is necessary as an acid to neutralize the baking soda in the quick bread formulas.) When using eggs, always use large grade.

Temperature: Temperature, like time, is an important ingredient in bread baking. With the exception of water, all ingredients should be at about room temperature when you use them (unless otherwise specified). If the ingredients are too cold, a longer mixing time may be needed to achieve the desired dough temperature. This could oxidize the flour and adversely affect flavor. If the ingredients are too warm, however, you may have to shorten the mix time, which could be detrimental to the gluten development. Because the ideal temperature range for a mixed dough is usually 76° to 80°F, cool water helps control the mix time to achieve the proper time and temperature balance. (Dough temperature increases about one degree per every minute of kneading or two degrees per minute if kneading in a medium-speed mixer.)

Water: Regular tap water makes good bread as long as it is not overly chlorinated or hard with minerals. In such cases, use bottled or filtered water.

Yeast: As a "new generation" baker, I am partial to instant yeast. I have found it the most dependable of the three types. It is readily available in supermarkets, and it keeps for up to a year in the freezer. It is also more potent than other yeasts, which means you can use less of it.

Instant yeast works best in most breads if stirred in with the dry ingredients. The one exception is in dry doughs, such as bagels, where even instant yeast needs to be hydrated in warm water in order to fully activate, as there is not enough moisture in the dough to completely dissolve the grains.

Fresh, or compressed, yeast has a shorter shelf life, but many bakers still prefer it because it has a longer history (in other words, they initially learned how to bake with it, just as their predecessors did). Fresh yeast can be added directly into the dough without rehydration, though it will activate quicker if first stirred into lukewarm water.

Active dry yeast also performs best if rehydrated first. The grains are bigger and coarser than instant yeast, so they may not completely hydrate and fully activate if added directly to the dough.

The master formulas generally call for instant yeast, but any yeast will work if you make the proper substitution. The ratio is as follows: 100 percent fresh yeast equals 40 percent active dry yeast equals 33 percent instant yeast. In other words:

- Multiply the amount of instant yeast by 3 for the equivalent amount of fresh yeast.

- Multiply the amount of active dry yeast by 2.5 for the equivalent amount of fresh yeast.

- Multiply the amount of instant yeast by 1.25 for the equivalent amount of active dry yeast.

Here's an example:

CONVERSION CHART			
	Fresh Yeast	Active Dry Yeast	Instant Yeast
Percentage	100	40	33
Weight	1 oz.	0.4 oz.	0.33 oz ($^1/_3$ oz.)
Dry Measure (crumbled)	1 tblsp.	1.25 tsp.	1 tsp.

MEASURING

The formulas indicate both weight and dry measures. Professional bakers prefer weighing ingredients because it is much easier to vary batch sizes when using the baker's percentage system, which is based on weight. Weighing is also more accurate than scooping, since almost everyone scoops dry ingredients differently. However, when ingredients are in very small amounts, such as $^1/_8$ teaspoon, dry measures are preferable. Most scales have a margin of error of about $^1/_4$ ounce and are not accurate at these minute levels. For this reason, you may find yourself using weight measures for part of a formula and dry for another.

For dry measuring using measuring cups or spoons, spoon the ingredient into the measuring tool to over-full and then scrape off the excess with a knife or spatula so that the ingredient is level with the top of the tool. Don't scoop the measuring cup into the flour or you will compress the flour too much.

For weight measures, excellent digital platform scales are available for $30 to $75 through cookware catalogs, as well as at many kitchenware shops. Classic balance scales, using counterweights on two platforms, are the best of all measuring tools and never break or wear out. Professional scales are too expensive for most home bakers, ranging from $350 and up. However, the Baker's Catalogue from King Arthur sells a small balance scale for about $90 (see page 199).

MIXING AND KNEADING

Although kneading by hand is one of
the joys of baking bread, many people
prefer to use a machine. If so, you may use
either a mixer with a dough hook attachment or a food processor with a plastic or
metal blade (see page 18). You may also
use a bread machine for kneading only,
and then shape the loaf by hand and bake
it in the oven.

It is hard to overmix a dough by hand
but easy to do so with a machine, so monitor dough temperature and cell structure
closely when using a mixer or food processor. Most doughs are at their best when
kneaded to between 76°F and 80°F, and
just long enough for the gluten to develop
(see page 29).

Kneading has three purposes: to disperse the ingredients, to hydrate the yeast
and grain and thus initiate the fermentation process, and to develop the gluten or
protein bonds that give the bread
strength and structure. With kneading,
most flours set up—that is, the gluten
strands bond—within 8 to 15 minutes. If
the dough gets too warm or is overmixed,
the gluten bonds break down and the
dough can be ruined. This usually happens only when an electric mixer has been
left on for too long and the dough has
heated up from the friction against the
bowl.

To knead by hand, use the heels of
your hands to press down and away for a
couple of strokes. Turn the dough a quarter turn and repeat. Continue this as long
as it takes for the dough to set up, which
means the gluten/protein develops a
strong elastic texture, tested by gently

1. When making bread dough by hand, begin by mixing all the ingredients in a bowl, until the dry ingredients are hydrated by the wet ingredients and form a coarse, soft ball of dough.

2. Transfer the coarse dough to a floured counter and knead with the heels of your hands to accomplish the three purposes of kneading: distribution of ingredients, gluten development, and initiation of fermentation. Dust your hands with flour from time to time to prevent sticking.

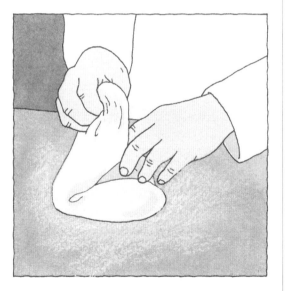

3. After a few kneading strokes, fold the dough over itself, give it a quarter-turn, and knead some more. Continue this kneading cycle till the dough is smooth and supple.

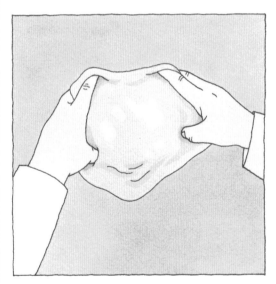

4. To test for gluten development, stretch a piece of the dough by gently pulling and turning it till a section stretches into a thin, translucent membrane, or windowpane. If the dough cannot hold the membrane, continue kneading for another minute or two.

stretching a small piece of dough to see if it can maintain a paper-thin, translucent membrane or windowpane (see page 29). If the dough is sticky, flour your work surface and your hands. If the dough is too stiff, add small amounts of water or other liquid and continue kneading. Keep the dough close to you; reaching across a table is hard on the back. Hand kneading usually takes 12 to 20 minutes, slightly longer than it takes by machine. The ball of ingredients will change before your eyes from a coarse mixture into a smooth, soft, elastic, and springy dough.

FERMENTING

Leavened bread and beer have a common ancestry; both are made from fermented grain. When yeast, a living single-celled fungus, feeds on the sugars and starches in bread dough, it creates two major by-products, alcohol (ethanol), which flavors the dough and then bakes off in the oven, and carbon dioxide (CO_2, or carbonic gas), which is trapped in the dough, forcing it to rise. As diastatic amylase enzymes, which live in the flour, facilitate a breakdown of the ingredients into simpler forms of sugar, thus making them more available

---

MIXING WITH A FOOD PROCESSOR

Hand kneading is one of the great pleasures of bread making, but mixing dough in home food processors is becoming popular. Processors work well and quickly, especially for wet, rustic bread doughs. The blade works the dough more diligently and efficiently than a dough hook or mixer paddle, but it is much rougher on the dough. You sacrifice a degree of control and increase the possibility of error when using a high-powered tool like a processor, but with precautions and practice, you can make it your ally. Here are some guidelines:

❏ When dough is mixed by hand or with an electric mixer, the ingredients are able to absorb the liquid gradually. Food processors are so efficient that they outpace the hydration process, so you must mix in two stages.

❏ In the first stage, use a short series of pulses to gather the ingredients and initiate hydration of the flour and yeast. Stop when the ingredients gather themselves into a ball.

❏ Let the dough rest for about 20 minutes. During this period, a number of chemical changes take place similar to those in the autolyse described on page 45.

❏ In the second stage, pulse the dough once or twice and then use the "on" button to mix it for no more than 45 seconds. Use a probe thermometer and the windowpane test (see page 29) to check for temperature and gluten development, then mix again for an additional period of no more than 45 seconds, and only if necessary. The dough should reach a temperature of 77°F to 80°F. If it heats up beyond that before it windowpanes, let it rest a few minutes to cool down. Then pulse a few more times and check again.

❏ If the dough is too bulky for the food processor, mix it in smaller batches and finish it off by hand on the counter.

❏ Do not add textured ingredients such as seeds, nuts, raisins, and other dried fruits until the final few pulses, or they will get chewed up.

as food for the yeast, fermentation increases and more complex flavors develop. This organic chemical activity affects the flavor, color, and texture of the bread.

The first rise, which varies according to the type of bread, is called the *primary* or *bulk* fermentation. During this stage, most of the flavor develops. The final rise, called the *proofing* stage, is primarily for lightness and texture, though flavor continues to develop. Some breads can sustain longer fermentations than others, depending on the ingredients. By extending fermentation to the appropriate limit, the baker elicits the fullest flavor from the grain (if overproofed the yeast may die, giving off a distasteful ammonia-like taste similiar, not surprisingly, to stale beer). Proper fermentation of the grain is the major skill of the bread baker's craft.

The dough techniques in many of the master formulas use refrigeration to stretch the fermentation time. This is called *retarding* the dough, and allows the home baker to replicate the qualities of world-class bread without attending to, or *building,* the dough throughout the day as is done in many bakeries, where refrigeration space is at a premium. Retarding is a key technique, allowing the home baker to create bread of professional quality.

SCALING AND BENCHING

The best way to know if your dough has proofed enough is to know in advance how high it should be. *Scaling* the pieces to specific weights allows you to determine how big the loaves will be and what size pans or baskets to use. In my bread classes, I insist that the students weigh out the dough even if the recipe says to divide it into so many equal pieces. This way you can visually determine if the dough has risen enough based on weight. With experience, you will learn what a 1-pound loaf of various doughs should look like when risen and how high it should be in a pan or basket. For small pieces like rolls, scaling is necessary to achieve uniformity of size; eyeballing the pieces can be misleading.

When making dinner rolls, you can weigh out a large piece of dough, from 8 to 16 ounces, then cut off equal-looking pieces and shape them into rolls (an 8-ounce dough will make four 2-ounce rolls; a 16-ounce dough makes eight 2-ounce rolls—which will bake down to $1^1/2$ ounces, the perfect size for dinner rolls).

Whether you are making loaves or rolls, the dough needs to be scaled above the finished weight because a few ounces of moisture will evaporate while the bread is baking. A $1^1/2$-ounce dinner roll should therefore weigh almost 2 ounces before it is baked. A finished baguette weighing 16 ounces should weigh 19 ounces before baking. A pan loaf planned for $1^1/2$ pounds (24 ounces) should be scaled to 28 ounces.

The best way to scale dough, regardless of the type of scale used, is to cut a piece larger than needed, weigh it, and then cut or snip off pieces till you achieve the desired weight. After doing this a few times, you will get pretty good at identifying approximate sizes. If your piece is underweight, it is perfectly okay to add more dough, but the fewer small pieces of add-on dough, the better for the final piece.

After scaling the pieces for larger loaves, you need to shape them into balls and let the gluten relax for 5 to 20 minutes (depending on the dough) so they can be further shaped. This is called *benching*. Benching allows the dough pieces to be extended into their finished shape, because the relaxed gluten does not resist the shaping.

In addition to rising in pans and baskets, loaves can rise free-form on sheet pans. I recommend lining the pans with baking parchment and dusting semolina, cornmeal, or polenta on the paper. If you do not have parchment, lightly mist the pan with an oil spray. If you want to bake free-form loaves directly on a baking stone or oven tiles, you can set them up on the back of the sheet pan and simply slide them onto the stone, parchment and all, when ready for the oven.

SHAPING

There are many bread shapes and many ways to do the shaping. Regardless of the method, be sure to seal any seams in the loaves so they do not open up while proofing or baking.

Rolls are fun and easy to shape. Take the scaled piece in your hand and roll it with a circular motion on a dry, unfloured surface, exerting just enough pressure with the heel of your hand to make the piece spring into your curled fingers. With a little practice you will be able to do this with both hands simultaneously. If the dough slides around too much, wipe it lightly with a damp towel. This will help it to stick to the work surface, generating enough friction to make it pop up in your hand. The bottom of the roll should have a little dimple, created by the circular shaping motion, which you should pinch closed with your fingers.

Boules, or large round loaves, can be shaped in the same way as rolls, though you may have to use two hands to rotate the dough because of its larger size. Or you can roll the dough in one direction, as for a torpedo-shaped *bâtard,* turn it one-quarter turn, and roll again, creating a round. Quickly finish it off by pinching closed the seams created while rolling the dough. As

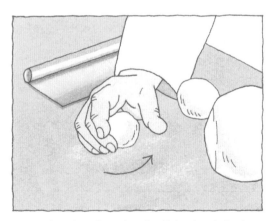

Using the edge of your hand, roll the dough firmly in a circular motion, curling your fingers to create a mold. The dough should pop up into your palm, having formed a tight, smooth skin.

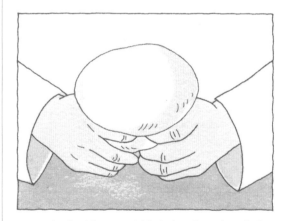

For a *boule,* lift twice-folded dough and pull the creased edges down to the bottom of the ball, creating a tight, smooth skin with all creases converging at the bottom.

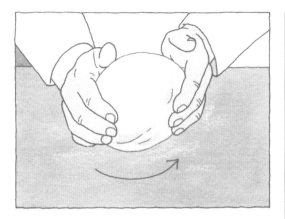

Roll the ball on the counter with both hands to smooth and round it before transferring the dough to a sheet pan or proofing basket.

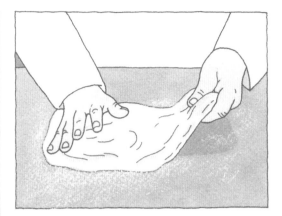

To make most bread shapes, transfer weighed dough pieces to a lightly floured counter and very gently (to minimize any de-gassing of the dough) pat each piece into a 1-inch-thick rough rectangle.

with rolls, the seams will converge on the bottom, where they can be pinched closed. (If the seams are not pinched closed, the ball will have a tendency to open up, or unravel.)

Bâtards*, torpedoes, logs, and sandwich loaves* all start out the same, by first gently forming the scaled dough into a rough square or oblong. Do not squeeze out all the air, because retaining the trapped gas produces a better finished loaf with a properly irregular hole pattern. Press the dough just enough to make the shape. It can then be rolled up like a cigar or folded letter style, again keeping the seam in one line on the bottom, where it can be pinched closed. The ends should also be pinched closed.

When using this torpedo shape for sandwich loaves, it is important to gently extend the shaped dough to the length of the loaf pan so that the ends touch the end walls of the pan. Do this by gently rolling the torpedo out from the center while your hands move out towards both ends (see il-

lustration for baguettes on page 22). It is also important to make the torpedo even in diameter, rather than thicker in the middle and tapered at the ends. This tapered look is attractive in *bâtards*, but in sandwich loaves you want all the slices to be the same size.

Baguettes are the most challenging of the basic shapes because they are so long and the dough tends to resist being extended. Unless the dough is extremely relaxed and extensible, it may take two or three resting periods between efforts to achieve the desired length. Try not to squeeze out all the air or to handle the dough any more than necessary, since excessive handling dries out the surface, causing a mottled or wrinkled look that mars the beauty of the finished loaf. Surface tension is necessary to keep the dough from spreading sideways while it proofs; you want it to retain its cylindrical shape rather than flattening out.

To make a baguette, first gently make a round, being careful not to squeeze out all the air. Cover and let the dough relax,

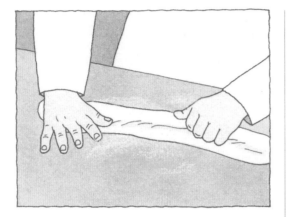

For baguettes or *bâtards*, use your thumbs or the edge of your hand to seal the dough at the crease, being careful not to de-gas or compress any more of the dough than necessary. This "thumbing" or sealing of the crease stretches the skin of the dough, creating surface tension and a tight, smooth surface. For *bâtards* or torpedoes, the loaf is now ready to proof. For baguettes or longer loaves, move to the next step.

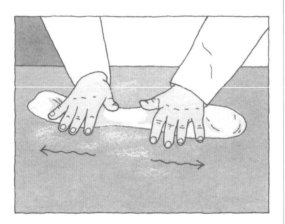

For baguettes, work from the center of the dough and gently rock and roll the dough back and forth, while gradually moving your hands out toward the ends of the dough. When the dough begins to fight this extension, by springing back like a rubber band, cover the dough and "bench" (rest) it for 3 to 5 minutes to relax the gluten. Then, repeat the extension process. (Note: You may bench the dough at this point for as long as 20 to 30 minutes without harm, but always take care not to press too hard when extending, to preserve the air pockets already in the dough.)

allowing it to sit for 20 minutes. Shape it into a *bâtard* or torpedo, then cover and relax the dough an additional 3 minutes. Then, extend the dough by gently pressing it into a rectangle (but not squeezing out all the air) and rolling up the dough by folding it as you would a letter, bringing the long bottom edge up to just above the center and then folding the top edge down to the bottom. (This is called the *letter fold.*) The seam should now be facing you in a left-to-right direction. Use the pinky edge of your hand to press down on the full length of the seam line to seal it between your hand and the table, and also to tighten the skin of the dough. (Or use your thumbs to seal the seam. This is called *thumbing.*) Turn the dough so the seam is now on the bottom and then, with slightly cupped hands, gently roll the dough out from the center to extend the length, by rocking it back and forth as your hands move apart in opposite directions to the outer ends. The dough should extend to about 9 to 12 inches. Let the dough rest for 3 more minutes and then repeat the process of gently flattening it into a plump rectangle, folding as described above, sealing the seam with the edge of your hand and extending the loaf by rocking and rolling it as your hands move from the center to the ends. The dough should extend up to about 18 inches. When the dough shrinks back because of its elasticity, stop shaping (if you try to force the dough, you will squeeze out all the air and rip the surface skin). Cover the dough, and allow it rest for 3 to 5 minutes to relax the gluten. You can then continue extending from the center out, as before, until the loaf reaches the desired length. (The length of your baguette is, by necessity, limited by the size of your oven. Most home ovens can handle only an 18-inch baguette, while commercial ovens can go up to 24 inches and beyond.)

Another method of extending the dough is to dangle the loaf by holding it with one hand from one end, allowing gravity to lengthen the piece while you run your other hand up and down the seam, simultaneously sealing it and gently stretching the loaf. Be sure to reverse direction, dangling and smoothing the loaf from the other end, to keep it even. As soon as the dough resists and shrinks back to its former length, stop, wait 3 to 5 minutes for the gluten to relax, and then make another pass at extending it.

There are fancier shapes that are not within the scope of this book, but regardless of shape, the principles are the same: Handle the dough as quickly and as little as possible; keep the seams sealed, and let the dough rest and relax if it resists shaping. Start with *bâtards* and torpedo shapes, and move on to baguettes and fancier styles as confidence in your shaping technique grows.

PROOFING AND SCORING

Proofing is the final rise before baking. Breads customarily complete their proofing in 60 to 90 minutes, but in many of the master formulas we will be both proofing and retarding the loaves, holding them overnight in the refrigerator before baking, to improve flavor, color, and texture.

The dough should be covered while it proofs to keep the surface from drying. A light mist of vegetable oil cooking spray over the dough allows any covering, plastic or cloth, to be peeled off without sticking. It is discouraging to get this far and have the loaf deflate because the top of it stuck to the cover wrap. (If it does deflate you can still bake it, though it will be smaller and denser than the ideal loaf.)

I am a strong advocate of cooking spray for home bakers. There are a number of brands of such sprays, and they are all acceptable. The main advantage of these canned sprays is that you can mist a very small amount, far less than if applying by hand or with a brush. Besides allowing you to cover your loaves without risking deflation, cooking spray allows home bakers to protect and retard doughs for long periods without fear of drying them out. Professional bakeries use large racks with plastic or canvas covers, and their refrigerated retarders (cold boxes with low airflow) are designed keep the breads from drying out. A home baker needs to improvise to replicate the advantages of a bakery, and cooking spray is an invaluable aid.

Since most homes do not have a proof box (a temperature- and moisture-controlled chamber used by most bakeries), I recommend proofing at room temperature. If your house is colder than 65°F, you may use a slightly warmed oven (heat it to just over 100°F but make sure the heat is off before proofing) or a warm spot such as the top of the refrigerator, but don't put the loaf out in the sun. You may also use large metal or glass bowls to cover your rising loaves, rather than plastic wrap or bags. These help keep in warmth as well as keeping the dough from drying out.

Dough will normally increase in size by 75 to 100 percent during final proofing. It should not spring back quickly when poked but should take 10 to 15 seconds to rebound. If you are not sure when to stop the proofing process, it is better to catch the loaf on the upswing, rather than after it has fully risen, so that it doesn't deflate when you score it. The loaf should grow 10 to 20 percent in the oven (this growth is called *oven spring*), but if it is overproofed, it will fall when scored and then barely recover its size, yielding a good but less-than-perfect loaf.

Doughs can be proofed in molds such as greased bread pans or floured proofing baskets (called *bannetons* in French) or freestanding on sheet pans. Molds are usually filled about halfway, and the dough is ready to bake when it fills the mold completely. When making freestanding loaves such as baguettes, if the dough is too slack to hold its shape, try laying it out on well-floured cloths, linen napkins, or tablecloths (called *couches* in French) and supporting it with walls made by bunching up the cloth between the loaves. You can also simply proof and bake these on flour-dusted parchment, knowing that the loaves will spread out as well as up.

In many of the master formulas, you will proof the dough for a while and then retard it overnight. Assuming that your refrigerator is set at around 40°F, the doughs should stop rising shortly after you put them in (sometimes within minutes). The retarding stage is a way to extend the fermentation period and develop more flavor without overproofing the dough.

The proofing times in the formulas are just guidelines. If your dough is moving faster or slower than the instructions indicate, you will need to adjust accordingly. Wait, if necessary, for the dough to rise to the suggested size before retarding. Otherwise you will have a much longer wait the next day, after you remove the dough from the refrigerator, for it to wake up and climb to its full size. Eventually you will get a feel for this timing, but it may take a little practice.

Scoring, also called *cutting, docking,* or *slashing,* is the strategic cutting of dough to improve its appearance and to enhance oven spring. Scoring releases some of the gas trapped inside the dough and allows you to control exactly where the bread will open, or bloom. It is almost always better to score at a 45-degree angle, rather than straight down into the bread, to get the most attrac-

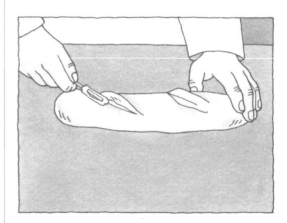

Scoring dough is best done with a sharp razor, either straight or curved on a wooden coffee stirrer (see page 25). You can also purchase a true lame or use a serrated knife. The cuts should be about 1/2 inch deep, and made at a 45° angle, rather than straight in. Baguettes have up to five parallel cuts, *bâtards* either one long or two shorter cuts, and *boules* may be scored either in a tic-tac-toe pattern, asterisk pattern, parallel lines, or with a spiral toward the top.

tive and open bloom. You can use a serrated knife, a straight razor, or a curved razor blade called a *lame.* (You can make a serviceable *lame* by carefully sliding a narrow wooden coffee stirrer through the end slots of a double-edged razor blade, which forces the blade to curve.) The cuts should be about $1/2$ inch deep in most instances. Some breads should be scored before proofing, but to insure the fullest bloom and most attractive appearance, the vast majority call for scoring just prior to baking.

OVEN TECHNIQUES

Here is where a few tricks can really make a difference. The key to a great crackly crust is steam in the oven. This softens the outside of the loaf, allowing it to expand during the first few minutes of baking.

Here's how to set your oven up for steam: Direct bottom heat from a professional stone hearth or deck oven can be replicated with a baking or pizza stone, or with unglazed ceramic tiles (available at garden or pottery shops). Ceramic tiles are usually placed on the floor of a gas oven or on the lowest rack of an electric oven, where you can leave them permanently. Rather than tiles, I prefer a 1-inch-thick pizza stone, available in many kitchenware departments, because the stone holds more heat and does not slide around as tiles do. It can be placed on any shelf in the oven, though I put mine in the bottom third of my electric oven to insure enough headroom for tall loaves. In a gas oven I would simply put it on the oven floor. If you do not have a baking stone, you can invert a regular sheet pan, turning it into a quasi-deck or hearth. It does not hold heat as

well as a stone but will work in a pinch.

Use a baking peel (wooden or metal, see page 32) to transfer loaves to the oven, handling them gently to transfer from the baskets, cloths, or parchment. Score them on the peel just prior to sliding them into the oven. If the dough is very soft and slack it will take a lot of semolina, cornmeal, or

---

CONVECTION OVENS

Convection ovens are far more efficient than conventional ovens because they use internal fans to circulate the heat. They are used in most commercial bakeries and can produce beautiful, evenly baked loaves of bread in a relatively short time. However, the moving air dries the crust faster, reducing its ability to expand.

The temperatures given in the master formulas are for conventional ovens because that's what most home bakers have. If you happen to have a convection oven, here are a few pointers for adapting the instructions:

❏ Set the temperature 50°F lower than stated, except when instructed to turn the oven up as high as it will go.

❏ Reduce the baking time by one-fifth to one-quarter.

❏ Rotate the bread, as usual, halfway through the bake. Many convection oven manufacturers claim that their ovens cook evenly, but I have yet to find one without hot spots.

❏ If your oven has a separate control for the convection fan, make sure to turn it on.

❏ If your oven allows you to bake with or without convection, try the bread both ways to find out which you prefer.

To transfer proofed dough onto the stone, use either a baking peel dusted with semolina or cornmeal, or the back of a parchment-lined sheet pan as a peel. Jiggle the pan to make sure the parchment will slide (sometimes condensation causes it to stick to the pan). Slide the dough, paper and all, onto the stone. Work quickly to minimize heat loss from the oven.

other dusting flour to keep it from sticking to the peel. Be generous. You may also use the back of a sheet pan lined with baking parchment as a quasi-peel. I strongly suggest you buy a supply of baking parchment from a kitchenware shop or directly from a local bakery. It will make baking and cleaning far easier.

Place an empty sheet pan or cast-iron frying pan on a lower rack while the oven is preheating (if baking on the oven floor, you can use the top rack, leaving enough headroom for the loaves). The initial temperature is usually higher than that needed for the final bake to compensate for the heat loss from steaming. As soon as the bread goes into the oven, pour 1 cup of hot water into the pan. This creates an instant cloud

of steam as well as some lingering vapor. Then, immediately use your spritzer to spray the oven walls with water to create more steam. Also spray the breads themselves (be sure not to spray the oven light-bulb; it may break). Close the oven door. Two minutes after the first spritz, spray the oven walls and loaves again. Open the oven door for only a brief instant to minimize heat loss. Once the oven has recovered from the shock of the steaming, adjust the oven setting down to the final bake temperature.

While the loaves are in the oven, check them periodically to be sure they are baking evenly. You will probably need to rotate them one or more times during the bake. Sometimes a 180-degree turn is sufficient; in my home oven four quarter turns are necessary for even coloring. Very few home ovens (or professional ovens, for that

As soon as the dough is transferred to the stone, pour 1 cup of hot water into a pan or cast-iron skillet that has been preheated on a different shelf. Quickly spray the oven walls and the dough with a spritzer and shut the door. Two minutes later, repeat the spritzing.

matter) bake evenly. Turn the loaves only when necessary; each time you open the oven door, as much as 50°F of heat are lost.

Most rolls and sandwich breads are fully baked when the internal temperature reaches 185° to 190°F. The wheat starch begins gelatinizing (thickening by full moisture absorption) just below this temperature. If you prefer a harder crust, allow the temperature to reach 200°F to 205°F, driving out more moisture. Loaf-pan breads need to reach 185°F. Lean hearth breads should reach 205°F if you want to retain the crisp crust. Some types, such as *ciabatta*-style rustic breads, can go as high as 210°F, which fully gelatinizes them and creates a shiny, almost translucent interior crumb.

Use a probe thermometer to read the internal temperature. If you don't have one, use the thwack test, thumping the bottom of the hot loaf and listening for a hollow sound. The sides of the loaf should be golden rather than white, firm to the touch rather than soft and yielding. If the loaf is still too soft, return it to the oven immediately. You can remove loaf-pan bread from the pans if they are nearly done and finish baking them freestanding on a sheet pan. They brown very quickly when removed from their pans, usually in 3 to 4 minutes.

CLOCHES

A cloche is a single-loaf-sized domed clay oven that replicates in miniature a brick or adobe hearth oven. Cloches cost about $50 and are becoming more and more popular. The Sassafras Company makes both round and oblong-shaped models under the name La Cloche.

The bottom of the cloche is like any ceramic hearth but the dome adds an element not found in home ovens: It traps the steam and gives the crust a beautiful sheen and a thick, chewy texture. The slow heat penetration also creates additional oven spring. The result is a loaf of uncommon beauty. The only drawback is that a cloche can hold only one loaf at a time.

To use a cloche, mist the base and dome of the cloche lightly with pan spray and sprinkle the base with semolina or cornmeal. Proof the dough either on the cloche base or as you normally would. Arrange the oven racks so that one is about one-third of the way from the bottom or near the center (you need enough room at the top to accommodate the dome). Preheat the oven to 50°F higher than for normal baking, around 500°F in most cases (or as indicated for the specific bread). When the dough is ready to bake, score it and then spritz the dough and the inside of the cloche dome with water. Place the dome over the dough and put the entire cloche in the oven. If you have an electric oven with an exposed coil, place a sheet pan on a lower rack to shield the cloche so that the bottom doesn't bake too quickly.

After 35 minutes, carefully lift the dome (use a good pot holder; the clay will be very hot!) to release some of the steam and to check for evenness of baking. If necessary, rotate the cloche a quarter or half turn. Replace the lid and continue baking until the bread is done. Baking time will be 20 to 30 minutes longer than on the hearth to allow extra time for the heat to penetrate the clay. If the bottom of the loaf appears to be baking faster than the top, remove the dome for the final 4 or 5 minutes, and the loaf will quickly brown.

DEFINITELY READ THIS BEFORE MAKING ANY OF THE MASTER FORMULAS

Baking and dough techniques will be discussed in the context of the various formulas. Once you have gathered your tools and ingredients and read the previous pages, you will be ready to begin building your doughs. I suggest you begin with one or more versions of French bread, trying both methods. If you want to skip ahead to other types, be sure to see what type of preferment is required and make it in advance. The sourdough starters, both barm and mild *levain,* take a number of days to make but can be kept indefinitely in the refrigerator after ripening. Don't get impatient and use the starters before the wild yeast is potent and the lactobacilli have created enough flavor—it will take five days to make a potent barm starter. If you already have a strong, healthy starter made by another method, it can be substituted for the ones described.

Beyond any information I can impart about the bread-making process, there is one essential skill I cannot give you. It is "feel." Since I will not be in your kitchen while you make your doughs, I have done everything possible to detail the processes for your success. However, many variables affect the final results, such as the brand and age of your flour, the temperature of your room and water, the intensity of your kneading, and the fermentation pace of your dough. The remedy for this is to develop a feel for the dough that comes only with practice and experience. Even in my classes, where I monitor each step of my students' progress, everyone's loaves require adjustments and come out different. The two most valuable ingredients in your bread, as I repeat over and over to my students, are time and temperature, the final controls that enable you to tweak a bread dough to that ultimate level we call *world class.* If you find that the doughs are not performing exactly as the formula indicates, manipulating time and temperature is the most valuable method to bring about the desired results. For example, sometimes a dough that is supposed to be ready for the next step in three hours may take as long as six if the room is cool and drafty or the dough is a little stiffer than ideal (or everything may move faster than indicated if it is a hot day).

Feel means an intuitive sense that a dough is exactly as it should be: properly hydrated, supple, lively and springy, mixed long enough to develop the gluten but not so long that the beta-carotene flavor and color oxidize away, and finally, fermented at a temperature and in a time frame conducive to the particular bread. When shaping your pieces, are you heavy-handed, squeezing out all the carbonic gas, or are you gentle, preserving the gas pockets to bring forth a properly irregular hole structure? These are all aspects of feel.

If you already think you know how to make bread but find that some of these concepts are new, please realize that many of us are just beginning to understand bread in a new way, at a world-class level. Do not assume you already know how to make bread this good; take these principles to heart, and please read the introductory pages as if learning for the first time. Then, when you begin making your dough, keep thinking about the elements of feel. Do this until you no longer have to think about it because you have internalized it. Once you have the feel of dough, your ability to adjust the formulas to serve your purposes will become intuitive. Then, and only then, will you be a true bread revolutionary.

WHAT IS WINDOWPANING?

The best way to know if your dough has been mixed enough is to use the windowpane test, also called the *membrane test*. After you have tried it a few times it will become easy, and you will make it part of your bread-making routine. Before you can use the test, though, you need to understand something about gluten.

Most breads should be kneaded or mixed just until the gluten sets up. What does this mean? Gluten is formed by the combination of the two proteins, gliadin and glutenin, that exist in flour (more so in wheat flour than in other grains). When these fragments are hydrated with water (or milk) they bond with each other, creating a large protein aggregate called gluten, which gives bread its structure and strength. The longer you knead the dough—up to a point!—the stronger the gluten becomes, and the dough feels springier and more elastic.

However, the friction of mixing causes the temperature of the dough to rise. If you work the dough too long and hard, the gluten begins to break apart, and the dough becomes irretrievable. This is one of the pitfalls of using an electric mixer or food processor, but it seldom happens with hand kneading.

The amount of hydration and kneading needed to achieve maximum gluten development varies with the type of flour, but doughs made with most bread and all-purpose flours set up in anywhere from 6 to 15 minutes when kneaded by hand or with a home mixer.

Here is how to do the windowpane test: After kneading for 6 to 8 minutes, or when the dough feels supple and stretchy, pinch off a small piece and stretch it slowly apart, gently pulling and rotating it. You are trying to stretch the dough into a thin, translucent membrane or windowpane. If it tears easily before reaching this state, knead for a few more minutes and try the test again. If the dough has not set up within 15 minutes, it may be too wet or too dry, in which case you will have to add more flour or water, as needed.

If after long mixing the dough suddenly becomes stringy and stretchy and sticks to your hands like bubblegum on a warm day, the dough is probably overmixed and broken. This is not the same as being too wet. It takes a long time for dough to break down from overmixing, and it stays sticky and gummy no matter how much extra flour you add. There's nothing to do if you overmix but throw the dough out and start over.

TERMS YOU SHOULD KNOW

All-purpose flour: Preferably unbleached, it has 9 to 11 percent gluten proteins, making it useful for quick breads, pancakes, muffins, and many other baked goods.

Aspect: The overall quality of a loaf, including bloom, crumb (webbing), aroma, and flavor.

Autolyse: A rest period in the mixing cycle that allows the gluten proteins to bond. Shortening the mixing time minimizes oxidation of the dough, preserving the flavor of the natural beta-carotene in unbleached flour. (See page 45 for a fuller discussion.)

Baguette: A long, thin, cylindrical hearth bread, usually French bread (*pain ordinaire*), though other doughs can be shaped this way.

Baking stone: An insert placed in a home oven that serves as a hearth. Thick pizza stones absorb and radiate heat the best. Unglazed ceramic tiles also work well. An inverted sheet pan will do in a pinch.

Banneton: A round or oblong basket, usually made of wood or wicker and sometimes lined with canvas, used for raising bread dough to give it a distinctive shape and to keep the dough from spreading sideways while proofing.

Barm: An English term for sourdough starter, usually made from a base of whole-wheat flour.

Bâtard: Literally "bastard," a *bâtard* is a short, torpedo-shaped loaf that is somewhere between a baguette and a *boule*. It can be made from many types of dough.

Benching: Resting fermented dough just before shaping so that the gluten relaxes, making it easier to form.

Biga: An Italian-style pre-ferment usually made with commercial yeast. It is added to dough to improve flavor and leavening.

Bloom: The external aspect of a loaf; bloom includes crust coloration and flowering at the cut points.

Boule: Round loaves, often raised in round *bannetons* but sometimes freestanding.

Bran: The exterior layer of a wheat berry or other grain. Bran is primarily cellulose, good for digestion, and contains enzymes and wild yeast, which make it a good addition to sourdough starters.

Bread flour: Unbleached white flour with a gluten-forming protein content of 11.5 to 13 percent. It is ideal for hearth breads and rolls, providing structure yet a degree of tenderness. It is the flour most often recommended in these formulas.

Build: The process of creating a bread dough, beginning with a starter or pre-ferment, elaborating with intermediate starters, and ending up with the finished dough.

Caramelization: The browning caused when sugar reaches 325°F. It is the main cause, along with the Maillard reaction, of crust colorization in bread.

Chef: Another name for a wild yeast starter before it is elaborated into an intermediate starter. Also called the *mother culture* or *mother*.

Cloche: A bell-shaped ceramic mini-oven used at home to replicate a brick oven.

Convection oven: An oven that uses moving air to intensify the heat. It bakes most products much faster than a conventional oven.

Cooking spray: Vegetable oil in a spray can, used to grease pans and mist the tops of loaves to prevent plastic wrap from sticking.

Cornmeal: Coarse corn flour, somewhere between flour and polenta. Aside from its uses as an ingredient, it also makes a good dusting flour on peels and beneath hearth loaves.

Couche: A type of linen used for raising hearth breads, especially those too long or too slack for *bannetons*. Bunching the cloth around the loaves provides a nonstick structure to help rising loaves retain their shape.

Crumb: The interior of a loaf, defined by its hole structure (webbing), the gelatinization of the starch, and its flavor.

Deck: The shelf of an oven, or another name for a stone or brick shelf oven.

Direct method: Mixing a dough in one step, without a pre-ferment, adding all ingredients, including the yeast, and mixing till ready.

Dock: To dock bread means to score the top of a loaf before baking. Docking can also refer to poking holes in a pie dough to prevent it from bubbling.

Ears: Scored pieces of crust that separate themselves from the loaf during baking and develop a beautiful, wavy appearance.

Elaboration: Building a starter into an intermediate dough.

Elasticity: The ability of a dough to stretch and be molded into shapes.

Endosperm: The starchy part of a wheat berry, as distinct from the germ and the bran. It represents about 85 percent of a wheat berry and is the primary ingredient in flour.

Enriched dough: Bread dough made with the addition of fat, sugar, eggs, or dairy. Heavily enriched doughs are called *rich doughs*.

Enzymes: Diastase and amylase protein fragments in flour and malted grain that activate in doughs, triggering a breakdown of starches, freeing their sugar molecules. These sugar molecules, in turn, become food for the yeast, thus enhancing fermentation.

Extensibility: The ability of a dough to stretch without tearing or springing back and to expand during fermentation.

Fermentation: The process in which yeast digests the sugars in dough, creating alcohol and carbon dioxide as by-products. Fermentation is what causes dough to expand and develop flavor. Also, another type of fermentation occurs in sourdough breads, caused by lactobacillus organisms that flavor the finished loaves by creating lactic and acetic acids.

Firm starter: An intermediate piece of sourdough starter, elaborated from a mother starter, used to build flavor and structure in sourdough breads.

Floor time: The first or primary fermentation, when the dough undergoes its bulk rise.

Gelatinization: The thickening and full hydration of bread starches. When the internal temperature of a loaf reaches between 180°-185°F the bread is considered gelatinized, though many breads are baked to a higher temperature.

Gluten: The major protein aggregate of bread, created by the combination of two proteins, gliadin and glutenin. Gluten gives bread its structure and strength. Wheat is the primary source of gluten and the only grain with enough gluten to make breads with a large, open-holed texture.

Hearth: A deck upon which loaves can be baked. It usually refers to deck or hearth ovens, which can be replicated in home ovens following the instructions on page 25.

High-gluten flour: White flour made from hard spring wheat with at least 13 percent to 14.5 percent gluten-forming protein. It is best used in conjunction with other grains and flour to provide more structure.

Hydration: The absorption of liquid, primarily water, by the other dough ingredients. Flour must be hydrated in order for gluten to bond. Yeast needs to hydrate to initiate fermentation. Starches must also hydrate in order to gelatinize.

Indirect method: Making bread dough in stages, usually by making a pre-ferment or sponge and building a dough after it has fermented.

Intermediate starter: A pre-ferment, usually made from a wild yeast starter, used to build a dough. It adds flavor and structure to the finished dough.

Kneading: Working a dough by agitating the ingredients with the heels of the hands. The purpose is to disperse the ingredients, initiate fermentation, and hydrate the flour so that the gluten can develop. Kneading can also be done by machine (see page 16).

Lactobacilli: These are the bacteria that give flavor to bread. They live in harmony with yeast in a dough and are cultivated in wild yeast starters such as barm or *levain*. Some of the bacteria create lactic acid and others create acetic acid, both of which are present in complexly flavored sourdough breads.

Lame: A curved razor blade used to score, or slash, bread dough.

Lean dough: Bread dough made without enrichments such as fat and sugar. The most well known is *pain ordinaire*, or French bread.

Levain: Either an intermediate starter or a type of bread, *pain au levain*, made from the starter.

Maillard reaction: A type of caramelization caused by the production of simple sugars through fermentation and enzyme activity. It contributes, along with normal caramelization, to crust colorization of yeasted breads.

Malt: Sprouted grain that has been dried to preserve the natural maltose sugars created during the sprouting process. If the diastase enzymes are still alive (diastatic), malt is a good food for sourdough starters and breads. If the enzymes have been killed by roasting (non-diastatic), the malt can still be used to add flavor. The most common malt comes from barley, but wheat malt (made from sprouted wheat flour) may also be used. Malted barley flour is often added to commercial flours.

Mixing: Combining the ingredients of a dough by hand or with a mixer or food processor. Mixers with paddle dough hook attachments are most commonly used for this purpose.

Old dough: Also called *pâte fermentée* or *pâte vieille*. This is dough held back from a previous batch and used to add flavor and leavening to a new dough.

Oven spring: The final rise a dough makes when put in the oven. As the bread warms, the yeast activity speeds up, boosting the loaf size and creating the blooming effect and ears of a loaf.

Paddle: The oval mixer attachment (not the dough hook) used for mixing batters and slack bread doughs.

Pâte fermentée, pâte vieille: See *old dough*.

Parchment paper: Baking paper that protects pans, reduces cleaning, and has a nonstick quality. It is available at most supermarkets.

Peel: A thin, long-handled wooden or metal shovel used to load dough or pizza onto a hearth or baking stone.

Polenta: A coarse cornmeal used both as an ingredient and to dust under hearth loaves.

Poolish: A French-style pre-fermented sponge made with a small amount of commercial yeast. The ratio of flour to liquid varies, but the sponge is usually wet rather than firm.

Pre-ferment: Any pre-dough used as a portion of the finished dough to initiate fermentation. It contributes leavening and flavor to bread, allowing the dough to endure an extended fermentation, which brings out the most flavor.

Proofing: When referring to dough, *proofing* means the final rise before baking. When referring to yeast, it means hydrating it to wake it up and prove that it is active and alive (the water-yeast mixture will bubble after a few minutes if the yeast is alive).

Punching down: Also called *turning*, punching down is a short kneading that deflates the dough so that it can undergo another rising cycle.

Push: The ability of a dough to continue rising after a number of fermentation cycles. Some doughs, if overfermented or underleavened, run out of push, their yeast exhausted, while properly leavened doughs exhibit strong push all the way through the baking cycle.

Refresh: Feeding a starter with flour and water to keep it alive. Refreshment schedules vary according to the needs of the starter and are indicated in their respective formulas.

Retard: To slow down fermentation by cooling the dough, usually in a refrigerator. Yeast goes to sleep at 40°F, allowing a dough to be kept for up to three days before baking. Commercial bakeries have special retarders with low airflow to prevent the surface of doughs from drying out, making it possible to store them without covers. In a home refrigerator, the dough must be covered.

Rich dough: Dough that has been enriched with butter, sugar, and/or eggs. Brioche is a classic example.

Round: Can mean both the process of shaping a dough into a round shape or the finished shape itself.

Scaling: Weighing ingredients, and later, pieces of dough to precise sizes.

Score: To cut, dock, or slash a dough prior to baking in order to give it a special look and to control its expansion during the oven spring.

Semolina: Gritty flour made from hard durum wheat, used both as an ingredient and as a dusting flour on peels.

Sourdough: Any bread made from wild yeast, but especially those that exhibit complex sour flavors.

Sponge: A pre-ferment used to give flavor, added leavening, and structure to dough. There are many ways to make sponges.

Spritzer: A spray bottle used to mist loaves and oven walls with water in order to create steam.

Starch: The main ingredient in bread, derived from the endosperm of wheat or any grain. It is composed of complex carbohydrate molecules that gradually break down during fermentation to release their sugars. Bread is not fully baked until the starch gelatinizes.

Starter: A sponge or piece of pre-ferment made with either commercial or wild yeast. It is used as leavening in the finished dough and may be made by any number of methods.

Straight dough: Also called the *direct method,* in which dough is made without a sponge or pre-ferment, with all the ingredients added in one mixing cycle.

Tolerance: The ability of a dough to endure handling variations during the fermentation process. Some doughs exhibit a large margin for temperature and time variations while others are more temperamental.

Turning: See *punching down.*

Webbing: The cell structure of the crumb, including the hole pattern and gluten skeleton.

Whole grain: Any grain that is used in its whole state, including the bran and germ, regardless of the fineness of the milling.

Windowpane: A test to check if the gluten has set up. By slowly stretching the dough till it forms a translucent membrane, you can determine if the dough has been mixed long enough (see page 29).

Yeast: A single-celled fungus that may be commercially produced or captured in its wild state on fruit, grain, and in the air. There are more than 125 strains. The two of most interest to bakers are *Saccharomyces cerevisiae* (commercially produced and also used in beer) and *Saccharomyces exiguus* (wild). Yeast initiates fermentation of the grain, resulting in leavening and flavor.

2

FOUNDATIONAL BREADS:
BUILDING THE LOAF

PRE-FERMENTS

The baker's challenge is to evoke the grain's fullest potential. The method for this is fermentation, and yeast is the alchemical agent by which fermentation is induced. As a general rule, long, slow fermentation draws forth the fullest flavors and the best results from dough. However, it is possible to overferment, which leads to off flavors and structural problems in the finished loaf. Finding the balance point is the key to the art and craft of baking.

The best way to increase fermentation time without overfermenting is to build the bread in stages (the indirect method) rather than by making it in one step (the direct, or straight-dough method). There are many ways to do this, but they all fall under the pre-ferment umbrella.

A pre-ferment can be either a dough sponge or a piece of old dough. A sponge consists of yeast and water but has only part of the flour required for the final dough. Old dough can be a piece left from a previous batch or it can be made specifically for the new bread. Whichever form pre-ferment takes, it is the seed for the final dough, boosting both the leavening power and the flavor by the addition of pre-fermented grain. The beauty of this method is that the bread can be made with the minimum amount of yeast, extending the fermentation time, which in turn improves the flavor and structure. Pre-ferments are essential for attaining world-class results in many types of breads.

Pre-ferments made with wild yeast include barms, sourdough starters, and *levains* (see pages 69–79). Yeasted pre-ferments, made with commercial yeast, include *poolish* (named for Polish bakers who first developed this technique in Vienna, where many of the so-called French breads originated), the Italian *biga, the* French *pâte fermente,* and the American sponge and "old dough" methods. Each pre-ferment has its own proportion of flour, water, and yeast. (Salt, while necessary in the final dough for flavor and texture, is rarely used in sponges because sodium is a yeast inhibitor.)

The following formulas, developed specifically for this book, cover a full range of yeasted pre-ferments and are the foundation for many of the breads that follow.

MASTER FORMULA:

POOLISH-STYLE (SPONGE) PRE-FERMENT

A *poolish* sponge is made by combining yeast with a small amount of flour and a large amount of water. Most finished breads have about three parts flour to two parts liquid, but a sponge has a much higher percentage of liquid, which yields a batterlike dough. In this wet consistency the yeast ferments and multiplies more quickly and easily because there is less resistance from the dough. By the time the remaining ingredients are added to the sponge, a healthy amount of fermentation has already developed. Some breads do not need more yeast at this point, while others require a small additional amount to boost or "spike" the final fermentation. Either way, the dough has been jump-started by the sponge. The complex starches and pro-

teins get a head start on breaking down to simpler sugars, creating more flavor and better coloration in the end product.

When making whole-grain breads, use some or all of the whole grain in the sponge, as the early fermentation conditions the flour, making the gluten molecules more extensible. Yeast loves to feed on the nutrients in the bran and germ of whole grains.

This sponge, almost like a crepe batter, is much thinner than that used by most professional bakeries. It pushes the limits of the low-yeast, long-fermentation principles and is especially good for rustic breads and for pizza and *focaccia* doughs.

Make the formula one to three days ahead of time so it will be on hand when you are ready to make your dough. (It will keep for up to three days in the refrigerator.) If you want to make bread the same day you make the sponge, make the sponge at least five hours in advance.

The sponge will be active and clean tasting for up to three days if kept refrigerated. This means that if you make the sponge on day one, you can make bread dough on days two, three, or four. After that, the sponge begins to lose strength and develop off flavors from the dying yeast cells.

COMMENTARIES

❑ This formula makes a large amount of *poolish,* more than is called for in the bread formulas that follow. Because of the tiny amount of yeast, it is difficult to make the formula much smaller. You could cut all the ingredients in half and use ⅛ teaspoon instant yeast if you can prefer. I suggest, however, that you make the full batch and plan for a few days of baking, or freeze the extra sponge for another time.

❑ I prefer instant yeast because it is strong and reliable, but other types will work (see page 14). Whatever kind you use, you can add it directly to the sponge without dissolving it first.

❑ The amount of yeast is so small that weight measurements are unreliable. For the same reason, the baker's percentage for yeast is too small to calculate, and the total weight does not include the yeast.

❑ The sponge will expand in the bowl, but because it is so wet, it will not be able to hold a rise. Instead it will bubble, foam, and collapse. This is a sign that the sponge is active and ready to use. Using overnight retardation, you can put the sponge in the refrigerator before it collapses, which is okay, as it will continue to develop, very slowly, while it cools.

❑ If you want to make bread the same day, allow the sponge to ferment for 5 to 6 hours at room temperature. If it is a warm day and the sponge is growing more rapidly than expected, refrigerate it as soon as you see the foaming, before it rises and collapses, to prevent it from developing too quickly (in which case it could have off flavors). Whether refrigerating or not, always wait a minimum of 5 hours before using the *poolish,* or as is preferred, until the next day. This allows for flavor enhancements to take place from starch-sugar conversions.

❑ You can freeze unused *poolish* and save it for another time, if you do so just before or after refrigerating it on the first night. If you wait much longer, the added fermentation will make it less reliable coming from the freezer. Transfer the *poolish* from the freezer to the refrigerator 24 to 36 hours before you intend to use it so that it can defrost gradually. Take the *poolish* out of the refrigerator 1 hour before using it to take off the chill.

INGREDIENT	%
Unbleached flour or whole-wheat flour	100
Water	178
Yeast	N/A

MAKES JUST OVER 3 POUNDS

4 cups (18 ounces) unbleached bread flour (or whole-wheat flour if making whole-wheat bread)

4 cups cool water (65° to 70°F)

$1/4$ teaspoon instant yeast, or $1/3$ teaspoon active dry, or $3/4$ teaspoon fresh, crumbled yeast

=*Approximate Weight: 50 ounces (3 pounds, 2 ounces)*

1. Combine all the ingredients in a mixing bowl large enough to hold the batter after it has doubled in volume.

2. Beat or whisk for about 1 minute, until the batter is well mixed and quite smooth. (Any remaining small lumps will dissolve when the final dough is mixed, if not before.)

3. Cover the bowl with plastic wrap and leave it at room temperature for 3 to 5 hours, or till foamy and bubbly.

4. Refrigerate the *poolish,* well covered, overnight.

MASTER FORMULA:

BIGA-STYLE (FIRM) PRE-FERMENT

Biga sponges are usually firmer than *poolishes*. As with *poolish, biga* comes in a wide range of styles, depending on the baker or the village. Stiffer pre-ferments take longer to develop than wet sponges because the thicker dough offers more resistance. For the same reason, they are easier to control, which is an advantage in bakeries where much is going on or in homes where baking schedules are unpredictable.

This pre-ferment will be active for up to three days if kept refrigerated, which means that if you make the *biga* on day one, you can make bread dough on days two, three, and four. As with the *poolish*-style sponge, this formula yields more than many breads require. You may freeze unused *biga* for up to six months. (It is best to freeze it on day two, as it accumulates more alcohol on subsequent days and will not hold up as well in the freezer.)

COMMENTARIES

❑ I prefer instant yeast because it is strong and reliable, but other types will work (see page 14).

❑ Using cool water allows the dough to mix thoroughly before the friction of the kneading raises its temperature to the optimal range of 78° to 80°F.

❑ You can also use an electric mixer with a dough hook or a food processor with a metal or plastic blade for the first two steps. An electric mixer takes about the same amount of time as hand kneading; a food processor takes only a few seconds (see page 18 for guidelines).

❑ Every brand of flour has a slightly different absorption rate. Because this is only a pre-ferment, the amount of liquid is not as critical as in the final dough, where adjustments can be made. The most important thing is to have enough water to hydrate all the flour.

❑ Because this dough will ferment for a long time and will be mixed again, it does not have to be kneaded as fully as a final dough.

❑ The fermentation time may need to be adjusted according to the room temperature. On hot days (above 80°F) you can cut an hour off the time; on cold days (if the house temperature is below 62°F) you may need to add an hour. The goal, remember, is to fully ferment the dough and build up the yeast.

❑ Retarding the dough in the refrigerator helps develop even more flavor, while slowing down the yeast activity. It also allows you to begin making bread dough the next morning that can be ready for dinner that night. Pull the *biga* from the refrigerator 1 hour before using to take the chill off.

INGREDIENT	%
Unbleached bread flour	100
Water	62.5
Instant yeast	0.7
Fresh yeast	2

3¹/2 cups (16 ounces) unbleached
  bread flour

1 teaspoon instant yeast, 1¹/4 teaspoons
  active dry yeast, or 1 tablespoon fresh,
  crumbled yeast

1¹/4 cups cool water (65°to 70°F)

=*Approximate Weight: 26 ounces
(1 pound, 10 ounces)*

1. Combine all the ingredients in a mix-
    ing bowl. Stir with a wooden or metal
    spoon until the dough forms a ball.

2. Transfer to a lightly floured work sur-
    face and knead for about 5 minutes,
    until the flour is fully incorporated
    and the dough is smooth and tacky
    but not sticky. Add a little more flour
    or water if necessary to achieve this
    consistency.

3. Place the dough in a clean bowl large
    enough to accommodate doubling.
    Cover the bowl with plastic wrap or
    enclose it in a plastic bag, and allow
    the dough to rise at room temperature
    for about 3 to 5 hours, or till the
    dough increases in size at least
    1¹/2 times.

4. Use immediately or punch down,
    cover with plastic wrap (or put it back
    in the plastic bag), and retard in the
    refrigerator overnight.

MASTER FORMULA:
PÂTE FERMENTÉE (OLD DOUGH) PRE-FERMENT

Adding a portion of old dough to a new
batch is a popular way of combining the
straight (or direct) and pre-ferment techniques. In this hybrid method, perfected
by Professor Raymond Calvel in France
(see page 180), the pre-ferment contains
all of the basic ingredients of the final
dough, including salt.

One advantage of this approach is that
every time you make bread, you can hold
back a piece of dough for the next time,
eliminating the need to make a separate
pre-ferment. The piece can be kept refrigerated for up to three days or frozen for up
to three months. (I always have a piece in
my freezer.)

The *pâte fermentée,* a simplified *pain ordinaire* dough, adds both leavening and
character to the final dough. Professor
Calvel has proven that it noticeably improves flavor and color and increases the
size of French bread by about 10 percent.

The following master formula is best
for pre-ferment use only; a more complete
French bread formula is given on page 43,
using this pre-ferment as an ingredient.
Once you start making bread this way you
will not need to remake the *pâte fermentée.*
Simply cut off one-third of each batch of
dough and save it for the next time.

COMMENTARIES

❏ French number fifty-five flour, the classic baguette flour, is unlike anything available in the United States. American flour is strong and elastic, while number fifty-five is extensible and able to stretch out without springing back. Our bread flour has too much gluten for this purpose, and all-purpose flour does not have enough. Blending the two, as in this formula, creates a reasonably happy medium (you can also make this with all bread flour if you'd prefer not to blend). American specialty flour companies, including King Arthur and Giusto's, are milling new blends that approximate number fifty-five; see pages 199–200 for mail-order information.

❏ Every brand of flour has a slightly different absorption rate. Because this is only a pre-ferment, the amount of liquid it is not as critical as in the final dough, where adjustments can be made.

❏ You may use the pre-ferment on the day it is mixed, in fact immediately, but it will lack the full flavor and texture that develops during retardation. Pull it from the refrigerator 1 hour before using so that it can warm up slightly.

INGREDIENT	%
Unbleached all-purpose flour	50
Unbleached bread flour	50
Salt	2
Instant yeast	0.7
Water	62.5

MAKES ABOUT 1⁵/₈ POUNDS

1³/4 cups (8 ounces) unbleached all-purpose flour

1³/4 cups (8 ounces) unbleached bread flour

1¹/2 teaspoons (0.33 ounce) salt

1 teaspoon (0.11 ounce) instant yeast

1¹/4 cups cool water (65° to 70°F)

Vegetable oil cooking spray

=Approximate Weight: 26.44 ounces (1 pound, 10.44 ounces)

1. Combine the flours, salt, and yeast in a mixing bowl.

2. Add the water, and stir with a large wooden or metal spoon till the flour is gathered and the dough forms a ball.

3. Turn the dough out onto a lightly floured work surface and knead the dough vigorously for about 10 minutes, until it is soft and pliable, tacky but not sticky. Knead in extra flour or water (just a few drops at a time), if necessary, to achieve this consistency. The dough is fully kneaded when it passes the windowpane test (see page 29) and is between 77° and 80°F (neutral to the touch).

4. Place the dough in a clean bowl large enough to hold it when it has doubled in bulk, and mist the dough lightly with cooking spray. Cover the bowl with plastic wrap or enclose it in a plastic bag, and let the dough rise for about 90 minutes. It should double in size.

5. Knead the risen dough for 30 seconds, form it into a ball, and re-cover the bowl with plastic.

6. Place the bowl in the refrigerator and retard the pre-ferment overnight. It will be ready to use the next day.

TWO FRENCH BREAD VARIATIONS

BASIC FRENCH BREAD (PAIN ORDINAIRE)

Making a great loaf of French bread (or *pain ordinaire* as it is understatedly called in France) is both an art and a science, and is all embodied in the principle of slow rise. Every baker has his or her own approach to slow rise—the term has become ambiguous from so many applications—but the unifying principle is that the longer and slower the fermentation, the better the bread.

Food scientists, like Harold McGee (who wrote the classic *On Food and Cooking*) and Professor Raymond Calvel (see page 180), quantify the chemical changes that occur during the fermentation process and explain how to control them to produce a consistent supply of great bread, thus demystifying the slow rise. It really does comes down to chemistry, plus that intangible quality called *feel*.

Kitchen temperature, kneading method, internal dough temperature, relative humidity, and water-absorption capacity of the flour are among the many factors that contribute to the chemical chain reaction that occurs during the fermentation or rising periods. The fact that dough usually doubles in size after about ninety minutes is a neat consolidation of all the drama that is going on inside that lump of dough.

Most home bakers, though, don't care about monitoring and charting the chemical activity of their dough. They just want great bread and the sense of accomplishment that accompanies a good, well-made loaf. Making bread is like operating a computer. Every keystroke triggers numerous yes/no commands through the system but the only thing that I, typing away, really care about is if the letter comes up on the screen. Those who have deeper interest in how the keystroke turns into a letter make great computer programmers, just as bakers with a keen interest in dough chemistry make great technicians and teachers.

I knew very little of the chemistry when I made my first successful loaf in 1978. I was simply following Julia Child's meticulous directions for French bread. Looking through various bread books of the time, I noticed that almost all other recipes for French bread instructed the home baker to form the loaves after the first rise and bake them after the second, just as with sandwich bread. (The notion, I think, was that home cooks wanted to get things done quickly.) But oh, what a difference Julia Child's extra rise made in the finished product.

Armed simply with the concept of slow rise, I became a baking fool, making bread every chance I got. The following year I entered my French bread in a county fair and won $100 and a best-in-show ribbon. The year after that I entered a whole-wheat French bread, following the same simple steps, and won again. My baking career was launched.

Since that time, I have learned other ways to achieve that perfection of crust and color, the creaminess of the inner crumb, and the loveliness of the open bloom. And with access to great bread from local artisan bakeries and better information from more sophisticated bread books, more and more home bakers are discovering the possibilities of good, hearth-style French bread. *Vive le* slow rise!

The following master formulas include a basic French bread recipe, following the classic slow-rise principle, and an advanced method, similar to the technique developed by Professor Calvel, using pre-fermented dough. Both give great results. You will soon be hearing the sound of crust, and once you hear it, you will never be able to settle for less.

MASTER FORMULA:
FRENCH BREAD I

Bread tastes its absolute best at the moment when the crumb has completely cooled, and will hold this quality for about two hours. After that, the staling process begins its inexorable march. Chances are, though, that the bread will have been consumed by then.

COMMENTARIES

❏ For a discussion of classic baguette flour and mail-order alternatives, see page 39 and also page 199. You can use all bread flour if you'd prefer not to blend with all-purpose.

❏ Malted barley powder is a natural sugar that enhances the flavor of bread, lends color to the crust, and feeds the yeast. It is available at beer- and wine-making supply stores. Ask for diastatic malt, which means that the diastase enzymes are still active. These enzymes are like vitamin pills for the fermentation process if used in small quantities. (Nondiastatic malt, or malted barley in which the diastase enzymes have been cooked, is used in larger quantities as a flavoring agent in some bread recipes.) Brown sugar is an acceptable substitute.

❏ See pages 37 and 39 for a discussion of water absorption. Adjusting the flour and water is part of the fun and challenge of making bread. Let the dough dictate your needs, not the formula.

INGREDIENT	%
Unbleached all-purpose flour	50
Unbleached bread flour	50
Salt	2
Malt powder	0.5
Instant yeast	0.5
Water	66

3¹/₂ cups (16 ounces) unbleached
all-purpose flour

3¹/₂ cups (16 ounces) unbleached
bread flour

2¹/₂ teaspoons (0.66 ounce) salt

1 teaspoon (0.17 ounce) malt powder or
brown sugar

1¹/₂ teaspoons (0.17 ounce) instant yeast

2²/₃ cups cool water (65° to 70°F)

Vegetable oil cooking spray

=*Approximate Weight: 54 ounces
(3 pounds, 6 ounces)*

1. Combine the flours, salt, malt, and
   yeast in a mixing bowl.

2. Add the water, and stir with a large
   wooden or metal spoon till the flour is
   gathered and the dough forms a ball.

3. Turn the dough out onto a lightly
   floured work surface and knead vigorously for about 10 minutes, until the
   dough is soft and pliable, tacky but
   not sticky. Knead in extra flour or
   water (just a few drops at a time) if
   necessary to achieve this consistency.
   The dough is fully kneaded when it
   passes the windowpane test (see page
   29) and is between 77° and 80°F.

4. Place the dough in a large, clean bowl
   that will hold it when it has doubled
   in bulk. Mist the dough lightly with
   cooking spray. Cover the bowl (not the
   dough) with plastic wrap or enclose it
   in a plastic bag, and let it rise for

about 30 minutes. It should just begin swelling.

5. Knead the dough for 30 seconds, form
   it into a ball, and re-cover the bowl
   with plastic. Allow it to rise for 90
   minutes, or until doubled in size.

6. Scale, bench, and shape the dough
   into loaves or rolls as described on
   pages 19–23. Place them on pans or
   in baskets (see page 24). If using pans,
   line them with parchment paper and
   dust with cornmeal or semolina for
   texture; if using baskets, mist them
   with cooking spray and dust them
   with rice flour or bread flour to prevent sticking.

7. Lightly mist the top of the shaped
   dough with cooking spray to prevent
   sticking, and place the pans or baskets
   inside a large plastic bag. Let it rest
   for 15 minutes.

8. Place the shaped dough in the refrigerator overnight, making sure the bag
   is loose but closed to prevent drying.

9. The next day, remove the dough from
   the refrigerator but leave it in the
   bag. The dough should be 50 percent
   to 75 percent larger than when it
   went in. If so, let the dough sit out
   for 1 hour to take off the chill. If not
   fully risen, let it sit at room temperature for 2 or 3 hours, until it com-
   pletes its rise.

10. Prepare the oven for hearth baking as
    described on page 25, making sure to
    place the empty steam pan on a lower
    rack. Preheat the oven to 475°F (allow

about 35 minutes for it to heat fully).
Make sure your spritzer bottle is filled
with water.

11. Remove the pan of dough from the
plastic 15 minutes before baking, to
allow the surface of the dough to dry
slightly. Just before baking, score the
bread as described on page 24. Put
the loaves or rolls in the oven, either
on sheet pans or by peel directly on
the stone (page 25). Then pour 1 cup
of hot tap water into the empty
steam pan, quickly spritz the oven
walls and the bread with water, and
close the door.

12. After 2 minutes, quickly spray the
oven walls and the bread again. Repeat
in 1 minute. Then, lower the oven
temperature to 450°F.

13. Wait 10 minutes and check the bread.
(Check rolls after 5 minutes.) Rotate
the bread, front to back, if it seems to
be baking unevenly. (If baking on
more than one oven rack, rotate the
bread top to bottom as well.)

14. When the bread has developed a rich,
golden brown color—this will take
about 25 minutes for loaves and 15
minutes for rolls—turn off the oven
(or lower it to 350° if you plan to bake
again). Leave the bread in the oven an
additional 5 to 10 minutes, until it
seems on the verge of overbrowning.

15. Remove the bread to a cooling rack
and allow it to cool thoroughly before
eating, 60 to 90 minutes for loaves,
20 minutes for rolls.

MASTER FORMULA:

FRENCH BREAD II (WITH PÂTE FERMENTÉE)

Using pre-fermented dough allows you to
achieve a great loaf without retarding.
There is also the advantage of having a finished loaf on the same day. However, the
long, slow rise of overnight retarding produces a more spectacular loaf, richer in
color with a dramatic blistered crust.

COMMENTARIES

❑ If you use all the dough, you can make four
1-pound baguettes. However, by saving a piece
as *pâte fermentée* for future doughs, you will still
have enough to make three loaves.

❑ See page 41 for a discussion of malted barley
powder. It is available as diastatic malt at beer-
and wine-making supply stores. Brown sugar is
an acceptable substitute, though malt is superior because it provides enzymes.

❑ If you do not have a scale, 16 ounces of pre-
ferment should fill a 4-cup measure when gently pressed into it. A little more or less will not
adversely affect the finished bread.

❑ To make this bread by hand, combine all the
ingredients in a mixing bowl, and follow steps
1, 2, and 3 in the formula for French Bread I on
page 42.

INGREDIENT	%
Unbleached all-purpose flour	50
Unbleached bread flour	50
Malt powder	0.5
Instant yeast	0.4
Water	66
Salt	2
Pre-fermented dough	50

3¹/2 cups (16 ounces) unbleached
all-purpose flour

3¹/2 cups (16 ounces) unbleached bread
flour (or use all bread flour)

1 teaspoon (0.17 ounce) malt powder or
brown sugar

1¹/4 teaspoon (0.14 ounce) instant yeast

2²/3 cups cool water (65°to 70°F)

2¹/2 teaspoons (0.66 ounce) salt

4 cups (16 ounces) pre-fermented dough
(*pâte fermentée,* page 38)

Vegetable oil cooking spray

=*Approximate Weight: 70 ounces
(4 pounds, 6 ounces)*

1. In the bowl of an electric mixer, com-
    bine the flour, malt, yeast, and water.
    Using the dough-hook attachment,
    mix on low speed for 4 minutes, or till
    a coarse dough has formed. Rest the
    dough for 20 minutes.

2. Cut the *pâte fermentée* into smaller
    pieces. Add the salt and the *pâte fermen-
    tée,* 1 piece at a time, with the mixer
    running on low speed. Mix for 4 to 6
    minutes, or till the dough is soft and
    pliable, tacky but not sticky. Mix in
    extra flour or water (just a few drops at
    a time) if necessary to achieve this con-
    sistency. The dough is ready when it
    passes the windowpane test (see page
    29) and is between 77° and 80°F (neu-
    tral to the touch). If your machine is
    not big enough to handle a dough this
    large, complete the kneading by hand.

3. Place the dough in a bowl large
    enough to allow it to double in size.
    Mist the dough lightly with cooking
    spray. Cover the bowl (not the dough)
    with plastic wrap, or enclose it in a
    plastic bag, and let the dough rise for
    about 30 minutes. It should just be-
    gin to swell.

4. Turn the dough out onto a lightly
    floured surface and knead by hand for
    a few seconds.

5. Cut off 1 pound of the dough for a
    future *pâte fermentée,* if you desire. Put
    it in a covered bowl or in a plastic bag
    and refrigerate or freeze it.

6. Shape the remaining dough into a ball
    and put it back in the bowl. Mist the
    dough lightly with cooking spray.
    Cover the bowl with plastic wrap or
    enclose it in a plastic bag, and let it
    rise for 90 minutes or until doubled.

7. Scale, bench, and shape the dough into
    loaves or rolls as described on pages
    19–23. Place them on sheet pans or in
    baskets (see page 24).If using pans,
    line them with parchment paper and
    dust with cornmeal or semolina for
    texture; if using baskets, mist them
    with cooking spray and dust them
    with rice flour or bread flour to pre-
    vent sticking.

8. Lightly mist the top of the shaped dough with cooking spray to prevent sticking, and enclose the pans or baskets inside a large plastic bag. Let the dough rise for 15 minutes and then retard overnight in the refrigerator as directed in steps 8 and 9 of French Bread I on page 42.

9. Prepare the oven for hearth baking as described on page 25, making sure to place the empty steam pan on a lower rack. Preheat the oven to 475°F (allow about 35 minutes for it to heat fully). Make sure your spritzer bottle is filled with water.

10. Remove the pan of dough from the plastic 15 minutes before baking, to allow the surface of the dough to dry slightly. Just before baking, score the bread as described on page 24. Fill a measuring cup with 1 cup of hot tap water. Put the loaves or rolls in the oven, either on sheet pans or by peel directly on the stone (page 25). Then pour the hot water into the empty steam pan, quickly spritz the oven walls and the bread, and close the door.

11. After 2 minutes, quickly spray the oven walls and the bread again. Repeat in 1 minute. Then, lower the oven temperature to 450°.

12. Wait 10 minutes and check the bread (check rolls after 5 minutes). Rotate the bread, front to back, if it seems to be baking unevenly. (If baking on more than one oven rack, rotate the bread top to bottom as well.)

13. When the bread has developed a rich, golden-brown color—about 25 minutes for loaves, 15 minutes for rolls— turn off the oven (or lower it to 350°F if you plan to bake again). Leave the bread in the oven an additional 5 to 10 minutes, until it seems on the verge of overbrowning.

14. Remove the bread to a cooling rack and allow it to cool thoroughly before eating: 60 to 90 minutes for loaves, 20 minutes for rolls. The bread will taste best if eaten within 2 hours of cooling.

THE AUTOLYSE

Using a 20-minute rest period when mixing dough with a machine minimizes mixing time, thus decreasing oxidation. Oxidation, caused by beating air into the dough, bleaches the flour, nullifying the positive flavor and aroma of the beta-carotene in the unbleached flour. This rest period is called the *autolyse*. While the dough rests, the protein fragments, glutenin and gliadin, continue to bond into gluten molecules, giving the dough its necessary structure.

The salt is added after the autolyse to allow the dough to hydrate more quickly (salt slows down hydration as well as fermentation). The pre-fermented dough is also added after the autolyse because it is already mixed and developed. You want it to have only enough additional mixing to incorporate it fully into the final dough.

RUSTIC BREADS

Ever since bagels hit the mainstream, prognosticators have been looking for the next big bread bust-out. World-class bread is clearly the general category, but which among the many great breads will capture the public's fancy? My guess is it will be the rustic-style breads, the best known of which is *ciabatta* (pronounced cha-BAH-tah). Because *ciabatta*-type breads are made from very wet doughs, they are difficult to mass-produce, but some commercial machines already exist and more technological advances are inevitable. My hope is that as volume bakers begin to accept the inescapable reality that slow-rise, long-fermentation processes create better, more marketable bread, the overall standard will continue to rise.

One of the best loaves of bread I ever tasted was at the 1996 Grainaissance Faire in Glen Ellen, California. The famous oven crafter Alan Scott (see page 100) had built a wood-fired brick oven for the event, a celebration of microbreweries and artisan bakeries. Peter Conn, the talented executive baker for the Il Fornaio restaurant group, made up a number of *ciabatta* loaves and focaccia and baked them in Alan's brick oven. The long wait for the wood to burn down to coals, for the baker to sweep out the ashes, and for the oven to cool down to a usable temperature added extra fermentation time to the already long-rising dough. The first batch of bread burned to cinders in a matter of minutes, as the oven was still over 800°F. An hour later, with the oven still a very hot 600°F, Peter

tried again. Both the *ciabatta* and focaccia picked up the smoky flavor of the residual madrone and oak ashes, sprung about 25 percent in size, and tasted so good that I couldn't stop eating them. I forgot about the great microbrews on display and kept returning to the oven for another taste. The bread was simply astounding. Peter finally gave me a whole loaf to take home, which barely survived the drive. I saved just enough for my wife to taste and she, too, was smitten. The bread was as good as it gets, and I was inspired to spend the next two months perfecting my own rustic bread technique.

Ciabatta means "slipper," so named because the loaf reminded someone from the Lake Como region of Italy of, well, a slipper. It looks like a circus clown's slipper to me, a floppy, oversized shoe. There is no other bread quite like it. Wet, slack dough, fermented with just a hint of yeast for long periods, produces amorphous loaves with big holes in the webbing. The crumb has a shiny, gelatinous appearance, with spider-web-like strands of gluten barely holding the loaf together. Sometimes the strands stretch beyond their ability to hold and then snap, leaving a big tunnel-like hole, or "room." (Some old-timers call it "the room where the baker sleeps.")

The big, open crumb exposes the gluten/protein to deep roasting, at the same time fully gelatinizing the starches. This gives the webbing its shiny, almost radiant aspect. The wide-open crumb also means that rustic breads stale quickly. Like most breads, they are best eaten within one or two hours of being removed from the oven, when they have completely cooled but still retain the buttery, toasty, nutty texture of the baked grain.

The same qualities—minimal yeast, maximum hydration (lots of water!), long fermentation, an inability to hold a defined shape (slack dough), big oven spring, large holes and a spiderweb crumb with a rich, deep-roasted flavor showcasing the natural sweetness of the wheat grain characterize *ciabatta's* cousins, *pugliese, francese, stirato,* and *rustico.*

Mastering these challenging doughs has far-reaching applications. With a few additional ingredients rustic doughs form the basis of spectacular focaccia and pizza, serve as a wonderful showcase for shiitake and wild mushrooms, and make an excellent low-fat substitute for buttery croissants and Danish pastry. Rustic breads will also really impress your friends and family, converting those few stragglers who have not yet joined the bread revolution.

The following formulas for *ciabatta* and other yeast-leavened rustic variations produce sticky doughs that require care and a little practice to master but are well worth the effort. Feel free to improvise on them, making substitutions where you think they will produce the qualities you seek. Milk, for instance, will soften or tenderize the crumb, as will oil or butter. My preference is always for the fewest conditioners I can get away with, so these formulas are about as simple as doughs of this style get. Where I substitute complexity is in the extralong fermentation, which adds qualities no conditioners can produce.

CIABATTA (SLIPPER BREAD)

Overnight retardation of the dough is crucial to the success of this bread. You need to plan several days ahead: day one for making the sponge, day two for mixing the bread dough, day three for shaping and possibly baking, and day four for baking any remaining loaves. A loaf can even be held over for baking on day five.

COMMENTARIES

❏ Unbleached flour is more flavorful than bleached (see page 13). This bread needs the strongest flour you can find. Look for one that specifies "high gluten."

❏ Make and refrigerate the pre-ferment the day before baking. Measure it and let it sit out for an hour before using to take the chill off.

❏ Because this dough is so wet, it works best to initially mix it with a paddle attachment, then switch to the dough hook. The next best choice would be to mix the dough in a food processor for 2 minutes. (See page 18.) If you choose to mix the dough by hand, it will take about 12 to 15 minutes of vigorous beating with a strong spoon to develop and stretch the gluten.

❏ It is amazing how well it works to dip your hands in water when working with wet dough. The dough just slides off. The more traditional method of dipping your hands in flour, on the other hand, gets you pretty gunked up after awhile. Either way, though, you will have to keep wiping your hands between stages, so have a wet towel handy.

❏ The extra cup of water added to the steam pan before baking extends the moisture time, helps to promote expansion, and gives the bread a shiny crust.

❏ Do not succumb to the temptation of eating the bread while it is still hot. You will taste mostly heat and will miss the subtle nuances of the grain. The flavor will be at its peak the moment the bread is completely cool.

INGREDIENT	%
Unbleached bread flour	100
Malt powder	1
Salt	2.8
Instant yeast	N/A
Water	44.5
Poolish-style sponge	67

MAKES 4 LOAVES

6 cups (27 ounces) unbleached bread flour

1¼ teaspoons (0.25 ounce) malt powder or brown sugar

3 teaspoons (0.75 ounce) salt

¼ teaspoon (0.02 ounce) instant yeast

1½ cups cool water (65° to 70°F)

2¼ cups (18 ounces) *poolish*-style sponge (page 35)

Vegetable oil cooking spray

=Approximate Weight: 58 ounces (3 pounds, 10 ounces)

1. Combine the flour, malt, salt, yeast, water, and *poolish* in the bowl of an electric mixer with a paddle attachment.

2. Mix on low speed for 1 minute, then on medium speed for 5 minutes. The dough will be sticky. Some will be pressed against the bowl and some bunched around the paddle. Dip a rubber spatula in water and scrape all the dough down into the bowl. Switch to the dough hook for another 7 minutes on medium speed. The dough will be very wet and stretchy. If not, add a few drops of water, as needed.

3. With a wet spatula, scrape down all the dough, cover the bowl with plastic wrap, and let the dough rise for 3 hours at room temperature. It will rise slowly, almost imperceptibly. Refrigerate it, covered tightly, overnight.

4. When you are ready to prepare the loaves the next day (or up to 2 days later), set out 3 sheet pans, parchment paper, cooking spray, a pastry cutter or knife, a bowl of cold water, a damp towel for wiping your hands, and semolina or bread flour for dusting. (I prefer the grittier semolina because it doesn't cake on the bottoms of the loaves.)

5. Invert the pans, cover the bottoms with parchment (cut it to fit if necessary), and mist the parchment with cooking spray. Liberally sprinkle the parchment with semolina and your work surface with flour.

6. Dip your hands into the water and transfer the dough to the work surface. Liberally sprinkle more flour over its surface. Dip a pastry cutter or knife into the water and cut the dough into 3 equal pieces. Flour your hands and lift each of the pieces, pulling them to almost the width of a sheet pan. When you lay them down they may shrink in a little but should

retain an oblong shape. (Another way to do this is to gently fold the flour-dusted pieces into thirds—a letter-fold—with well-floured hands. The dusting flour streaking through the loaves becomes part of the texture of the finished loaves, a common look with rustic breads.)

7. With either floured or wet hands, transfer 1 piece to the first sheet pan, gently pulling it to the desired length. Repeat with the other pieces, placing them on separate sheet pans. Lightly dimple each piece all over with moistened fingers, pressing gently to break up any air pockets.

8. Mist the tops of the loaves with cooking spray. Enclose each pan inside a plastic bag, and let the dough rise for about 4 hours at room temperature. The loaves should swell noticeably, as if ready to burst at the seams, nearly doubling in size. You may then bake the loaves. (If refrigerating them overnight, put them in the refrigerator after just 1 hour.)

9. Prepare the oven for hearth baking as described on page 25, making sure to put an empty steam pan on the bottom rack. Preheat the oven to 500°F.

10. Carefully slide the pans out of the bags, slowly peeling the bag off if it has settled on the dough. Allow the dough to warm to room temperature while the oven is preheating (it takes at least 30 minutes for most ovens to reach 500°F). Lightly dimple any noticeable air pockets (or pop them with a toothpick).

11. If baking on a stone, slide the dough, parchment and all, from the back of the sheet pan directly onto the stone, or carefully lift the parchment, lay the dough on a lightly floured peel, and transfer the dough to the stone. If not using a stone, simply place the sheet pan in the oven. Do not attempt to score this bread.

12. Spritz the bread and the oven walls with water, and pour 2 cups of hot water into the empty pan. Shut the oven door, wait 2 minutes, and spritz the oven walls again.

13. After 5 minutes, reduce the oven heat to 450°F. Bake for about 30 more minutes, or till the crust is a deep, rich brown and feels very crisp.

14. Turn off the oven and open the oven door, but leave the bread in for an additional 5 to 10 minutes. The goal is to bake it as long as possible without burning, so that the crust sugars deeply caramelize and the interior crumb develops a nutty flavor. The bread is done when the internal temperature of the loaves reaches 205° to 210°F, and the loaf feels light and airy, almost hollow, when lifted off the paper (the bread will soften as it cools).

15. Remove the parchment from the bottom of the bread and let it cool on a rack for at least 1 hour before eating.

MASTER FORMULA:
MUSHROOM CIABATTA

This is a challenging bread to make, but done properly, it is one of the most remarkable you will ever taste. This formula is a variation of a bread introduced by Carol Field; it applies slow-rise principles to a recipe in her wonderful book, *The Italian Baker.* You need to make the pre-ferment the day before. The garlic and mushrooms have a weakening effect on the gluten, so it is best to bake the bread the same day you make the dough.

COMMENTARIES

❏ Because this dough is so wet, it works best to mix it initially with a paddle attachment, and then switch to the dough hook. The next best choice would be to mix the dough in a food processor for 2 minutes. (See page 18.) To mix the dough by hand takes about 12 to 15 minutes of vigorous beating with a strong spoon to develop and stretch the gluten.

❏ The long primary fermentation is due to the small amount of yeast in the dough. The longer it develops, the better the bread will be.

❏ Stretching the dough one last time before the final rise extends the hole structure and gives the loaf more of a rustic bread look.

❏ The extra cup of water extends the moisture time and helps to give the bread a shiny crust.

❏ Rustic breads are so inherently moist that any additional oven time you can buy helps bake them more deeply and keeps the crust from softening too much.

❏ The bread continues to cook for quite a while after it comes out of the oven, and the mushroom and garlic flavors permeate the dough as it cools. Like other breads, this one tastes best when completely cool.

INGREDIENT	%
Unbleached bread flour	100
Biga-style pre-ferment	50
Fresh mushrooms	50
Dried mushrooms	N/A
Olive oil	7.5
Garlic	1
Salt	4
Instant yeast	0.4
Water (approx.)	80

MAKES 3 LOAVES

2 cups (8 ounces) *biga*-style pre-ferment (page 37)

6 dried porcini or dried shiitake mushrooms

2 cups simmering water

2 tablespoons plus 1 teaspoon (1.2 ounces) olive oil

2 cups (8 ounces) sliced fresh brown crimini or shiitake mushrooms

1 teaspoon (0.17 ounce) minced fresh garlic

3 1/2 cups (16 ounces) unbleached bread flour

2 1/2 teaspoons (0.66 ounce) salt

1/2 teaspoon (0.06 ounce) instant yeast

Vegetable oil cooking spray

> =*Approximate Weight: 50 ounces (3 pounds, 2 ounces)*

1. Measure the refrigerated *biga* and let it sit out for 1 hour before using, to take the chill off. Cut it into small pieces.

2. Soak the dried mushrooms in the hot water for 1 hour. Drain them well, saving all the water, and chop them into bite-size pieces. Strain the water to remove any grit and set it aside to cool to room temperature.

3. Heat 2 tablespoons of the oil in a skillet over medium heat. Sauté the mushrooms and garlic until the mushrooms give up their juices and begin to brown on the edges. Take care not to burn the garlic.

4. Drain the mushrooms and garlic completely, straining the juices into the reserved mushroom water.

5. In the bowl of an electric mixer with a paddle attachment, combine the flour, salt, yeast, *biga,* and enough of the mushroom water to make a soft, sticky dough. (You will probably not need all of it.)

6. Mix on slow speed for 1 minute, then on medium for 10 minutes. The dough should be very sticky but should not stick to the sides of the mixing bowl, only to the bottom. (This is called "cleaning the bowl.") Add the rehydrated dried mushrooms (but not the fresh mushrooms) and mix for 2 minutes more. Dribble the remaining teaspoon of olive oil down the side of the bowl during the final seconds of mixing to coat the dough and make it easier to remove later. Cover the bowl with plastic wrap and let the dough rise at room temperature for about 3 hours, until it swells noticeably. (The amount of expansion may vary as this is a slow-moving dough.)

7. Line 3 inverted sheet pans with parchment paper, mist the parchment with cooking spray, and sprinkle it with semolina or flour. Flour your work surface and hands generously and have more flour ready; the dough is sticky, and you will need to reflour your hands often.

8. Turn out the dough onto the work surface and toss it in the flour to coat it. Divide it into 3 equal pieces.

9. Gently pull each piece into a rectangle about 12 inches long. Spread one third of the sautéed mushroom mixture on each rectangle and press it into the dough.

10. Roll up each piece of dough jelly-roll fashion, then turn it and roll it in the other direction, forming a ball. Seal the edges to make as smooth a ball, or *boule,* as possible.

11. Place the dough balls on the prepared pans, mist them with cooking spray, and dust them with more flour. Enclose the pans in plastic bags, and let the doughs relax for 20 minutes.

12. Remove the pans from the plastic bags. Flour your hands again, and gently pull each dough ball into a rectangle about 12 inches long. Mist and flour the dough again, and return the pans with dough to the plastic bags and re-seal. Let them rise for 2 to 3 hours, till the loaves are plump and seemingly bursting at the seams. Like other rustic loaves, these breads are not scored prior to baking.

13. Prepare the oven for hearth baking as described on page 25, making sure to put an empty steam pan on the bottom rack. Preheat the oven to 500°F.

14. Slide as many loaves as will comfortably fit onto the baking stone, keeping in mind that they will rise about 25 percent more while baking. If you don't have a stone, place the sheet pan directly into the oven.

15. Spritz the bread and the oven walls with water and pour 2 cups of hot water into the empty pan. Close the oven door. After 2 minutes, spritz the loaves again.

16. After 10 minutes, reduce the oven heat to 425°F. Bake for about 30 minutes more, rotating the pan front to back after 15 minutes to ensure even browning.

17. When the loaves are golden brown, turn off the oven and open the oven door, but leave the bread in for an additional 5 to 10 minutes, to finish off the interior. (If you plan to bake a second batch, just turn the oven down to 350°F.)

18. Remove the parchment from the bottom of the bread and let the bread cool on a rack for at least 1 hour before eating.

UNIVERSAL RUSTIC BREAD

Pugliese, francese, stirato, rustico, ciabatta, stretch bread: these shiny, big-holed loaves are especially great for picnics. There are many names for these rustic breads and many ways to make them. The following formula builds the loaves in stages that, in turn, bring forth qualities not attainable otherwise. While not conforming to the style of any specific rustic bread, this formula incorporates the most extensive fermentation technique, and so is true to the spirit of rustic bread, by whatever name you call it.

COMMENTARIES

❑ For a sourdough version of this formula, substitute an equal amount of firm starter made from barm (page 72).

❑ I use milk in this formula because milk softens the crumb and promotes browning. I prefer buttermilk (see page 14), but you can use low-fat, nonfat, regular milk, or even yogurt. If you prefer your bread dairy free, substitute water.

❑ Olive oil also tenderizes the crumb. You can omit it, however, if you prefer to keep the bread lower in fat.

❑ Because this dough is so wet, it works best to mix it first with a paddle attachment, then with the dough hook. The next best choice would be to mix the dough in a food processor for 2 minutes. (See page 18.) If you choose to mix the dough by hand, it will take about 12 to 15 minutes of vigorous beating with a strong spoon to develop and stretch the gluten.

INGREDIENT	%
Unbleached bread flour	100
Biga-style pre-ferment	100
Sugar	3
Salt	3
Instant yeast	0.37
Milk	25
Olive oil	5.25
Water	50

MAKES 3 LOAVES

4 cups (16 ounces) *biga*-style pre-ferment (page 37)

3^1/$_2$ cups (16 ounces) unbleached bread flour

1 tablespoon (0.5 ounce) sugar

2 teaspoons (0.5 ounce) salt

^{1}/$_2$ teaspoon (0.06 ounce) instant yeast

^{1}/$_2$ cup (4 ounces) milk, at room temperature

2 tablespoons (1 ounce) olive oil

1 cup cool water (65° to 70°F)

Vegetable oil cooking spray

=Approximate Weight: 46 ounces (2 pounds, 14 ounces)

1. Make the *biga* the day before baking. Measure it and let it sit out for an hour before using, to take the chill off. Cut it into small pieces. Combine it with all the other ingredients in the bowl of an electric mixer with a paddle attachment.

2. Mix on slow speed for 1 minute and then switch to the dough hook and continue mixing on medium for 8 minutes. You may have to stop once or twice to scrape the dough down into the bowl. The dough will be batterlike and very sticky. Cover the bowl with plastic wrap and allow the dough to rise at room temperature for 4 hours, until it swells visibly, to about 1^1/$_2$ times its original size.

3. The dough will have stiffened somewhat. Scrape it onto a heavily floured counter, flour your hands, and roll the dough in the flour to coat it.

4. Divide the dough into 3 equal pieces and gently round each piece into a loose ball. Leaving the pieces on the counter, mist the tops with cooking spray, dust with flour, and loosely cover with a plastic bag or plastic wrap. Let the dough rise at room temperature for 1 hour.

5. Invert 3 sheet pans, cover them with parchment paper, and mist the parchment with cooking spray. Sprinkle the parchment with semolina or flour.

6. Sprinkle the dough with more flour, and with floured hands, gently stretch the pieces into rectangles 8 to 12 inches long. Take care not to squeeze them too hard, which will de-gas them; you want to keep the holes that are beginning to form for the characteristic rustic look. Transfer the dough to the sheet pans.

7. Dip your hands in cold water and gently dimple the loaves to break up any large air pockets. (If left, these will turn into tunnels when the bread is baked.) Do not flatten the bread; press gently so the loaf retains its shape.

8. Again, mist the tops with pan spray and dust with flour. Seal the pans of dough in large plastic bags and let them proof at room temperature for 2 hours or more, until the loaves are at least double their original size (They will spread out more than up.)

9. Prepare the oven for hearth baking 40 minutes before baking, as described on page 25, making sure to place the empty steam pan on a lower rack. Preheat the oven to 500°F.

10. Do not score the loaves, but pop any large surface bubbles with a razor or toothpick. Slide the loaves, parchment and all, onto the baking stone. Or place the sheet pans directly in the oven if you do not have a stone.

11. Spritz the loaves and the oven walls with water and pour 2 cups of hot water into the steam pan. Close the oven door. After 2 minutes, spritz the oven again. After 5 minutes, reduce the heat to 425°F.

12. Bake for about 30 minutes, or till the loaves are golden brown, the crust is hard, and the internal temperature is 205°F.

13. Turn the oven off, open the door, and leave the bread in the oven for about 10 additional minutes, until it seems that the loaves just cannot go a minute longer without burning. You will be rewarded with a shiny, creamy crumb.

14. Remove to a cooling rack, peeling off the parchment as you do. Cool for 1 hour before eating.

SWEET RUSTIC BREAD

I love croissants and other *viennoisserie*-style breakfast breads, but I do not like filling my already portly frame with so much butter (well, I like it at the time, but not when I have to spend extra hours at the gym working it off). Sweet rustic bread provides the comfort and satisfaction of rich breads without the fat.

The inspiration for this bread comes from the wonderful New York City bakery Ecce Panis, where they make a bread called sweet *fougasse.* I have only been in Ecce Panis once, but it was a memorable visit. The breads there were simply stunning. *Fougasse* is usually a plain or herbed yeasted flatbread in the shape of a ladder or a tree, but the sweet *fougasse* I had at Ecce Panis was wedge-shaped, without the customary slits and lattice patterns. It was dusted with powdered sugar and had the delicate texture and crumb of *ciabatta* or *pugliese,* with a creamy webbing that was nearly transparent. It was every bit as satisfying as a croissant. It has been so long since my inspirational visit to Ecce Panis that I'm not sure how much my bread resembles theirs, but I do know you will find it immensely satisfying.

Because this bread is a little sweeter than regular rustic bread, it is ideal for breakfast or snacking. You can bake the bread without overnighting it, but the results will not be quite as good. You may also hold unbaked doughs in the refrigerator for two or three days, making it possible to have freshly baked loaves each day. You may think that six to eight loaves are a lot to make at once, but they do make great gifts for your neighbors. You can, of course, cut the formula in half.

COMMENTARIES

❏ Because this dough is so wet, it works best to initially mix it with a paddle attachment, then switch to the dough hook. The next best choice would be to mix the dough in a food processor for 2 minutes. (See page 18.) If you choose to mix the dough by hand, it will take about 12 to 15 minutes of vigorous beating with a strong spoon to develop and stretch the gluten.

❏ Turning—briefly kneading, as in step 4—stiffens the dough further. The rest period allows for additional flavor and structure development.

❏ The most common error made with rustic doughs is to bake them before they reach the bursting stage (step 8), but this is the key to a fully opened crumb.

INGREDIENT	%
Unbleached bread flour	100
Poolish-style sponge	79
Granulated sugar	12
Salt	2.5
Instant yeast	0.3
Olive oil	5
Water	39.5
Confectioners' sugar	N/A

2 cups (16 ounces) *poolish*-style sponge (page 35)

4$^{1}/_{2}$ cups (20$^{1}/_{4}$ ounces) unbleached bread flour

5 tablespoons (2.5 ounces) granulated sugar

2 teaspoons (0.5 ounce) salt

$^{1}/_{2}$ teaspoon (0.06 ounce) instant yeast

2 tablespoons (1 ounce) olive oil

1 cup cool water (65° to 70°F)

Confectioners' sugar for dusting

Vegetable oil cooking spray

=*Approximate Weight: 49 ounces (3 pounds, 1 ounce)*

1. Measure the refrigerated *poolish* and let it sit out for an hour before using, to take the chill off.

2. Combine all the ingredients in a mixer with a paddle attachment.

3. Mix on slow speed for 1 minute and then switch to the dough hook and mix on medium for 8 minutes. You may have to stop once or twice to scrape the dough down into the bowl. The dough will be batterlike and very sticky. Cover the bowl with plastic wrap and let the dough rise at room temperature for about 3 hours, until it swells, increasing in size about 1$^{1}/_{2}$ times.

4. The dough will have stiffened somewhat. Scrape it onto a heavily floured counter, flour your hands, and roll the dough in the flour to coat it, kneading

gently for a few seconds. Round it into a loose ball, and dust it with more flour. Cover the ball of dough loosely with a plastic bag or plastic wrap, and let it rise at room temperature for 1 hour.

5. Invert 3 sheet pans, cover them with parchment paper, and mist the parchment with cooking spray. Sprinkle the parchment with semolina or flour.

6. Flour your hands and dust the dough again with flour, folding and kneading it for a few seconds. Gently pat the dough into a thick disk about 6 inches in diameter, and cut it into 6 to 8 wedges with a knife or pastry blade (for smaller breads, cut it into more wedges). Dip the blade in cold water between each cut to allow it to slide through the dough without sticking.

7. Keeping your hands floured, transfer the wedges to the prepared pans. Do not stretch them, and make sure there is plenty of space between the pieces. Mist the tops of the wedges with cooking spray, dust with flour, and loosely cover or enclose them in a plastic bag. Let the dough proof at room temperature for 2 hours, until the pieces increase to about $1^{1}/_{2}$ times their original size. Refrigerate them overnight.

8. Remove the pans from the refrigerator 2 hours before you plan to bake, or until practically bursting (about double their original size). Prepare the oven for hearth baking 40 minutes before baking, as described on page 25, making sure to put an empty steam pan on the bottom rack. Preheat the oven to 475°F.

9. Do not score the loaves. Slide them directly onto the baking stone, parchment and all, or cut the parchment between the doughs with scissors and transfer the loaves one at a time, still on the parchment, to a peel and slide them onto the baking stone.

10. Spritz the loaves and the oven walls with water, and pour 2 cups of hot water into the steam pan. Close the oven door. After 2 minutes, spritz the oven again. After 5 minutes, reduce the heat to 425°F.

11. Bake the loaves for about 20 more minutes, rotating the breads front to back, when halfway through, for even baking.

12. When the loaves are golden brown and register 205° to 210°F on a probe thermometer, transfer them to a cooling rack.

13. Fill a small strainer with confectioners' sugar. Mist the tops of the hot loaves with cooking spray. Holding the strainer just above the breads, tap the side of it, sifting a dusting of the sugar onto the oiled tops. Let them cool for 40 minutes before eating; the crust will soften considerably as it does.

YEASTED BAGELS

Bagels are the fastest growing bread product in America. Originally an ethnic bread associated with Jewish immigrants from Poland and Russia, the bagel is now about as mainstream as white sandwich bread. The distinctive aspect of a bagel is the chewy, shiny crust and tight, springy crumb, achieved by poaching the dough in simmering water for a minute or two before baking it in a hot oven.

For many years, commercial bagels were hand formed by rolling out pieces of dough into 6-inch ropes, looping them into a donutlike shapes, and pinching the ends to close the circles. The hand labor was, as you might imagine, the most costly part of the process. In the late 1950s, Harold Atwood invented the first bagel machine, laying the foundation for today's bagel boom. At least five companies now make bagel machines, some of them capable of forming 20,000 bagels per hour! Thousands of bagel machines are sold each year, and bagel shops seem to be opening on every corner.

Another manufacturing breakthrough was the development of steam-injected rack ovens to replace kettle boiling. These ovens greatly reduce production costs by eliminating a time-consuming step and are probably the key to the explosive growth of the industry. Many bagel makers, however, believe that unless the dough is poached it should not be called a bagel, but others insist that steaming has an equivalent effect. Some retail bagel shops proudly display their kettles where customers can see them, while other shops receive racks of frozen, unbaked bagels from a central commissary for baking on-site in steam-injected rack ovens. Amazingly, at least to those of us who grew up on authentically kettled bagels, steamed bagels are now more popular, probably because they are softer and easier to chew.

For people like me who grew up with smoked salmon (lox), whitefish, sturgeon, and kippers, the bagel has an iconic place in the taste-memory hall of fame. In our family, the Sunday brunch ritual was built around a platter of beautifully displayed fish, sliced tomatoes, onions, and lemon wedges—with a dish of cream cheese and a plate of warmed bagels on the side. My parents were always pleased to find another source of lox. "This is the best yet, not as salty as so-and-so's, and the belly lox is even better than the Nova Scotia." I loved going to the City Line Bagel Shop in Overbrook, Pennsylvania, an early prototype of the stores now sweeping the country. Last year I drove by and was pleased to see that it is still there, an independent bakery holding its own against the franchises.

MASTER FORMULA:
YEASTED BAGELS

Bagel dough is simply a variation of lean French bread, made with little or no fat or dairy products, a touch of sweetness, and less fermentation. It is much stiffer than hearth bread dough, which slows down the rise and creates the characteristic denser crumb. There is no question that boiling, or, more properly, poaching the dough produces a superior product, which is good news for home bakers without powerful steam-injected ovens.

The following formula is a variation of a recipe I developed for a company that is now selling bagels nationwide with great success. The difference between this formula and those used by most bagel companies is the thin, *poolish*-style pre-ferment, which uses a minimum amount of yeast to produce maximum grain fermentation. It incorporates the slow-rise principle used in other world-class breads, yet is as easy as the simplest direct-method bagel recipe. Besides improving flavor, the added fermentation extends shelf life.

You must start this formula one or two days ahead because you need both a sponge and an overnight retarding of the formed bagel dough. You can make the sponge and dough the same day by making the sponge at least five hours in advance, but the longer, slower method yields the best results.

COMMENTARIES

❏ Because the dough is very dry, this is one of the rare formulas where lukewarm water is necessary to rehydrate the instant yeast. If you don't use warm water, specks of yeast in the dough will create brown "hot" spots on the surface of the finished bagels.

❏ You may substitute up to 1 cup of whole-wheat flour for the bread flour to give the bagel a light whole-grain texture (or replace 1/4 cup of the bread flour with an equal amount of wheat bran or wheat germ). If you do so, you may need to add an additional tablespoon or two of water when mixing the dough.

❏ I suggest honey in this formula because most home bakers have it on hand. Malt is the usual sweetener for bagels, and if you have access to malt syrup, by all means substitute an equal amount. It is not quite as sweet as honey and lends a firmer chew to the bagel. You could also substitute 1 1/2 tablespoons of malt powder and a few drops of water. Don't use sugar or the result will be noticeably inferior.

❏ The dough temperature for this formula is higher than in other formulas because the dough does not undergo the customary primary, or bulk, fermentation.

❏ Scale the dough to any size from 2 to 4.5 ounces (the bagel will lose 10 to 15 percent of this weight to oven evaporation). I prefer larger bagels because they stay fresh longer, but mini bagels are popular for snacking.

❏ My method of forming the bagels is a departure from the old rope-and-loop method. I prefer it because it results in more evenly formed bagels that don't come apart when poached. It is also a bit gentler on the dough, resulting in a lighter, more flavorful bagel. However, you may find the rope-and-loop method more to your liking.

❏ If the dough doesn't float to the surface within 15 seconds when you poach it, it isn't sufficiently proofed. If you bake the bagels this way, the holes will close up too much in the oven, puckering into something resembling a belly button.

INGREDIENT	%
Unbleached bread flour	100
Poolish-style sponge	50
Instant yeast	0.4
Water	25
Salt	3.1
Honey (or malt)	6.2

MAKES 6 TO 14 BAGELS

1 cup (8 ounces) *poolish*-style sponge (page 35)

1/2 teaspoon (0.06 ounce) instant yeast

1/2 cup lukewarm water (approximately 85°F)

31/2 cups (16 ounces) unbleached bread flour

2 teaspoons (0.5 ounce) salt

11/2 tablespoons (1 ounce) honey or malt syrup (or 1 tablespoon malt powder)

=Approximate Weight: 29 ounces (1 pound, 13 ounces)

1. Measure out the sponge and let it sit at room temperature for an hour before using, to take the chill off.

2. Stir the yeast into the water to dissolve it, and let it sit for 3 minutes.

3. Combine the sponge, flour, salt, and honey in the bowl of an electric mixer with a dough hook or in a mixing bowl. Add the water-yeast mixture.

4. If making by machine, mix for 1 minute on slow speed and for 10 to 12 minutes on medium speed. (Warning: Stiff doughs can be hard on electric mixers. If your machine struggles, re-move the dough and finish kneading by hand.) If making by hand, mix all the ingredients in a bowl till they form a ball and then knead on a lightly floured surface for about 15 minutes. The dough should be dense and fairly dry (satiny) to the touch, smooth and stretchable. It should be between 82° and 85°F (warm to the touch) and pass the windowpane test (see page 29). Add a little more water or flour, if necessary, to achieve the desired texture.

5. Immediately cut the dough into 6 to 14 equal pieces, depending on the size bagel you want. (A typical commercial bagel is scaled to 4 to 41/2 ounces.) Roll the pieces into balls, as if making dinner rolls. Cover them with plastic wrap or a clean towel, and let them rest on a clean counter for 5 minutes.

6. Line a sheet pan with parchment paper and dust it lightly with cornmeal.

7. To form the bagels, poke a hole in the center of one piece of dough with your thumb. Keeping your thumb in the center, work the dough around, expanding the hole and making an even circle. Put your other thumb in the hole, too, and gently expand the circle till the hole is about 11/2 inches across for a large bagel and at least 3/4 inch across for a smaller bagel. If the dough resists or tears, let it rest for a few minutes while you move on to another piece and finish shaping when the gluten has relaxed. Another shaping method is to roll out the ball of dough to a 6-inch "rope" and loop it around your hand, with the ends meeting

between your thumb and forefinger. Roll the connecting ends on the counter to seal.

8. Place the shaped pieces about 2 inches apart on the prepared pan. Enclose the pan in a plastic bag and let the dough rise for about $1^1/2$ hours, until it has increased in size about 25 percent. To test the dough, drop 1 piece into a pan of cold water. It should float within 15 seconds. If it doesn't, let the dough rise a little longer and test again. (Return the floater to the pan with the others.)

9. Make sure the bag is closed, and refrigerate the dough for at least 6 hours, or preferably, overnight.

10. Position an oven rack in the middle of the oven and preheat to 475°F. Lightly grease a sheet pan or line it with parchment. Sprinkle semolina or cornmeal on the pan and then mist with cooking spray. Remove the pan of shaped dough from the refrigerator half an hour before you plan to bake the bagels. Fill a large pot with at least 4 inches of water and bring it to a boil. (You can use a hotel pan or other oversized pan across 2 burners if you have one, but be sure the water is deep enough for the bagels to fully submerge before bobbing to the top.) Reduce the heat till the water simmers and shimmers.

11. Working in batches, gently drop the pieces of dough into the water. Be careful not to crowd the pan; the pieces need enough room to float face up without touching. They should sink and then bob to the surface within 15 seconds.

12. After 1 minute, flip the bagels over with a slotted spoon and poach them on the other side for 1 minute more.

13. Remove the bagels with a slotted spoon, allowing all the water to drip back into the pot. Place them 2 inches apart on the prepared pan. Sprinkle on seeds or other toppings if you like.

14. Bake the bagels for 10 to 12 minutes, till lightly browned. Check them halfway through, and rotate the pan front to back if they are browning unevenly.

15. Transfer the bagels to a rack and let them cool for at least 30 minutes before eating. To freeze bagels, cool completely, 60 to 90 minutes, and seal tightly in a freezer bag.

BAGEL VARIATIONS

I grew up with a few basic bagel variations: pumpernickel, black and white (half dark rye and half regular), raisin, and egg. Toppings were confined to onion, garlic, poppy seeds or sesame seeds, and kosher salt. Now that bagels have gone mainstream, they appear in all sorts of incarnations: blueberry, pizza, sundried tomato and basil, granola, and on and on. Obviously, the rules have changed—in fact, there are no rules—so feel free to create your own variations. Here are a few guidelines:

For seeds and other toppings, figure on about 1 teaspoon per bagel.

Finely chopped and sautéed fresh onion or garlic is better than dried, but if using dried, soak it in warm water for about 15 minutes first to rehydrate.

Besides the usual poppy and sesame seeds, consider using nigella (black onion seed), flax, sunflower, or fennel seeds.

For a light coating, sprinkle on the topping after the bagels have been poached, just before baking. Spritz the toppings with additional water to hold them on.

For a thick coating, dip the just-poached bagels in a bed of the topping ingredient.

For rye bagels (generally called pumpernickel, though this is an imprecise use of the name), substitute coarse rye flour for up to one-third of the bread flour; if you like, add 2 cups of raisins per pound of flour at the end of the mixing cycle.

You may add up to 1 cup of marinated sun-dried tomatoes and/or herbs toward the end of the mixing cycle.

For egg bagels, replace 3 ounces of water with 2 eggs per pound of flour.

For a thinner crust and a breadier texture, omit the poaching step and bake the bagels following the hearth baking instructions on pages 25–27.

For an even chewier bagel, poach the dough for an additional 2 minutes.

FREEZING AND CUTTING BAGELS

Bagels freeze very well and can be kept for weeks or months, to be pulled out individually whenever the urge strikes. If you slice them before freezing, you can pop the frozen halves into a toaster without waiting for them to defrost. Preslicing diminishes bagels' freshness slightly, but the convenience is worth it. (Hard-core bagel lovers insist that a bagel should not be toasted but merely warmed. You will be able to taste more of the grain quality in an untoasted bagel, but if you plan to slather it with cream cheese, butter, or jam, that's probably irrelevant.)

Do not try to slice a frozen bagel, and never hold one upright between your fingers when slicing (bagel-cutting injuries are a leading cause of emergency-room visits!). Let unsliced frozen bagels thaw for at least an hour before cutting. Do not try to speed them along in a warm oven or they will dry out. If you do not have one of the popular bagel-slicing tools, lay the bagel flat and press down gently but firmly from the top. Cut parallel with the tabletop, using a very sharp, serrated knife. Do not push down too firmly or the knife will not be able to move sufficiently. If you plan to freeze the bagel after cutting it, leave a thin hinge to keep the top and bottom together.

WHITE BREAD

For all the knocks it takes from bread revolutionaries, white sandwich bread is still the most popular bread in this country. I know a wonderful guy named Herb Ernest who was in charge of a mobile army bakery during World War II. He and his men set up and tore down huge portable ovens and transported large mixers throughout northern Africa and western Europe right up to the end of the war. His bakers, some of whom were German prisoners, cranked out 20,000 two-pound loaves a day for the troops. It may not have been the world's best bread because of the poor flour quality, but it was probably the most revered at the time. White loaf bread, marching across Europe; what an image: the true Wonder Bread!

The French, for their part, have long been fond of a loaf they call *pain de mie* ("bread of the crumb"), a tight-grained white bread used for canapés and small sandwiches, but it never really caught on here. In this country the general buying public prefers soft white bread with an even, medium-size crumb. It could be made much better if the crumb were opened all the way and irregular hole patterns accepted, but then it would go stale more quickly on the shelves, a definite marketing concern for large and small bakeries alike.

MASTER FORMULA:

WHITE SANDWICH BREAD

As home bakers we do not, thankfully, have to be concerned about shelf life, so this master formula takes white bread to its zenith: It has fully developed flavor from long fermentation yet is soft and airy, perfect for any kind of sandwich. I have yet to find a better white bread.

COMMENTARIES

❑ Although this formula is for two loaves, you can also make smaller sandwich loaves, dinner rolls, or soft, hoagie-style submarine rolls from this multipurpose dough.

❑ Make the pre-ferment the day before, and use the full amount in this formula. Because this bread has a higher percentage of pre-ferment than flour, you can bake it the same day you mix it and achieve full flavor.

❑ Punching down or "turning" the dough for a second rise, as in step 4, promotes fermentation and gluten development, which enhance the flavor and structure of the bread.

❑ You can use different size pans, but do not fill the pans any fuller than two-thirds, or the loaves will appear ready for the oven before they actually are. If you put too little dough in the pan, the loaves will not develop the proper dome.

❑ Be sure to allow the loaf to cool. You will crush this relatively soft bread if you try to slice it before it cools completely; its creamy texture and flavor will reward your patience.

INGREDIENT	%
Unbleached bread flour	100
Biga-style pre-ferment	100
Salt	3.1
Sugar	9.3
Instant yeast	0.9
Whole milk	37.5
Unsalted butter	25

MAKES 2 LOAVES

4 cups (16 ounces) *biga*-style pre-ferment (page 37)

3¹/2 cups (16 ounces) unbleached bread flour

2 teaspoons (0.5 ounce) salt

3 tablespoons (1.5 ounces) sugar

1¹/4 teaspoon (0.15 ounce) instant yeast

³/4 cup (6 ounces) whole milk, at room temperature

¹/2 cup (4 ounces) unsalted butter, softened

Vegetable oil cooking spray

=*Approximate Weight: 31 ounces (1 pound, 15 ounces)*

1. Cut the *biga* into small pieces. Combine it with all the other ingredients in a mixing bowl or in the bowl of an electric mixer with a dough hook.

2. If making by hand, stir the ingredients together till they form a ball, then knead on a lightly floured work surface for 12 to 15 minutes. If making by machine, mix for 1 minute on slow speed and for 10 to 12 minutes on medium speed. The dough is ready when it is soft and supple, between 77° and 80°F, and passes the windowpane test (see page 29). Add a small amount of water or flour if necessary to create the right texture.

3. Round the dough, and put it in a clean bowl large enough to hold it when it has risen. Mist the dough lightly with cooking spray, cover the bowl with plastic wrap, and let the dough rise for about 1 hour at room temperature. It should rise to about 1¹/2 times its original size.

4. Remove the dough and knead it again, by hand, for 5 minutes. Round it into a ball, return it to the bowl, re-cover and let the dough rise for an additional hour, until it again increases about 1¹/2 times in size.

5. Divide the dough into 2 equal pieces, and shape them into rolls or sandwich loaves as directed on pages 20–21.

6. Grease two 5 by 9-inch bread pans. (Cooking spray works well for this.) Place the shaped doughs in the pans and mist them lightly with cooking spray. Cover the pans loosely with

plastic wrap or enclose them in a large plastic bag. Let the loaves rise in a warm spot or at room temperature for 60 to 90 minutes, till nearly doubled in size. The dough should crest above the rims of the pans but not mushroom over the sides. If the dough shows signs of mushrooming, bake it immediately.

7. When the dough is nearly ready, place an oven rack in the center of the oven and preheat to 350°F. (Make sure there is enough headroom for the loaves. If not, lower the rack a notch.)

8. Remove the pans from the plastic and bake the loaves for about 45 minutes, rotating them front to back after 20 minutes to promote even browning. The bread is done when it is golden brown all around and has an internal temperature of 190°F. If you don't have a probe thermometer, carefully remove a loaf from the pan and thwack the bottom; it should make a hollow sound.

9. Turn the loaves out onto a rack, and let them cool for at least 2 hours before slicing.

3

THE STAFF OF LIFE:
4,000 YEARS OF BREAD

Beer is liquid bread and bread is solid beer. I've been using this analogy for years to illustrate the simple nature of bread: baked fermented grain. The conventional wisdom is that leavened bread appeared in Egypt about 4,000 years ago, probably as an afterthought of beer making. Beer, though, was not the beverage we now drink but a thick gruel of fermented grains eaten, or slurped, as a nutritious meal full of healthful penicillin-making fungi, as well as proteins and carbohydrates. The prevalent grain was an ancestral strain of wheat called *emmer*.

Bread, however, did not simply begin at the foot of the pyramids in a vacuum; most of the world has been eating unleavened bread for as long as civilization can be charted. Even now, unleavened flatbreads are far more common than risen wheat breads in equatorial cultures where cassava,

or tapioca flour derived from the detoxified root of the manioc plant (or yucca cactus), is the primary ingredient. Barley, corn (maize), and oats are also bread grains. There is no gluten in cassava, and very little in barley, corn, or oats, so breads made exclusively from these grains are by necessity flat, whether they have yeast in them or not.

The Egyptians, though, are credited with applying yeast fermentation to wheat-type grains and developing a baking process, including a kneading method using their feet, that produced what we now call leavened bread. They used individual earthenware containers, not unlike cloche clay ovens (page 27), and rolled them over hot coals till the wet dough inside was baked.

See the January 1995 issue of *National Geographic* for an article about rebuilding an ancient bakery and recreating this early

Egyptian-style bread using emmer and wild yeast captured in the area by Dr. Ed Wood, a serious collector of world sourdough strains.

The Egyptians were known by their rivals in the ancient world as "The Bread Eaters." Bread was not only their principal food but, along with beer, a form of currency.

The ancient Greeks and, later, the Romans furthered the craft, making yeasted breads from wheat, barley, and other grains. The Greeks are often credited with inventing the prototype of the modern bread oven: a domed chamber with a door that opened and closed. For centuries, their everyday bread was barley *maza* (flatbread), with wheat breads allowed only on feast days. But by the time of the Golden Age of Pericles, *artos,* or wheat breads, could be bought daily at bakeries. During this era, bakers began creating bread in different shapes to denote special occasions: mushroom-shaped breads (*boletus),* rustic breads (*almogaeus),* braided loaves (*streptice),* rye (*syncomiste),* spelt (*chondrite),* and the crescent-shaped *hemiarton,* made in Ephesus to honor Artemis, the goddess of the moon. More than eighty types of bread were produced throughout the Greek countryside. No wonder that, even today, per capita bread consumption is higher in Greece than in any other country—double the rate in France and four times the rate in the United States. Bread roots go deep.

By the time of Jesus, there were 329 bakeries in Rome alone, most of them run by Greeks with assistance from Gaulish immigrants who had learned the art of skimming foam from beer and using it as leaven. These bakers belonged to an exclusive guild, one that was as hard to get out of as it was to get into; God help any baker's son who did not want to follow in his father's profession. During the time of the Roman Empire, bread baking developed into an industry with the harnessing of water for milling, the application of bolting (straining out the bran and germ to make white flour), and the mechanization of kneading with horse-driven mixers. Loaves were usually baked in rounds, sometimes scored with petal designs, sometimes filled with dried fruit. Bolted flour breads (called *siligineus),* light in texture, were made for the patricians while the coarser whole-grain breads (*plebeius* and *sordidus)* were baked for the masses.

As the Roman Empire disintegrated, baking moved into homes. Bread from the home hearth became the foundation of meals, as soup was poured over a slice that was eaten at the end of supper. (The word *supper* derives from the Frankish *suppa,* or later, the English *sop.*) Thick slices of bread eventually served as plates, or *trenchers,* which soaked up the juices of a meal and were often shared by two people (*companions,* that is, "sharers of bread"). It became fashionable for the wealthy to give their gravy-soaked trenchers to the poor or to the dogs.

Bread became intertwined symbolically with the Judeo-Christian influences that dominated much of civilization. From the Jewish *maza* flatbread or matzoh, to the eucharistic wafer, to the various festival breads associated with St. Joseph, Michael the Archangel, and the Virgin Mary, bread is at the core of many religious celebrations. The name of Jesus' birthplace, Bethlehem, means "house of bread"; Jesus declared himself "the bread of life"; Christmas, Michaelmas, Easter, and Lenten breads all have their symbolic renderings.

In the late Middle Ages, communal village ovens, located far from the wooden houses and kept watch over by the town's official baker, became common. This responsibility increased the baker's importance as baking evolved into a trade and a craft. As in Egyptian times, bread became a form of currency and a form of credit. Bakers were powerful credit brokers, "loaning" out bread, keeping tally by notching wooden tablets with a knife, and collecting grain and services as payment.

In France, the king himself was in charge of all bread, delegating supervision to the grand provost of Paris, who in turn delegated it to local provosts. King Louis IV recognized the importance of bread when he said, "He who controls a nation's bread is a greater ruler than he who controls their souls." His descendant, Louis XVI, known as the Bread King when he ascended to the throne, paid the ultimate price for this expectation when he and his wife, Marie Antoinette (who mythically declared, "Let them eat brioche!"), failed to keep the public trust.

Baking guilds and systems of apprentice training flourished between the twelfth and seventeenth centuries. (In one ritual, an apprentice would be elevated to full membership in the fraternity after declaring to the local master baker, "Master, I have served and completed my four years.") Over this period, the patron saint to whom bakers swore an oath of dedication changed from St. Peter to St. Lazarus and finally to St. Honoré.

The standard wild yeast method of bread making, in which old dough was used to ferment and leaven new dough, was challenged in the early 1600s, when bakers rediscovered that beer yeast made lighter breads. They found that adding milk made bread even lighter and that a small amount of salt, then a very expensive item, greatly improved the taste of the bread. Soon bakers developed a whole line of soft luxury breads. When these breads (like brioche!) became scarce during the reigns of Louis XV and XVI, the lack contributed greatly to the general agitation leading to the French Revolution.

In the United States we have had our own ebbs and flows of interest in bread. In 1829 Sylvester Graham, a Presbyterian minister from Massachusetts, warned Americans against the evils of white bread. (He also attacked mustard, catsup, pepper, condiments in general, meat, and fats.) He promoted a coarse whole-wheat flour that for years was known as graham flour. It was excellent for making Graham crackers, though I have a feeling they were nothing like the ones I use in my favorite cheesecake crusts or s'mores.

In 1850 there were 2,017 bakeries in the United States. Washington, D.C., alone, with a population of only 40,000, had 123 bakeries. However, ours was still primarily a rural and pioneer society, and 90 percent of the bread was baked at home. By 1910 the amount of home-baked bread had fallen to a still substantial 70 percent, but the shift to an urban-based culture was accelerating.

In 1927 Continental Baking introduced Wonder Bread in a balloon-decorated wrapper. The same year, Lender's Bagel Bakery was founded by Polish immigrant Harry Lender. (His sons, Murray and Marvin, later moved into flash-frozen bagels, which dominated the market until recently.) In 1930 Continental Baking figured out how to preslice Wonder Bread. Interestingly, Toastmaster introduced the automatic toaster the same year, and toast became a very hot item. Around the same time, a Texas farmer named Hickman Price developed equipment enabling him to harvest 600,000 bushels of wheat from 23,000 acres at a cost of twenty-five cents per bushel, but by 1936, the Texas dust storms rendered his acreage almost useless.

ITT took ownership of Continental Baking in 1968. In 1984, Ralston-Purina bought Continental. The same year, Lender's Bagels was bought by Kraft Foods (they sold it in 1996 for about $100 million). In 1995 Interstate Bakeries of Kansas City announced it would purchase Continental Baking from Ralston-Purina for $461 million in stock. Meanwhile, most artisan bakeries struggled to achieve annual sales of $250,000 to $1 million, while a few, like La Brea in Los Angeles and Acme in Berkeley, were selling up to $5 million worth of bread a year. Surveys by bakery trade journals indicate that specialty and artisan breads represent a small but growing segment of the bread industry, about 5 percent. Wonder Bread is still, as you read these words, the largest selling brand of bread in the United States.

The organic movement has spawned new interest in both whole-grain flours (Sylvester Graham would be pleased) and improved strains of flour. Giusto's in San Francisco is now milling a small amount of Parisian-style flour, similar to the classic French baguette flour, number fifty-five, hitherto unavailable to American bakers. King Arthur Flour Company of Norwich, Vermont, sells a white whole wheat flour with the nutritional values of whole wheat but a flavor closer to unbleached white flour. Technology and cereal chemistry, sciences only intuited by previous generations, have produced wonderful breakthroughs in yield and performance but at the same time have denuded whole valleys trying to keep pace with consumer demand.

The story of bread is, in many ways, the story of humankind. Whether we interpret it culturally, religiously, or historically, we see the interconnectedness of people and their daily bread. While bread has symbolized the presence of God in the world, it has also served as the currency of daily commerce and the primary foodstuff of many peoples. Money, another indispensable creation with all sorts of symbolic dimensions, has long been synonymous with bread. The reason is clear: They both represent energy, the convergence and exchange of forces. If we are, as I have proposed, in the midst of a paradigm shift in the world of bread, if we are gradually, grudgingly, gruelingly reclaiming some of the turf dominated by the Wonder Breads of the world, then perhaps we are in the midst of a paradigm shift of even greater implications as well. Who knows? If we follow the progress of bread in this unfolding story, which is really our story, perhaps we will find clues to what else lies ahead.

THE BARM SPONGE STARTER

Whether you call your starter *levain, desum, barm,* or *sourdough,* it is a wild yeast starter and the oldest way to make leavened bread. The various names denote particular methods of creating the starters and also indicate the level of acidity and complexity. However, they are all made by the same strain of wild yeast, called *Saccharomyces exiguus,* and by a varied collection of lactobacillus organisms (i.e., bacteria). These organisms live in a symbiotic relationship within the flour-liquid medium, mutually supporting each other's existence.

I call my starter a barm because that is what Monica Spiller calls it, and she taught me how to make it. Monica is a microbiologist who specializes in mycology, the world of fungi and mushrooms. Yeast is the smallest member of the mushroom family, and Monica fell under its spell. She's English, though she now lives near San Francisco, a yeast fanatic's fantasy land. Readers of Elizabeth David's *English Breads and Yeast Cookery* know that in England starters are called *barms,* and Monica felt it her British duty to revive the good name, overshadowed as it has been by the French *levain* and Italian *biga.* Her method for making a sourdough starter is so simple and foolproof that I was inspired to join in her barm crusade.

Monica loves whole-grain breads, especially those made purely with whole wheat. While that has been the focus of her bread making, I have found all sorts of applications for her starter in the wider world of breads. Much to her surprise, I successfully weaned my pure Spiller barm starter from whole wheat to unbleached bread flour and shortly thereafter won the James Beard Foundation's National Bread Competition with the bread formula I am about to teach you.

There is nothing esoteric about this starter. A lot of misinformation about sourdough has been passed from generation to generation and now from Internet user to Internet user. In the old days, as people figured out how to make or keep a starter, they passed on their method as if it were the one true way, and that is how sourdough cults were born. Despite such claims, some of which are now being promulgated through "sourdough electronic chat rooms," there are many ways to make a starter and keep it going. Some of them are quite elaborate and incorporate unnecessary steps or ingredients, but the following method, adapted and modified from Monica's original barm method, is a proven winner. It is easy to make and maintain, as hundreds of my students can attest.

SOURDOUGH CRASH COURSE

Before beginning the formula, a few introductory comments about sourdough: The two main bread yeasts are *Saccharomyces cerevisiae* and *Saccharomyces exiguus* (also called *Saccharomyces minor*). *S. cerevisiae,* commercially cultivated on molasses and other nutrients, is the yeast used in beer and yeasted bread. It is fast-acting, strong, and aggressive. *S. exiguus* is a wild yeast that lives on plants, fruits, and grains. It is the white bloom on grapes, plums, and other fruit, and it also lives on the outside of wheat berries. *S. exiguus* is slower acting and not as aggressive as the commercially produced *cerevisiae.*

Yeast and bacteria feed on sugars. Flour only contains small amounts of sugar, but large amounts of starch. Fortunately for the yeast and bacteria, starches can be broken down through a natural chemical action triggered by enzymes (some of which are called *amylases* and *diastases*) that also exist in the grain. This process causes the starch to release its sugar components. Yeast and bacteria also provide their own enzymes, further releasing the sugar molecules trapped in the starch. What this means is that bread dough is a perfect habitat in which yeast and bacteria can live and work. The dough supplies an unfolding cache of food for the hard-working and always hungry organisms.

The by-products of yeast activity are alcohol and carbon dioxide (carbonic gas, also called CO_2). In bread, the alcohol bakes off; in beer, it stays in the soup, as does the CO_2. Beer, then, really is liquid bread and bread is, to a lesser extent, solid beer. The yeast activity is called *fermentation*; it both flavors and leavens the dough as the CO_2 is trapped in the gluten structure of the dough, forcing it to expand. The image I have is of thousands of yeast cells eating and then burping.

Fermentation occurs quickly in commercial-yeast breads but takes longer in the slower-acting wild yeast breads. The benefit of this slower process is that it allows the lactic bacteria to add their flavor-enhancing influence. There are a number of strains of bacteria that add pleasant flavor tones to fermenting dough, including *Lactobacillus plantarum* and *Lactobacillus brevis.* In San Francisco there is a bacterium unique to the area called *Lactobacillus sanfrancisco,* which gives San Francisco sourdough its unique flavor. What happens is that the bacterial activity, a second type of fermentation, creates its own by-products: lactic and acetic acids. These acids lower the pH level of the dough, and eventually, create sour flavors. Breads that have a proper balance of lactic (buttery flavor) and acetic (vinegary flavor) acids are the ones that taste the best. This is where the skill of the baker comes in.

The bacteria take longer to do their work than the wild yeast does. (Fortunately, wild yeast likes the acidic medium, unlike commercial yeast, which prefers more neutral conditions.) Leavening is possible within a few hours after making the dough, but the bread will not develop its fullest flavor. As the yeast exhausts the available nutrients—all the while fermenting the dough and creating alcohol and CO_2—the bacteria slowly produce their lactic and acetic acids. Since our goal is to evoke the fullest potential from the grain, we must extend the fermentation to bring out more flavor. We build the loaves in stages through a series of feedings, called *refreshments* and *elaborations.* The general terms for this are the *build* or the *elaboration.*

Bakeries have different systems for building doughs. Some use six-hour feeding cycles in which the dough is tended round the clock by shifts of bakers; others use a daily system with less frequent feedings. Some bakeries may follow a six-stage build while others use just two. The James Beard competition loaf you are about to learn is a San Francisco-style sourdough that I call a wild yeast *boule* or *bâtard* (in competitions it is prudent to throw in a few European terms). It is made by a three-stage build with long retarding cycles. This allows for the best flavor with a minimum of disruption of your life.

One of the important insights Monica passed on to me is the value of natural enzyme nutrients for the yeast. Enzymatic action is what frees up the sugar molecules trapped in the starch bonds; enzymes are as responsible as yeast for the chemical change in dough. One of the best sources of enzymes is sprouted grain. The sprouting process, also called *malting,* converts grain starches to malt sugars and greatly increases the presence of diastase enzymes, similar to amylase. This is the reason malted barley, or malt, is so often added to flour and bread formulas. Monica believes that flour made from malted wheat berries is an even better way to supplement dough because it is of the same grain as the flour. When you feed malt to a sourdough starter, the starter responds very positively; it is like giving it a vitamin pill. Wheat malt is available in some natural food stores as sprouted wheat flour. Both wheat and barley malt are available from beer- and wine-making supply stores, and either one can be used in this formula.

One final note: Monica sells a barm starter kit and a book that includes detailed instructions and more elaborate information than I have given you here. Her kit, which comes with a jar of sprouted wheat flour and a dried concentrate of wild yeast and lactobacillus, can get you up and running with a barm starter in a very short time. I encourage you to consider writing to her (see "Alton-Spiller," page 199).

You can accomplish the same results in just a few extra days, however, by using the method in the following master formula. You can create a strong starter and begin building doughs by the fifth day, though it will take two or three weeks for the full complexity of flavors to develop. The first few batches will taste similar to those made from a mild *levain* starter (page 79), but the sponge medium encourages the development of sour flavors, and these will eventually come forth.

Your barm starter must be refreshed at least three days before you plan to start making bread. However, should you want to take a break from bread making, you do not have to keep feeding the barm to keep it alive. The organisms will go dormant in the sponge if kept cold. The sponge can even be frozen; enough yeast and bacteria will survive a long dormancy to reactivate when the refreshment cycles begin again. The acidity in the sponge destroys the gluten bonds after about a week, so a long-dormant sponge will have the consistency of smooth, thick soup rather than stringy bread batter. I throw out all but one cup and begin building it up over a three-day period to restore the structural strength and revitalize the organisms.

Armed with this knowledge, you are now ready to make a barm starter. You will not have to repeat this process, but can begin your builds with the same starter, kept vibrant by regular refreshments. After that, countless bread options will be available to you, including those in the master formulas ahead.

MASTER FORMULA:

BARM SPONGE STARTER

I refer to this starter throughout the book as barm to distinguish it from the milder *levain* starter. *Barm* is the English term for starter and is the root of the term *barmy,* which means "tipsy" or "ditzy." This is because the starter produces alcohol (ethanol, actually), which may rise to the top of the sponge if it is not stirred for a week or so. Alaskan gold miners used to skim off this alcohol and trade it with the local Indians for supplies. (I've been told it will give you a massive headache and hangover.) One of the tribes was called the Hoochinoo, and thus was born the term *hooch* as slang for whiskey.

COMMENTARIES

❏ The main reason to use organically grown wheat flour on the first day is to protect against the slight chance of contamination. I have seen many starters made with regular commercial flour and there is rarely a problem, but "purer is better" is a healthy rule. The first stage of building a starter is crucial because the various organisms are just getting established, so the healthier you can make the medium the better your chances for success.

❏ Whether using wheat or barley malt, it is important that the diastase enzymes are alive, as they are in diastatic malt. (When the malt is roasted to create richer flavors, the enzymes cook, creating nondiastatic malt; it is a wonderful flavoring agent and sweetener, but does not provide the enzymes needed at this stage.) Sprouted wheat flour, because it is not roasted, is diastatic. Beer-making supply houses are a good source for malt, as are natural foods stores and The Baker's Catalogue (see page 199).

❏ Honey is an excellent yeast food and is added in the first stage to encourage yeast growth. It is not necessary once the starter is up and running.

❏ I use raisin water on day one because raisins, like the grapes they once were, are a home for wild yeast cells. The yeast, which reveals itself as the powdery bloom on grape skins, loves to feed on the grape sugars. This is why grapes left on the vine beyond harvest time will ferment on their own. Wine grapes are popular for inoculating starters but they are not always available. Raisins, however, are available year-round and work just as well. Soaking the raisins in warm water (not hot, which would kill the yeast) draws both the yeast cells and some of the natural sugar into the water. This infusion of yeast helps jump-start the sponge. It will work, albeit more slowly, to use plain water because the wheat also provides yeast, as does the air. But the raisin water strengthens the presence of the *S. exiguus* yeast, making it difficult for other strains of yeast to establish themselves. If you have wine grapes, simply plunge them into the sponge and fish them out after about 10 minutes (it is not necessary to crush the grapes to release the juice; their prime purpose is to provide added yeast cells). As with flour, purer is better, so use organically grown raisins and grapes if possible.

❑ Both the wild yeast and lactobacillus organisms prefer a cool environment; 65°F is ideal. Warmer temperatures encourage other more acetic and less flavorful bacteria.

❑ Many brands of bread flour are already malted, meaning they have a small amount of barley malt flour in the blend (the ingredient list will say "malted barley flour"). This is great for your starter, but not essential. If your flour does not include malted barley, it will still work.

❑ On day two, the sponge will be made slightly thicker. The thicker sponge encourages more of the sweeter lactic acids, while still promoting sourness. As a rule, lactic acid-producing organisms prefer drier sponges and acetic acid (sour) producers like wetter, looser, more oxygen-rich sponges. This is a wet sponge because you want a truly sour sourdough (for a milder starter, see page 79). Later in the process, as you elaborate this barm sponge starter into an intermediate firm starter, it will develop more lactic flavors.

❑ By day three, the sponge should be double the size it was on the previous day. As you build the size of the sponge, you start using doubling as the standard feeding format (see page 75). Wild yeast starters like a consistent feeding pattern and adapt themselves to the rhythm you establish. The organisms need enough fresh nutrients to keep them busy for awhile. If they wipe out their supply, the cells begin to die and the starter develops a flavor like nutritional yeast (nutritional yeast, also called *brewer's yeast*, is just dead cells of the *cerevisiae* yeast strain, full of vitamin B but no longer alive to ferment bread or beer). Should you find yourself overwhelmed by the volume, you can also double your starter by discarding half and building back to the current level.

❑ By day four, the pace of development is beginning to pick up. You discard half to keep down the quantity. You also wean the starter from honey and malt supplements because there is now enough enzyme activity in the sponge to quickly break down the starches.

❑ By day five, the starter should bubble up much more quickly, and in larger quantities, take longer to cool in the refrigerator. This means it will continue to ferment for an hour or two after you put it away. The acidity takes up to two days to peak, but the leavening capability stays strong and steady for up to two days from the time of bubbling.

❑ During refreshment, it is important not to feed the starter more frequently than once every 24 hours; it needs time to use most of the new food first. As with people, overfeeding a starter can cause sluggishness.

❑ When building a dough, if the starter is cold your dough will be cold, extending the fermentation time. If time is not a concern, you can use the cold starter and give the dough longer rising time before moving to the next step.

❑ I like having a large supply of starter because I can make larger batches of bread. However, you need only 2 cups to make two to three loaves of bread, so 4 to 6 cups of starter is enough for most home bakers. The problem with a large batch is that if you do not use it, you have to throw away a lot when you refresh it.

❑ I have kept unused starters in both my refrigerator and freezer for six months and made great bread from them after just a few days of refreshment. Freeze a starter only if refrigerator space is an issue or you know it will be months before you plan to make bread again. The starter will probably last longer than six months, but I hate to make guarantees beyond what I have experienced.

DAY ONE

1 cup (4.5 ounces) organic
   whole-wheat flour

1 tablespoon (0.66 ounce) diastatic wheat
   or barley malt powder or liquid

1 teaspoon (0.25 ounce) honey

1 cup raisin water (see note)

In a clean glass or ceramic mixing bowl
(stainless steel is also acceptable; aluminum is not), mix all the ingredients till
they form a smooth sponge. Cover the
bowl with plastic wrap and allow the
dough to ferment at cool room temperature (65° to 70°F) for 24 hours.

   Note: To make raisin water, soak 1 cup
of raisins (organic if possible) in 2 cups of
warm water. Strain out the raisins after 15
minutes and measure out 1 cup of liquid.

DAY TWO

1 cup (4.5 ounces) unbleached
   bread flour

1/2 teaspoon (0.11 ounce) malt

1 teaspoon (0.25 ounce) honey

3/4 cup cool water (65°F)

You will see little or no signs of fermentation; this is to be expected. Whisk the day
two ingredients into the sponge. It will be
slightly thicker because you are reducing
the water-flour ratio. It is okay if the
sponge seems a little lumpy as long as all
the flour is wet and absorbed. Cover the

bowl again with plastic wrap and allow the
sponge to ferment at cool room temperature for another 24 hours.

DAY THREE

2 cups (9 ounces) unbleached bread flour

1/2 teaspoon (0.11 ounce) malt

1 1/2 cups cool water (65°F)

You will see the beginning of fermentation
as bubbles form on the sponge, but the activity will be minimal. Do not worry if the
sponge separates. Whisk in the day three
ingredients to make a smooth sponge double the size of the previous day's. Cover the
sponge with plastic wrap and again let it
ferment for 24 hours.

DAY FOUR

2 cups (9 ounces) unbleached bread flour

1 1/2 cups cool water (65°F)

You should see strong signs of fermentation, with lots of bubbling on the surface
of the sponge, and smell the aroma of light
vinegar. Discard half the sponge (or give it
to a friend who can carry on, following the
same instructions). Whisk in the day four
ingredients, cover, and allow to ferment
for another 24 hours. If the sponge is very
bubbly by the time you retire for the
night, refrigerate it. Otherwise, leave it at
room temperature.

DAY FIVE

4 cups (18 ounces) unbleached
   bread flour

3 cups cool water (65°F)

The barm is already capable of leavening bread, but I advise one final day of refreshment to enhance the flavor, so whisk in the day five ingredients. You will have more than 2 quarts of starter the next day, so you will probably have to transfer it to a larger container, such as a ceramic crock or a clean plastic bucket. Cover the container loosely to allow gas to escape, and let it ferment at a cool room temperature for 4 hours. It should be very bubbly at this point (allow more time if not bubbling). Put the sponge in the refrigerator till the next day. You will then be ready to start making bread.

REFRESHMENT
INSTRUCTIONS

1. When refreshing your barm you want to double the volume; anything less does not provide enough nutrients to keep it healthy. The amount of barm you keep should be enough to make bread and still leave you at least 2 cups from which to rebuild. If you make bread regularly, you should feed the barm every 2 days for optimal performance (the flavors peak on the second day). If you deplete it, you may feed it every day.

2. Follow the basic refreshment pattern of 4 parts flour to 3 parts water *by volume.* (This, interestingly, works out to the inverse, 3 parts flour to 4 parts water *by weight.*) For example, if you add 4 cups (18 ounces) of flour, add 3 cups (24 ounces) of water. After feeding the starter, let it ferment at room temperature for 4 to 6 hours. (The time may vary depending on how warm or cool it is; look for lots of bubbling action.) For best flavor, refrigerate the refreshed barm overnight before building it into a dough.

3. When building a dough, remove the barm from the refrigerator 1 hour ahead of time to take off the chill. You may also use slightly warmed water to compensate for the cold starter.

4. Here are some additional tips for working with your barm:

   If you go away or do not use the barm for a week or longer, discard some when you return and build it back with two or more cycles of refreshments.

   If the sponge separates, discard the grayish liquor that floats to the surface before refreshing. This "hooch" tastes more like vinegar than whiskey. Don't stir it back into the sponge; it is sourer than you want your breads to be. You may freeze the barm for up to 6 months, but allow for 3 refreshments to rebuild it (spread out over a 3-day period) after thawing and before using.

SOURDOUGH: SAN FRANCISCO AND OTHERWISE

The barm sponge starter is the best "mother culture" for building San Francisco-style sourdoughs. Calling a bread a San Francisco sourdough is technically incorrect if you are not using starter filled with *Lactobacillus sanfrancisco*, but the reality is you can make great sourdough with your local microorganisms. *L. sanfrancisco* does have a signature effect on crust formation and flavor, but some of the finest sourdough breads in North America come from places as diverse as Seattle, Minneapolis, Los Angeles, Austin, Portland, Washington, D.C., Philadelphia, and New York City—and those are just the ones I have tried. This method will work anywhere.

What makes this a San Francisco–style bread is a sour rather than mild starter, a wet rather than firm mother sponge (as in *pain au levain*, page 81), and an intermediate "build." Using both wet and firm starters develops a more rounded flavor. You could make a dough directly from the barm sponge but it will be slacker and spread out rather than up. It also won't have as much complexity of flavor. The firm starter makes a big difference; it allows you to step beyond good bread to incredible bread.

The following master formula is the same as the one I used when I won the James Beard National Bread Competition. By following the formula, you will produce a loaf that is both beautiful and delicious, with a blistery, golden brown crust and a classic irregular hole pattern. The most dif-ficult step is deciding when to put it in the oven. To get a feel for that perfect moment requires a little practice. Home conditions make it impossible to specify exact times, but you will soon figure out the rhythm of your kitchen and doughs. After that, you will not want to stop making this bread. It is simply extraordinary.

MASTER FORMULA:

SAN FRANCISCO SOURDOUGH

The intermediate starter used in this formula develops more lactic flavors and also strengthens the structure of the bread. It is, in effect, a sourdough *biga*-style starter. It is sometimes called the *levain* or *chef*.

COMMENTARIES

❑ The number of loaves this formula makes depends on how you divide the dough. A typical *boule* is 1.5 pounds, while American-style baguettes, log, and torpedo-type loaves are usually scaled to 19 ounces and bake down to 1 pound. (In France baguettes are closer to 12 ounces.) *Bâtards* can be scaled from 10 to 19 ounces.

❑ The firm starter usually comes together without any additional water, but you may need to add a few drops.

❑ This formula is for basic white sourdough. An even more complexly flavored "country" sourdough can be made following the same instructions but substituting one of the following for 2 cups of the bread flour: 2 cups whole-wheat flour; 1 cup whole-wheat plus 1 cup coarse rye; or any combination of whole wheat, rye, wheat bran (no more than $1/4$ cup), and polenta totaling 2 cups. If you are making this country bread substitution, I suggest using the strongest high-gluten flour you can get rather than regular bread flour. (You may be able to purchase high-gluten flour from your local bakery if your natural foods market does not have any.) This stronger flour (about 14.5 percent gluten) gives added structure not provided by the other grains. You may also need to increase the water by two to three tablespoons because whole-grain flours soak up more than white flour.

❏ The formula calls for malt (or sugar), but it is really optional. It does give the crust added sweetness and promotes deeper coloration. Some bread flours include malt as an additive, in which case you do not need to add any.

❏ When the starter is refrigerated overnight, the flavor develops while the bacteria continue to feed. The dough will not rise much in the refrigerator, but it will be ripe and ready to use; you may also hold it until the day after.

❏ Usually, the first fermentation is longer than the proofing stage after shaping; I use a relatively short first rise and a long proofing-retarding cycle. This is where my method diverges from others.

❏ Put only shaped dough into the refrigerator; unshaped dough will not have enough "push" left to rise again after an overnight retarding. By the same token, be sure to let your shaped dough rise sufficiently before refrigerating, or it will take a long time the next day to rise fully.

❏ If you did in fact refrigerate the loaves too soon, take them out 3 or 4 hours ahead of time. It will take 2 hours for the yeast to wake up and another 1 or 2 hours for the loaves to finish rising.

❏ Lots of steam in the first few minutes of baking allows the dough to spring as much as 10 to 20 percent and makes for a beautiful bloom.

❏ The cool-down period in the oven is to ensure a crisper crust, evaporating internal moisture without burning the crust. The sour flavor is much more noticeable after the loaves cool completely. Some connoisseurs believe the best flavor does not emerge till the second or third day, though the crust will be stale by then.

MAKES 3 OR 4 LOAVES

INGREDIENT (STARTER)	%
Unbleached bread flour	100
Barm sponge starter	178
Water	N/A

FIRM (INTERMEDIATE) STARTER

2 cups (9 ounces) unbleached bread flour

2 cups (16 ounces) barm sponge starter (page 71)

Room temperature water as needed

=Approximate Weight: 25 ounces (1 pound, 9 ounces)

INGREDIENT (DOUGH)	%
Unbleached bread flour	100
Firm starter	92.5
Salt	2.8
Malt	0.9
Water	59

DOUGH

Firm Starter (from above; use all 25 ounces)

6 cups (27 ounces) unbleached bread flour

1 tablespoon (0.75 ounce) salt

1 1/4 teaspoon (0.25 ounce) malt or sugar

2 cups cool water (70°F)

Vegetable oil cooking spray

=Approximate Weight: 70 ounces (4 pounds, 6 ounces)

1. To make the firm starter, stir together the flour and the barm in a mixing bowl until it forms a ball (add a few drops of water if necessary to make it come together).

2. Turn the dough out onto a lightly floured surface and knead for about 4 minutes, till all the flour is incorporated and forms a fairly smooth dough. It is okay if it is a little sticky, but it should not be stiff or dry.

3. Place the dough in a clean bowl, cover with plastic wrap, and allow the dough to rise at room temperature for about 6 to 8 hours, till the dough nearly doubles. Refrigerate it, well covered, overnight.

4. To make the dough, take the firm starter out of the refrigerator about 1 hour before using. Then break it into about 6 pieces. Mix the firm starter and all the other ingredients in the bowl of an electric mixer with a dough hook or in a mixing bowl. (If the firm starter is very cold you may use slightly warm water.) If using a machine, mix for 1 minute on slow speed and then 6 to 8 minutes on medium, till the dough is smooth and tacky but not sticky. It should pass the windowpane test (see page 29) and register 77° to 80°F on a probe thermometer. To knead the dough by hand should take 10 to 12 minutes.

5. Place the dough in a clean bowl, cover the bowl with plastic wrap, and allow the dough to rise at room temperature for about 4 hours. It will not rise very much but will just begin to show

signs of swelling. However, if it does rise more rapidly than indicated—as occurs in some cases—still allow it the full fermentation time.

6. Divide and weigh the dough into 3 or 4 equal pieces, and shape into baguettes, *boules,* or *bâtards* as directed on pages 20–23. Place them in floured proofing baskets (*bannetons*) or on the back of a sheet pan lined with parchment and dusted with cornmeal or semolina. Mist the tops of the loaves with cooking spray and cover with plastic wrap or enclose in plastic bags. Let proof at room temperature for 3 to 4 hours, or till 1 1/2 times the original size. Place in the refrigerator, well covered, overnight.

7. Remove the loaves from the refrigerator at least 1 hour before you plan to bake. Prepare the oven for hearth baking as described on page 25, making sure to place the empty steam pan on a lower rack. Preheat the oven to 475°F.

8. Transfer the loaves to a peel that has been dusted liberally with cornmeal or semolina (if making baguettes, you can use the sheet pan as a peel). Score the loaves as directed on page 24, and slide them onto the baking stone.

9. Spritz the oven and loaves and pour 1 cup of hot water into the steam pan. Close the oven door. After 2 minutes, spritz the oven and the loaves again and lower the temperature to 450°F.

10. Bake for about 30 minutes, rotating the loaves front to back after 15 minutes, if necessary, for even browning.

11. When the loaves appear done, with a rich golden crust, turn off the oven and let sit for 10 additional minutes before removing to a cooling rack. Let cool for 1 hour before eating.

MASTER FORMULA:

MILD STARTER

This is the starter for classic French *levain* breads and Flemish *desums*. It uses a firm mother rather than a sponge, which promotes the growth of the less sour lactic bacteria rather than the acetic bacteria that thrive in the wetter medium of the barm (see page 73). The mild starter has the full leavening power of a wild yeast starter but a milder, more neutral flavor.

The timetable will vary with your kitchen temperature, so it is important to check your dough regularly to determine when to make the next refreshment.

COMMENTARIES

❏ You will need only a portion of the starter to build *levain* bread using the formulas in this book. The unused portion can be kept in the refrigerator for up to three days and used as a "seed culture" to make other *levains*.

❏ If you will not be using it that soon, you can refresh it by repeating the day four process. Or you can freeze it for up to two months; allow two refreshment cycles after thawing to bring it back to full strength.

❏ Organic flour is preferable for this formula, though not required. The reason to begin with whole-wheat flour is that wild yeast, *Saccharomyces exiguus,* lives on the outside of the wheat berry and accompanies the flour through the milling process. The more yeast in the initial dough, the easier it will be for it to establish itself. Organic flour, due to the absence of pesticides, is an even better host for the yeast than treated wheat, strengthening the odds of making a clean-tasting, strong starter.

❏ The purer the water the less chance for off flavors. Some bakers insist on filtered or spring water. I have successfully made this starter with tap water, but if your water is very hard or full of chlorine, use filtered or spring water instead.

❏ Switch to white flour on day two now that the dough is inoculated with a growing colony of yeast. You want to wean the starter over to white flour because a white flour starter has more applications. You may continue to use whole-wheat flour if you plan to make only whole-wheat breads, but it is not necessary.

❏ It's unlikely there will be much rising after day one unless you have a 90°F proof box. On warmer days the yeast activity accelerates but, whether or not the dough rises, it will be ready to move to the next stage because the yeast has had time establish itself.

❏ The reason for discarding half the dough on day two is to control and monitor the starter. From this point on you do want to see specific growth.

❏ After day three, as the dough continues to feed on the fresh nutrients provided by the flour, it can grow to even four times its original size. More typically it will triple in 24 hours, which is a sign that it is ready for the next stage.

❏ The *levain* referred to at the end of the formula is leaven, not the type of bread called *pain au levain* or *levain* bread. To avoid confusion, some bakers refer to the *levain* starter as *the chef*.

❏ Be sure to save the extra piece of dough, which can be considered a backup so you do not have to recreate the starter from scratch. Once you have made a chef, you can keep it going when you make the final bread dough (the *pain au levain*) by removing some of the dough prior to adding the salt. This dough becomes the chef for the next batch.

DAY ONE

1 cup (4.5 ounces) whole-wheat flour

$1/3$ cup cool water (65° to 70°F)

Stir the ingredients together in a mixing bowl and then knead them on a lightly floured surface for a few minutes till a smooth ball of dough is formed. Press the dough into a glass or clear plastic 2-cup measure, and mark where the top of the dough is on the outside of the cup. Cover the cup with plastic wrap and set it in a warm spot in the kitchen (but not in the oven). Allow it to ferment for 24 hours.

DAY TWO

1 cup (4.5 ounces) unbleached bread flour

$1/3$ cup cool water (65° to 70°F)

Remove the dough from the measuring cup (it may or may not have risen; it does not matter). Cut it into 6 pieces.

In a mixing bowl, mix the bread flour and water with the pieces of old dough till they form a ball. Turn out the dough onto a floured surface and knead for just a few minutes, till it forms a smooth ball of dough.

Divide this into 2 equal pieces and press one of them into the measuring cup, to the same line as on day one. Cover with plastic wrap and set aside to ferment in a warm spot for about 24 hours. (You can discard the other piece of dough or give it to someone else to build their own starter.)

DAY THREE

1 cup (4.5 ounces) unbleached bread flour

$1/3$ cup cool water (65° to 70°F)

Do not remove the dough from the measuring cup until it has doubled in volume. This may take more or less time than 24 hours. When it has doubled, repeat the process from day two and press the finished piece of dough into the measuring cup to the original line. Cover and allow to rise another 24 hours, or till it triples in volume.

DAY FOUR

1 cup (4.5 ounces) unbleached bread flour

$1/3$ cup cool water (65° to 70°F)

When the dough triples in volume, you are ready to make the *levain* starter. Repeat the process as on the previous day but do not throw away any of this new dough. This piece is your *levain* starter or chef. Allow it to ferment in a covered bowl for 4 hours before using.

MASTER FORMULA:

BASIC AND COUNTRY LEVAIN (PAIN AU LEVAIN)

These are sourdough breads that are not supposed to taste too sour. In order to accomplish this, the loaves are built from mild starter (page 79). Mild starter is also called the *levain,* or leaven, and gives the bread its French name, *pain au levain.* The cleanly fermented flavors of this bread contrast dramatically with the pleasant but sour flavors of San Francisco–style sourdough. It is made in the same manner, but the mild starter gives it a far less acidic taste. For this reason, it is a good bread to have with wine, which explains its popularity in France and in the finer restaurants of this country. San Francisco sourdough, on the other hand, goes better with beer and strongly flavored foods.

The basic *levain* is made with bread flour, while the country *levain* contains a percentage of whole grains, giving it a more earthy, peasant-style character. You can make any number of variations from this master formula depending on the blend of grains.

COMMENTARIES

❏ To make country *levain,* substitute one of the following for 2 cups of the bread flour: 2 cups whole-wheat flour; or 1 cup whole-wheat flour, 1/4 cup wheat bran, 1/2 cup rye flour, and 1/4 cup polenta (or any combination adding up to 2 cups). If you substitute 2 cups of rye flour, the bread would be known in French as *pain au méteil.* If you increase the rye flour to more than the bread flour, it becomes known as *pain au seigle.*

❏ Instead of making two loaves, you can also make one large 3-pound loaf, in the style of some artisan bakeries, or smaller loaves and baguettes. This dough also makes wonderful hard dinner rolls.

❏ The firm starter in this formula is an intermediate step, or "build." In Europe it is called the *élaboration,* meaning an extension of the original seed culture.

❏ Unless you are using a piece of preweighed dough saved from a previous bake, you only need a small piece of the original mild starter for the firm starter in this formula. You can store the remainder in the refrigerator or the freezer (see page 79).

❏ There is no need to work the starter extensively when it is first mixed. It will be kneaded again in the final dough.

❏ The dough may rise faster or slower depending on the room temperature. If it is rising faster than you want it to, put it in the refrigerator to retard. If moving too slowly, wait it out or move it to a warmer place. The dough is fully risen when it takes about 15 seconds to spring back when poked. As you get used to working with baskets or other molds, you will be able to gauge when a dough has filled the mold to the appropriate level.

❏ The cool-down phase at the end helps dry out the internal crumb, allowing the crust to remain crackly for a longer period.

INGREDIENT (FIRM STARTER)	%
Unbleached bread flour	100
Water	66
Mild starter	89

FIRM STARTER

1 cup (4.5 ounces) unbleached
  bread flour

6 tablespoons room-temperature water

1 cup (4 ounces) mild starter (page 79)

=*Approximate Weight: 11.5 ounces*

INGREDIENT (DOUGH)	%
Unbleached bread flour	100
Water	67
Firm starter	48
Salt	2.75

DOUGH

5$\frac{1}{4}$ cups (24 ounces) unbleached
  bread flour

2 cups cool water (65° to 70°F)

Firm starter (from above; use all
  11.5 ounces)

2$\frac{1}{2}$ teaspoons (0.66 ounce) salt

Vegetable oil cooking spray

=*Approximate Weight: 52 ounces*
  (3 pounds, 4 ounces)

1. To make the firm starter, mix the starter ingredients in a mixing bowl. When they form a ball, turn the dough out onto a floured surface and knead just until all the ingredients are incorporated and the dough forms a smooth ball.

2. Place the dough in a clean bowl, cover it with plastic wrap, and allow it to ferment at room temperature for 4 hours. Then put it in the refrigerator overnight.

3. Remove the starter from the refrigerator 1 hour before making the dough, to take off the chill. Just before mixing, cut the starter into 6 pieces.

4. To make the dough, combine the flour, water, and the pieces of starter in the bowl of a mixer with a dough hook or in a mixing bowl. If using an electric mixer, mix on low speed for 1 minute, then on medium for 3 minutes. (If saving dough to be the chef or firm starter for another time, cut off a piece the same size as the original firm starter, about 12 ounces, and set it aside in a covered bowl for 4 hours to develop.)

5. Add the salt and continue mixing for another 4 minutes, or just till the gluten sets up. The dough should pass the windowpane test (page 29) and register 77° to 80°F on a probe thermometer. If you are mixing the dough by hand, it will take 10 to 12 minutes to reach this stage.

6. Put the dough in a clean bowl, cover the bowl with plastic, and allow the dough to rise at room temperature for about 3 hours, until it begins swelling in size (the amount it rises depends on the warmth of the room, but it does not need to rise much before proceeding to the next step).

7. Divide the dough into 2 pieces and round each into a ball (see page 20). Use a prepared *banneton,* basket, or mixing bowl, and place the smooth or top side down (and, thus, the bottom, or seam side, up). Or place the balls top-side-up on the backs of 2 sheet pans that have been lined with baking parchment and sprinkled with semolina, cornmeal, or polenta.

8. Mist the dough with cooking spray and enclose each piece and its container in a plastic bag. Let the dough rise at room temperature for about 4 hours, or till nearly doubled in size. You may either bake the bread at this point or retard it overnight in the refrigerator. If retarding, remove it from the refrigerator 1 hour before baking, to take the chill off. Note: If you retard the dough it will be slightly more sour in flavor.

9. Prepare the oven for hearth baking as described on page 25, making sure to place the empty steam pan on a lower rack. Preheat the oven to 475°F.

10. Transfer the loaves from the baskets to a peel that has been dusted liberally with cornmeal or semolina. (You can also use the sheet pan as a peel, or bake directly on the pans.) Score the loaves as directed on page 24 and slide them onto the baking stone.

11. Spritz the oven and loaves and pour 1 cup of hot water into the steam pan. Close the oven door. After 2 minutes, spritz the oven and the loaves again and lower the temperature to 450°F.

12. Bake for about 30 minutes, rotating the loaves front to back after 15 minutes, if necessary, for even browning.

13. When the loaves appear done, with a deep reddish-gold crust, turn off the oven (or lower it to 350° if you plan to bake again) and let the loaves sit for 7 to 10 minutes before removing them to a cooling rack. Let them cool for 1 hour before eating.

MASTER FORMULA:
SOURDOUGH BAGELS

While commercial bagels are not customarily made with wild yeast, there is no reason they cannot be. Unfortunately, many of the so-called sourdough bagels that are sold are made with sourdough powders and flavoring agents, rather than by traditional slow-rise methods. I have had great success with this formula, producing a deeply flavored yet authentically textured bagel. The method is similar to *levain* with a few bagel techniques added. The crumb is tighter than in regular bread, so it takes a little extra chewing to bring out the complex flavors, but that is no impediment to enjoyment.

COMMENTARIES

❏ You will need to make the starter a day or two before beginning the bagels. The firm starter represents a large percentage of the finished dough and gives the bagels a strong sour flavor.

❏ For more of a whole-grain texture, substitute up to 1 cup of whole-wheat flour or 1/4 cup wheat bran for an equal amount of bread flour. It may be necessary to increase the water by a few tablespoons.

❏ I list honey in the ingredients, but barley malt is more commonly used in bagels than honey. Both work well. If you have regular, diastatic malt powder, use 1 1/2 tablespoons plus 1 tablespoon of water. The bagels will not be as sweet with the malt but will have a nice chew and coloration.

❏ Be careful when mixing the dough. Bagel dough is stiffer than most breads. It is tough on a mixer and hard to knead by hand. If your mixer seems to be struggling, remove the dough and finish by hand. Or dribble a few tablespoons of water down the side of the mixer bowl to reduce friction. This allows the dough hook to work more easily, reducing wear on the motor.

❏ It takes wild yeast doughs longer to ferment than commercially yeasted doughs. Most of the sour flavor is developed during the rise in step 3 and the subsequent overnight retarding, so be patient.

❏ Bagels can range from 4.5 ounces down to 2 ounces. They will lose some weight during the bake due to evaporation. While the larger sizes are more common, there is a growing interest in 2-ounce mini bagels for snacks and such.

❏ Overnight retarding is the best way to make a flavorful bagel, yeasted or leavened. However, if you want to bake on the same day, allow a minimum of 5 hours in the refrigerator for the flavors to develop.

❏ Many recipes for bagels call for sugar, food-grade lye, salt, baking soda, milk, malt, or honey in the water, when poaching bagels. After experimenting with these, I found no improvement in the finished product. Plain water is sufficient.

❏ See page 61 for more on freezing and safely cutting bagels.

INGREDIENT	%
Unbleached bread flour	100
Firm (intermediate) starter	50
Salt	2
Honey	9
Water	50

2 cups (8 ounces) firm (intermediate) starter (page 77)

3¹/₂ cups (16 ounces) unbleached bread flour

1¹/₂ teaspoons (0.33 ounce) salt

2 tablespoons (1.5 ounces) honey or malt syrup (or 1¹/₂ tablespoons malt powder)

1 cup cool water (65° to 70°F)

Vegetable oil cooking spray

=Approximate Weight: 39 ounces (2 pounds, 7 ounces)

1. Remove the firm starter from the refrigerator 1 hour before mixing the dough to take off the chill. Break it into small pieces.

2. Combine the starter and all the other ingredients in an electric mixer with a dough hook or in a mixing bowl. Mix on low speed for 1 minute to combine the ingredients into a ball, then increase the speed to medium and mix for about 8 to 10 minutes, or till the dough is stiff but satiny, dry to the touch but stretchy. It should feel slightly warm to the touch (80° to 82°F on a probe thermometer) and pass the windowpane test (page 29). If you are kneading the dough by hand, allow 12 to 15 minutes for it to reach this stage.

3. Put the dough in a clean bowl, cover with plastic wrap or enclose in a plastic bag, and let the dough rise at room temperature for about 4 hours, until it begins to swell.

4. Cut the dough into 6 to 14 equal pieces, depending on the size of the bagels. Roll the pieces into balls, as if making dinner rolls. Cover them with plastic wrap or a clean towel, and let them rest for 5 minutes on a clean countertop.

5. Line a sheet pan with parchment paper, lightly mist the parchment with cooking spray, and dust it with cornmeal or semolina.

6. To form the bagels, lightly flour your hands and poke a hole in the center of 1 piece of dough with your thumb. Keeping your thumb in the center, work the dough around, expanding the hole and making an even circle. Put your other thumb in the hole, too, and gently expand the hole till it is about 1¹/₂ inches across for a large bagel and at least ³/₄ inch across for a smaller bagel. If the dough resists or tears, let it rest for a few minutes, while you move to another piece, and finish shaping when the gluten has relaxed. Or see page 59 for an alternate method.

7. Place the shaped pieces about 2 inches apart on the prepared pan. Enclose the pan in a plastic bag and let the bagels proof for 3 hours; they will rise only slightly. To test the dough, drop one piece into a pan of cold water. It should float within 15 seconds. If it doesn't, let the bagels rise a little longer and test again (return the floater to the sheet pan with the others).

8. Make sure the bag is tightly closed and refrigerate the dough overnight.

9. Take the formed dough out of the refrigerator 30 minutes before baking. Preheat the oven to 475°F. Lightly grease another sheet pan or line it with parchment. Dust it with cornmeal or semolina and mist with cooking spray. Fill a large pot with at least 4 inches of water and bring it to a boil. Reduce the heat to a simmer.

10. Working in batches, gently drop the bagels into the water without crowding the pan; the bagels need enough room to float fully face up without touching. They should sink and then bob to the surface within 15 seconds.

11. After 1 minute, flip the bagels over with a spoon and poach them on the other side for 1 minute more.

12. Remove the bagels with a slotted spoon, allowing all the water to drip back into the pot. Place the bagels 2 inches apart on the prepared pan. Sprinkle on seeds or other toppings if you like (see page 61).

13. Bake the bagels for 10 to 12 minutes, till lightly browned. Check them halfway through and rotate the pan front to back if they are browning unevenly.

14. Transfer the bagels to a rack and let them cool for at least 30 minutes before eating. To freeze the bagels, allow them to cool completely (60 to 90 minutes) and seal them tightly in a freezer bag.

4

THE QUALITY OF GRAIN: THE WHOLE-WHEAT RENAISSANCE

The whole-grain movement began thirty years ago as a voice on the counterculture fringe. It was a fascinating time, but before exploring it, we need to review a few basic wheat facts. A wheat berry, the seed of mature wheat grass, has three distinct parts: the outer layer, called the *bran,* which is almost pure cellulose; the inner germ, the seed of future life, which is full of natural oil and other nutrients; and in between, the starchy endosperm, from which we get white flour. Whole-wheat flour, as the name suggests, is ground from the whole berry and delivers the whole nutritional package.

That may seem straightforward enough, but the sixties were a highly passionate and politicized time. I remember intense late-night discussions about conspiracies to rob us of proper nutrition, the destruction of the integrity of flour, empty calories, the leeching of our body's vitamin B by white flour and white sugar, and the health and consciousness benefits awaiting us as soon as we purged our houses and bodies of those corrupting, refined substances and replaced them with whole wheat (preferably milled seconds before using) and honey (or maple syrup if we could afford it and wanted to prevent the exploitation of bees). I was a fervent convert, even though I had a real problem chewing some of the early whole-wheat breads that crossed our table.

For a brief time back then, I was part of a street theater troupe in Boston. We performed behind masks in slowly moving tableaux or used large, stick-manipulated puppets to express our opposition to the Vietnam War or our views on other important humanistic issues. The highlight of every performance was a closing ritual in which we passed out loaves of homemade whole-wheat bread and the cast and audience broke bread together. This theatrical recreation of the religious Communion experience always had a profound effect, deepening whatever response the play itself generated.

As a newcomer to the troupe, I was responsible for grinding the flour that was used for each evening's bread. We had a small hand-cranked grain mill, and it took me close to an hour to grind enough wheat berries to make six or seven free-form loaves. The only ingredients were flour, salt, yeast, and water. The loaves were kneaded and formed into rough, round shapes, without a primary fermentation and punch-down. We baked the loaves so they came out of the oven about the time the play was starting. It was not great bread but it was great theater.

I had previously experimented with the macrobiotic method of bread making, which was similar to the theater troupe's, except without yeast. My very first macrobiotic loaf came out of the oven with a thick chewy crust and a pastelike interior, underbaked by at least 10 minutes. Proud as could be—and unable to interest my friends in more than a crumb of the undercooked dough—I ate the whole thing. The resulting indigestion was minor compared to the sense of pride and empowerment I felt. If I could make my own bread then I could do just about anything. I have since marveled at how the mind can, at least temporarily, perceive something as good, even when it fails to meet the minimum standards of acceptability. Glee is a powerful energy.

This style of yeastless bread making was later perfected in a loaf called Essene Bread. The advancement was brought about by using ground wheat-berry sprouts rather than flour. The sprouting makes the wheat digestible, so even if the center of the loaf is doughy it will be easier to stomach than the version I made. The romance attached to this kind of bread is that it is both basic and guilt-free; it is, in today's parlance, politically correct. Unfortunately, I do not find it particularly enjoyable to eat because the flavor of the wheat is not properly showcased. Grassiness rather than the nuttiness of the grain comes through. It is akin to making wine from fine grapes and then drinking it before the nuances of the grapes have had a chance to emerge.

Alvarado Street Bakery, a neighbor of mine, took the sprouted wheat concept to another level, adding sweeteners and pure vital wheat gluten to create a light and tasty loaf. The bread seems to be made from flour, even though it is made from wheat sprouts. Alvarado Street Bakery is now the largest producer of certified, organically grown wheat bread in the country; and it has advanced the whole-grain movement by helping healthful bread escape the health food onus.

On my own journey through macrobiotic brick loaves and theatrical communions, I came across a few wonderful whole-grain breads and techniques that, years later, worked their way into the neo-traditional approach of Brother Juniper's Bakery. In 1971 I joined up with a group of counterculture spiritual seekers to open a vegetarian restaurant in Boston called the Root One Cafe. We commissioned two nearby hippie bakeries to make our bread.

One specialized in a salt-rising method that made a dense whole-grain loaf from wheat with a little corn and other grains (salt-rising breads are a variation of wild yeast breads, featuring a very long fermentation). It had to be sliced thinly in order to be enjoyed, not unlike some German-style breads with similar characteristics. It was hard to slice evenly, but it was delicious. The long fermentation brought forth the full flavors of the grains; there was a slight sourness that lent the bread a wonderful finish, or aftertaste, in the mouth. Finish is an important aspect of bread enjoyment and one reason why sourdough breads have such appeal.

The other bread we used was called Six Grain. It, too, was made by a long, slow, salt-rising method, but with less flour and a lot of cooked rice. It was too crumbly to work well for sandwiches. We tried slicing it thicker, hoping it would hold together, but it rarely did. The flavor, though, was wonderful; you had the sensation of eating a bowl of porridge with every slice. Years later, when developing Struan bread, I remembered the effect of the cooked rice and incorporated it into my formula, but in much smaller amounts. The rice adds a moistness and sweetness to the bread that cannot be duplicated with uncooked grains.

Toward the end of the seventies, whole-grain breads came into their own, not only through bakeries like Alvarado Street but also through franchises such as Great Harvest, who taught new bakers how to be entrepreneurs and masters of whole-grain baking. In the past fifteen years, Great Harvest has opened about 100 franchises throughout the country, and most of them have been quite successful. Their breads are dense but flavorful, often sweetened with honey or fruit syrup. The grain is ground into flour right in the bakery and made into bread the same day.

Two American bread books, written fifteen years apart, were seminal to the whole-grain movement. They were books with an agenda, both spiritual and material, written by people with a mission. The first was Ed Espe Brown's *The Tassajara Bread Book*. When I began baking bread in 1972, everyone I knew had a copy of it, and it remains a common reference point in bread discussions today. The hand-lettered pages became a model for many cookbooks of the seventies and eighties, and the simple, direct instructions gave confidence to a whole generation of bakers. The second important book was *The Laurel's Kitchen Bread Book* by Laurel Robertson, Bronwen Godfew, and Carol Flinders. When it was published in 1987, the field was ripe for detailed baking instructions and for a more direct understanding of the relationship between the food we prepare and the beliefs we profess—the interconnectedness of things. This book strengthened the voice of the whole-grain movement and kept it from being drowned out by traditional and neo-traditional bread partisans as the bread revolution moved ahead.

The most influential book in the whole-grain renaissance, however, was written in 1977 by an Englishwoman with no spiritual agenda other than a religious fervor to improve the quality of bread. Elizabeth David's *English Bread and Yeast Cookery* is a daunting treatise on the rise and fall of decent bread in England and a stirring appeal for a return to more health-ful breads. Because Ms. David was so highly regarded in the culinary world, in a class with M. F. K. Fisher and Julia Child, her words were taken to heart by those who read them, spawning a whole-grain renais-sance in Great Britain and inspiring bakers on this side of the Atlantic as well.

These baker-authors spurred advances in whole-grain technique that now make it possible for home bakers to create extraordi-nary whole-grain breads. Any type of bread is possible when you know how. While I might prefer a light crumb with big air pockets and a sweet finish, others may favor chewy bread with tightly packed holes and little or no sweetness. Allow yourself to taste a full palette of possibilities; learning what you like is part of the quest.

Your choices will be influenced by the nutritional benefits, the fullness of the wheat and other grain flavors, and the fin-ish, or aftertaste. The most important con-sideration is whether the bread is satisfying and enjoyable—whether you would eat it again, what price you would be willing to pay for it, what it goes well with, whether you would make a sandwich with it.

There are French bread bakers and purists like the brothers Max and Lionel Poilane who are convinced that the only true bread is that made from whole grains. Few of us may ever taste the Poilanes' in-ternationally renowned breads, but we can enjoy wonderful whole-grain breads made by our local artisan bakeries, and better still, by our own hands using these master formulas.

MASTER FORMULA:

100 PERCENT WHOLE-WHEAT BREAD

This bread incorporates a variation of the *poolish* pre-ferment method, but with whole-wheat rather than white flour in a thicker sponge. I prefer a medium-grind whole-wheat flour rather than fine-grind because it gives the bread a more interest-ing texture. You can also use a blend of fine and coarse grinds. (If you buy your flour from a natural foods store where it is sold in bins, you can usually choose from these grinds, as well as from hard and soft wheats; if buying packaged whole-wheat flour, check the label to be sure it is hard wheat, intended for bread rather than pastry.)

This bread is rich and moist, with full wheat flavor. When I developed it at Brother Juniper's Bakery, I thought it would appeal to a small segment of our cus-tomers and was surprised at how popular it became. Besides containing no refined flour, this bread has no dairy products or oil, which makes it ideal for people on lac-tose-restricted, as well as low-fat, diets.

COMMENTARIES

❑ Raisin juice concentrate is a wonderful yeast food and natural sweetener. It can be purchased at natural foods stores. You can also make your own by soaking 1 cup of raisins in 2 cups of warm (not hot) water for 1 hour. Either strain the water from the raisins and cook it down to a thick syrup or purée the raisins and soaking water in a blender or food processor. The extra will keep for months in a sealed container in the refrigerator.

- For the rice in this formula, save cooked rice from meals or make some ahead of time. Simmer 1 part brown rice in 2^1/$_2$ parts water till all the water is absorbed (usually about 40 minutes). Cool the rice before adding it to the bread dough.

- The fermented sponge at the end of step 1 is called a *mature* or *ripe* sponge. It is at its peak as a leavening agent and has pre-fermented the grain.

- Instead of using a loaf pan, you can shape the dough into a free-form round or other shape and place it on a greased sheet pan. If you are using a loaf pan, the dough should fill it at least halfway. If the dough seems to be too much for your pan (filling it three quarters or more before rising), cut some dough off and bake it separately as a roll or small free-form loaf.

- See page 23 regarding proofing technique. Bake the loaf while it is on the rise rather than overproofed. It will spring (i.e., rise) an additional 10 percent in the oven if it has not already reached its peak.

MAKES 1 LOAF

INGREDIENT (SPONGE)	%
Whole-wheat flour	100
Instant yeast	1.4
Water	100

SPONGE

1^3/$_4$ cups (8 ounces) medium-grind whole-wheat flour

1 teaspoon (0.11 ounce) instant yeast

1 cup cool water (65° to 70°F)

=Approximate Weight: 1 pound

INGREDIENT (DOUGH)	%
Whole-wheat flour	100
Sponge	400
Salt	4.25
Instant yeast	1.5
Honey	25
Raisin juice concentrate	25
Brown rice	75

DOUGH

^{7}/$_8$ cup (4 ounces) medium-grind whole-wheat flour

^{3}/$_4$ teaspoon (0.17 ounce) salt

^{1}/$_2$ teaspoon (0.06 ounce) instant yeast

1^1/$_2$ tablespoons (1 ounce) honey

2 tablespoons (1 ounce) raisin juice concentrate

6 tablespoons (3 ounces) cooked brown rice

2 cups (16 ounces) sponge (from above; use all)

Vegetable oil cooking spray

=Approximate Weight: 25.23 ounces (1 pound, 9.23 ounces)

1. Stir together the sponge ingredients in a mixing bowl till the flour is absorbed and the mixture forms a thick paste. Cover the bowl with plastic wrap and allow the sponge to ferment at room temperature for 4 hours. It should rise and then fall.

2. Combine all of the dough ingredients, including the sponge, in a mixing bowl or in the bowl of an electric

mixer with a dough hook. If making by hand, knead for about 15 minutes; if by machine, 10 to 12 minutes (1 minute on slow speed, 10 minutes or so on medium speed). The dough should be soft and elastic, tacky but not sticky. It will feel a little firmer and more textured than white bread dough, but should pass the windowpane test (see page 29).

3. Put the dough in a clean bowl, cover the bowl with plastic wrap, and allow the dough to rise at room temperature for 90 minutes, or till it doubles.

4. Grease a loaf pan (either 4 by $8^{1/2}$ inches or 5 by 9 inches). Shape the dough into a sandwich loaf as directed on page 21, and place it in the pan, seam side down. Mist the top lightly with cooking spray. Cover loosely with plastic wrap or enclose in a plastic bag. Allow the dough to rise at room temperature for 60 to 90 minutes, till it crests above the pan, doming but not mushrooming over the sides.

5. Position an oven rack in the bottom third of the oven but not on the bottom rung. Preheat the oven to 350°F.

6. Place the loaf in the center of the rack and bake for 20 minutes. Turn it front to back to insure even browning, and bake for 25 to 35 minutes more. The bread is done when the crust is a deep golden brown on all sides, the loaf sounds hollow when thwacked on the bottom, and the internal dough temperature is about 185°F. If the bread seems too soft, you may remove it from

the pan and finish it directly on the oven rack; it will brown very quickly.

7. Remove the bread from the oven to a cooling rack, and let it cool for at least 90 minutes before slicing.

USING DIFFERENT GRAINS

Using grains other than wheat for bread making is not a new concept. For centuries, grains such as spelt, rye, barley, and corn were as prominent. Traditionally, bread was made from locally grown grains. If this meant the breads turned out flat or dense, so be it; traditional societies adjusted to the limitations of their resources. Though wheat is not indigenous to many parts of the world—including North America—it has emerged as the predominant grain because it has the unique advantage of lots of gluten. It is really a modern phenomenon that any kind of bread can be made anywhere.

Wheat, which was brought to North America by the Europeans, now accounts for a huge proportion of our agricultural planting, and wheat grown in the United States and Canada is recognized as the heartiest and strongest in the world. Strains grown elsewhere excel in other qualities, but the strong gluten of American-grown wheat makes it the absolute best for combining with other, weaker grains.

Like most bread lovers, I want my bread to be dense with flavor yet light in texture. I have a bias in favor of grains that are indigenously American (North or

South) in origin, such as corn, quinoa, and amaranth, but have no problem incorporating international grains like rice, millet, oats, rye, and barley into my baking. Our bodies appreciate a cross-section of the grain kingdom, and the various flavors create endless options for the baker.

The trick, of course, is getting the proper balance between wheat and other grains in order to achieve a good texture. The multigrain breads, such as Boston Six Grain, that I described in the introduction to this chapter would probably not be as popular today as they were twenty-five years ago because of their crumbly texture.

Experimentation has led me to conclude that at least 65 percent of the grain must be wheat, preferably unbleached, high-gluten white flour. A strong, hard, whole-wheat flour will work if you are committed to exclusively whole grains (spring wheat is harder than winter wheat, if your market offers you a choice), but unbleached high-gluten flour does produce a lighter texture.

Beyond that, the rules for working with multigrains are simple:

1. When using rice or wild rice, cook the grain first; it will not soften in the dough otherwise. The same is true of steel-cut oats, buckwheat groats, millet, and other full-size grains.

2. Finely milled grains like cornmeal tend to disappear in bread and muddy the color. I prefer coarsely ground grains, such as polenta, grits, or rye meal. This grind does not usually require cooking or soaking; the uncooked grain absorbs moisture from the dough and softens nicely without losing its color or identity (though there is a soaker method, described on page 186, that is popular in Germany for softening the grain.)

3. Rolled grains such as oats and triticale flakes will almost disappear in the dough when baked. They are better used uncooked. Some people like making bread with leftover cooked oatmeal, but the finished bread will be denser and heavier than with uncooked oatmeal.

4. If you like the taste of the grains you use, then you will like the finished bread, but do not expect it to shine through as the predominant flavor. Oatmeal bread does not taste like oatmeal cereal; the flavor is much more subtle, tempered by the wheat flour. The one grain that does tend to hold its own is rye, which has a strong, distinct flavor (for more on rye breads, see page 104).

The following recipes use a wide variety of grains. You may substitute, or mix and match, as long as the grind is similar. When you find a basic formula you like, try it with different grain combinations to discover the flavor shades that each grain brings to the finished loaf.

YEASTED MULTIGRAIN BREAD

Be sure to make the pre-ferment for this recipe the day before, and take it out of the refrigerator at least 1 hour before using.

COMMENTARIES

❑ Loaf pan breads should always rise above their pans, but not overrise and mushroom over the sides. Bake them while still on the rise, assuming a 10 percent oven spring.

INGREDIENT	%
Unbleached bread flour	100
Biga-style pre-ferment	100
Multigrain blend	37.5
Brown rice	12.5
Brown sugar	12.5
Salt	3.1
Instant yeast	2
Buttermilk	50
Honey	18.75
Water	62.5

MAKES 1 LOAF

2 cups (8 ounces) *biga*-style pre-ferment (page 37)

1³/4 cups (8 ounces) unbleached bread flour

³/4 cup (3 ounces) multigrain blend (page 97)

2 tablespoons (1 ounce) cooked brown rice

2 tablespoons (1 ounce) brown sugar

1 teaspoon (0.25 ounce) salt

1¹/2 teaspoons (0.16 ounce) instant yeast

¹/2 cup (4 ounces) buttermilk

2 tablespoons (1.5 ounces) honey

10 tablespoons (5 ounces) cool water (65° to 70°F)

Rolled oats or poppy or other seeds for topping (optional)

Vegetable oil cooking spray

=*Approximate Weight: 31 ounces (1 pound, 15 ounces)*

1. Measure the refrigerated *biga* and let it sit out for 1 hour, to take the chill off. Cut it into small pieces.

2. Combine the *biga* with the other dough ingredients in a mixing bowl by hand or in the bowl of an electric mixer with a dough hook. If making by hand, stir until all the ingredients gather and form a ball. Then turn the dough out onto a floured counter and knead for about 12 minutes. If using a machine, mix on low speed for 1 minute, then increase to medium and mix for 10 additional minutes. As you mix or knead, the dough will lose its coarse, gruel-like texture and become smooth. The dough is ready when it passes the windowpane test (page 29) and feels neutral to the touch (77° to 80°F). It should be tacky but not sticky, with the grains dispersed throughout.

3. Put the dough in a clean bowl, cover with plastic wrap, and allow the dough to rise at room temperature for 90 minutes, or till it doubles in size.

4. Grease a loaf pan (either 4 by 8 ½ inches or 5 by 9 inches). Shape the dough into a sandwich loaf as directed on page 21, and place it in the pan seam side down (or follow the directions for a free-form loaf, page 20, and place it on a greased sheet pan).

5. If topping with rolled oats or seeds, fold up a wet, clean towel and roll it over the top of the loaf, then sprinkle on the topping; it will stick to the wet dough.

6. Mist the loaf lightly with cooking spray. Cover it loosely with plastic wrap or enclose it in a plastic bag. Allow the dough to rise at room temperature for 60 to 90 minutes, till it crests above the pan, doming but not mushrooming over the sides.

7. Position an oven rack in the bottom third of the oven, but not on the bottom rung. Preheat the oven to 350°F.

8. Place the loaf in the center of the rack and bake for 20 minutes. Turn the loaf front to back to insure even browning, and bake for 25 to 35 minutes more. The bread is done when the crust is a deep golden brown on all sides, the loaf sounds hollow when thwacked on the bottom, and the internal dough temperature is about 185°F. If the bread seems too soft, remove it from the pan and finish it directly on the oven rack; it will brown very quickly.

9. Remove the bread from the oven to a cooling rack, and let it cool for 90 minutes before slicing.

LEAVENED MULTIGRAIN BREAD

This is a sourdough version of multigrain bread, perfect for sandwiches or dinner rolls. It also makes a fine hearth bread, but it must be baked at the lower temperature used for sandwich and other semi-enriched breads because the milk and sweeteners caramelize too fast at the higher hearth temperatures. The crust is purposely soft, not crackly, making it a good choice for children. Feel free to experiment with different seed and grain combinations; this formula can be turned into dozens of different breads by changing one or two of the ingredients.

COMMENTARIES

❑ Use either the firm (intermediate) starter from barm (page 77) or the firm mild starter (page 79) for this formula. Be sure to make the starter the day before, and take it out of the refrigerator at least 1 hour before using.

❑ Multigrain breads take a while to absorb liquid (hydrate) because of the various size grains, so you will see the dough go through a gradual structural change from a lumpy gruel to a smooth, homogenized unit.

❑ The primary fermentation, in step 2, is where much of the flavor is developed.

❑ The dough's rise will slow down once it is placed in the refrigerator, so let it rise almost to the finished size first. You could bake at this point, but your bread will have more complex flavor and better color if you wait.

❑ After you remove the dough from the refrigerator, if it is overproofed, the dough will stay indented instead of gradually springing back.

If this is the case, do not attempt to score free-standing loaves or they will deflate. Determining when a dough has fully risen is one of the trickiest parts of making bread. You will get better at it with practice as you begin to recognize the appropriate size based on the weight of the dough.

INGREDIENT	%
Unbleached bread flour	100
Firm starter	100
Multigrain blend	50
Brown rice	19
Brown sugar	21
Salt	4
Honey	19
Buttermilk	50
Water	50

MAKES 1 OR 2 LOAVES

2 cups (8 ounces) firm starter (page 77) or mild starter (page 79)

1³/4 cups (8 ounces) unbleached bread flour

1 cup (4 ounces) multigrain blend (page 97)

3 tablespoons (1.5 ounces) cooked brown rice

3 tablespoons (1.5 ounces) brown sugar

1¹/4 teaspoons (0.33 ounce) salt

2 tablespoons (1.5 ounces) honey

¹/2 cup (4 ounces) buttermilk

¹/2 cup cool water (65° to 70°F)

Poppy, sesame, or other seeds for topping (optional)

Vegetable oil cookng spray

=*Approximate Weight: 32 ounces (2 pounds)*

1. Measure the refrigerated starter and let it sit out for 1 hour, to take off the chill. Break the starter into small pieces and combine it with the other dough ingredients in a mixing bowl or the bowl of an electric mixer with a dough hook. If making by hand, stir until all the ingredients gather and form a ball. Then turn the dough out onto a floured counter and knead it for 12 to 15 minutes. If using a machine, mix on low speed for 1 minute, then increase to medium and mix for 10 to 12 additional minutes. The dough is ready when it passes the windowpane test (page 29) and feels neutral to the touch (78° to 80°F). It should be tacky but not sticky.

2. Put the dough in a clean bowl, cover the bowl with plastic wrap, and allow the dough to rise at room temperature for about 3 to 4 hours, or till it swells slightly in size (it does not need to double).

3. Shape the dough into sandwich loaves, free-form loaves, or rolls (see pages 20–21). Place them in greased *bannetons,* baskets, loaf pans or on sheet pans. If you are using topping, fold a wet, clean towel and roll it over the top of the dough to make the seeds adhere better, and then sprinkle them on (if you are using a *banneton* or basket, wait till just before baking to top the loaves). Mist the top of the shaped dough with cooking spray and cover it with plastic wrap or enclose it in a plastic bag. Let the dough rise for another 3 to 4 hours, or till

almost doubled in size, then refrigerate it overnight.

4. Remove the dough from the refrigerator 1 hour before baking. Loaf-pan bread should be cresting above the rim of the pan, doming but not mushrooming over the sides. Free-standing loaves or rolls should be plump but not overrisen. They should slowly spring back when poked with a finger.

5. Position an oven rack in the bottom third of the oven, and preheat to 350°F. (If using a stone, place it on the rack.)

6. If garnishing basket-risen loaves with seeds, do so now. Remove them from the baskets, invert them, and spray or brush the tops of the loaves (the bottom in the baskets!) with water and sprinkle on the seeds. Transfer free-standing loaves or rolls to a peel or sheet pan that has been dusted with semolina, polenta, or cornmeal. Scoring the loaves is optional.

7. Bake the bread for about 20 minutes, then rotate from front to back and continue baking till done. Free-standing loaves should take a total of 30 to 40 minutes, pan bread 45 to 55 minutes. The loaves should have a rich golden crust and make a hollow sound when thwacked on the bottom. The internal temperature should be about 185°F.

8. Remove the loaves to a cooling rack and let cool thoroughly before slicing—45 to 90 minutes depending on the size of your breads.

THE MULTIGRAIN BLEND

Many combinations of grains produce good multigrain breads, but this is my favorite grain blend. (I use a smaller amount of wheat bran than other grains because it has a cutting effect on gluten.)

1 pound polenta (coarse, not finely milled, cornmeal)

1 pound rolled oats

$1/4$ pound wheat bran

This can be mixed ahead of time and kept in a storage container or in a plastic bag in the freezer. Other grains that can be substituted include triticale flakes, wheat flakes, amaranth, quinoa, and rye flakes. I prefer using just three or four grains so I know how each ingredient is contributing to the flavor and texture.

Large grains, such as rice, bulgur (cracked wheat), steel-cut oats, millet, buckwheat groats, or barley, must be cooked and cooled first, and can be added as an additional ingredient, staying within the flour-to-grain ratio (65 to 80 percent bread flour, 20 to 35 percent grain blend) described below.

As discussed on page 93, I do not recommend finely milled grains like rice flour, cornmeal, or rye flour in the multigrain blend, as they dull the bright color of the loaf.

Regardless of the blend, the key is to keep it in proportion to the rest of the dough. To retain the best structure, the dough needs 65 to 80 percent bread (or high-gluten) flour. The additional grain flavors are interesting but need to be complemented by sweeteners like honey or sugar to really come forth. Many health-conscious bakeries have learned the hard way that just because a bread has many grains in no way guarantees that it will taste good.

VARIATIONS OF MULTIGRAIN

You can vary these master formulas to create dozens of interesting breads. The following ingredients are examples of additions or substitutions you can make:

Cooked wild rice (substitute for cooked brown rice)

Seeds, including pumpkin, sesame, and poppy seeds (about 1 cup per loaf)

Nuts, including sliced almonds and walnut pieces (about 1 cup per loaf)

Raisins and other dried fruit (currants, chopped apricots, figs, etc.—1 cup per loaf)

Chopped fresh fruit like mango or apples (about 2 cups per loaf)

Chocolate chips or chunks (1 cup per loaf)

Dried or fresh chopped onion ($1/2$ cup dried or 2 cups fresh per loaf) or minced garlic (4 to 8 cloves fresh or 1 tablespoon dried minced garlic per loaf—see below for further instructions)

Chopped sweet red or green peppers (1 to 2 cups per loaf) or hot chiles (up to 1 cup per loaf)

Seasonings such as cayenne ($1/2$ teaspoon per loaf), black pepper ($1/2$ teaspoon per loaf), rosemary (1 teaspoon per loaf, fresh or dried), other herbs (1 to 3 teaspoons dried, $1/4$ cup fresh per loaf), and hot sauce (2 to 4 tablespoons per loaf)

Here are some additional guidelines:

1. Fresh or granulated garlic should be added only during the final 2 minutes of mixing, or rolled into the loaves during shaping, or it will adversely affect gluten development.

2. Onions, nuts, seeds, and fruits should also be added during the final 2 minutes so they do not get chewed up in the mixing process. Dried chopped onion, though, should be added at the beginning to allow it time to fully hydrate.

3. If making raisin bread, mix the raisins into the dough rather than spreading them on flattened dough and rolling it up; this will prevent them from falling out so easily after the bread is sliced. Try this method: Soak the raisins in lukewarm water for 1 minute to wash off surface yeast and sugars. Mix the raisins into the dough during the final 2 minutes of mixing. After the first rise, roll out the dough into a rectangle and spread it with a layer of cinnamon sugar (1 part ground cinnamon, 4 parts granulated sugar). Roll it up like a jelly roll to create an interesting spiral. Or you can top the loaves with the cinnamon sugar after they come out of the oven: Brush melted butter on the hot loaf top and then roll the top in cinnamon sugar to coat. It will form a nice crust as the loaf cools.

4. When adding big seeds like pumpkin or sunflower to dough, toast and cool them first. This brings out a deeper flavor as they get double-roasted during the final bake (this is not necessary with small seeds like sesame, nigella, or flax).

5. Likewise, when using onions, sweet red peppers, or hot chiles, you can sauté or roast them ahead. If you want them to retain their crunch, though, use them raw in relatively large pieces.

6. If garnishing the tops of the loaves with seeds, moisten the top of the dough first so they won't fall off after the bake (see pages 96–97, steps 3 and 6).

A NOTE ABOUT NONWHEAT BREADS

I know a number of people who have difficulty handling gluten. By that I mean that as a result of celiac disease, environmental illness, or some other condition, they get physically or emotionally ill if they eat conventional bread. I received many calls at Brother Juniper's Bakery asking me to create a nongluten bread. It may be difficult to understand if you have never suffered bread deprivation, but there was a sound of desperation in the pleas, and they touched me deeply.

Lori Starr Brown, a woman who has celiac disease, called to tell me she had substituted rice flour for the wheat and made a few other adjustments in some of the recipes from my first bread book and had created a nice array of nonwheat breads. Because of the lack of gluten, her breads couldn't attain the height and texture of wheat breads, but they made nice English muffins and small loaves. Since then we have worked together to create a number of wheat-free, gluten-free breads. We hope eventually to publish them in a book of their own. In the meantime, you can create your own variations by substituting rice flour for the wheat and other grains. Add 1 teaspoon of xanthan gum per loaf; use a commercial egg replacement where eggs are called for, and avoid malt and low-gluten grains like barley, rye, and oats. Be prepared to work with sticky doughs. See the resource section on page 195 for more recipe and product information.

5

THE ROMANCE OF WOOD-FIRED BRICK OVENS, AND A FEW ADVANCED TECHNIQUES

Master Formula: Yeasted Rye ; Master Formula: Naturally Leavened Rye Bread;
Master Formula: German Five-Kern Bread

About a year after my wife, Susan, and I opened Brother Juniper's Cafe, we were visited by a short, sinewy fellow with an English accent and an aura I can only describe as character. His name was Alan Scott. He showed us blueprints for a wood-burning brick oven that he thought would make a marvelous addition to our little bakery cafe. He seemed totally undaunted by the fact that our cafe was barely 800 square feet, including the kitchen, and was hidden inside an arcade building with four other shops. He regaled us with stories about how people were using these ovens as centerpieces in their establishments and how wonderful the bread was, *real* bread, he called it, made from freshly ground wheat and mixed with an ancient sourdough starter called *desum*. He sold the loaves himself from the back of a truck near Point Reyes National Seashore in Califor-

nia to a steady group of loyalists devoted to wood-fired breads. I loved the imagery and the romance of such a picture and tried hard to figure out how I could incorporate it into my undercapitalized little operation. Alas, I never did solve the problem and spent the following years wondering what-if, while I followed Alan's career through newspaper articles as his beautiful, rustic ovens began showing up in backyards, restaurants, and bakeries across North America.

Recently, I have seen Alan's ovens in some pretty upscale places. The basic firing and venting system is the same as always, but the facades have become larger and classier, sometimes Italian themed, sometimes brassy. He has become a folk hero to a whole generation of bakers, presiding over oven raisings, similar to Amish barn raisings, wherein a group of baking enthusiasts gather to construct in one day an oven that might have taken a single craftsperson weeks to build. They then stage a ritual firing of the bricks and the first loaves are baked—pretty primal, and the stuff from which legends grow.

Alan is not alone in this wood-fired brick oven trend. Italian companies are selling prefab *forni* with entirely different firing systems. My friend Lou Preston, owner of Preston Vineyards in Sonoma's Dry Creek wine country, baked fresh bread daily to sell in his tasting room from an adobe *forno* of his own design. The secret, he told me, was adding horse manure and straw to the local adobe clay, which gave the dome enough strength to withstand the intense heat generated by the oak and madrone he burns on its deck. Sometimes it's better not to know. He now bakes in a new Alan Scott oven.

Karen Mitchell, who owns a wonderful cafe in St. Helena, California, called the Model Bakery, inherited two large brick ovens when she bought the bakery ten years ago. They are about one hundred years old; some of the bricks wiggle, but the oven works perfectly. Rather than build a fire in it each day, her bakers heat the bricks with large industrial torches, flamethrowers I call them. The bricks are flamed for 30 minutes, and then a steady stream of pizzas, breads, pies, cookies, and cakes are baked as the bricks gradually cool. When the time comes to bake again, the bricks are retorched. Customers come from miles around to see this show and to buy the delicious breads and pastries the bakery produces. Karen told me that there is so much residual heat in the bricks and surrounding sand that it would take nearly a month for the oven to cool down enough for someone to crawl in to make repairs.

Whether fueled by wood, coal, or flamethrowers, brick ovens are hot in more ways than one. They are now coming back into vogue, but the old Italian-style bakeries in cities like New York, Philadelphia, and San Francisco never stopped making bread in brick ovens. It may well be that, like some of the advancements in dough technology, modern gas-fired or electric ovens are as good or better than the old brick versions. Still, clay or brick decks encased in thick walls of hand-packed adobe and sand, heated by hardwood gathered in the nearby forest, project an image of bread baking that captures the timeless quality of the process and transcends technological innovations.

Modern ovens have computer controls that assure consistency; they have both stationary and moving brick decks, depending on the need. Some, called rotating rack ovens, lift an entire rack of bread off the floor and turn it like a rotisserie within a steam-injected chamber, baking evenly colored loaves with an efficiency and consistency never imagined a few years ago. One bakery in San Francisco has designed a system of extending baguette dough on felt-covered metal fingers, jiggling out the dough to its proper length much like a person would. Their baguettes are beautiful and appear handmade. Technology continues to improve upon itself, yet the image of the wood-fired brick oven persists. Romance is hard to overpower.

For the home baker, stuck with a built-in gas or electric oven, or if among the elite, a restaurant-grade range with a double-doored oven, the bread-baking challenge is this: how to replicate both the quality and romance of having an Alan Scott–type oven on the back porch, its tiny door opening its glowing, fiery mouth into the kitchen. Assuming that buying a blueprint from Alan or a kit from Italy is out, what are our options? We have discussed how to simulate a wood-fired oven at home, using baking or pizza stones and tiles (page 25) and even how to use the more symbolically ideal cloche (page 27). Now we will examine oven technique more deeply.

The first thing that a wood-fired oven does better than a home oven is to get really, really hot. When I watched Peter Conn of Il Fornaio burn his first batch of *focaccia* in one of Alan Scott's ovens at the 1996 Grainaissance Fair (see page 46), it was because the oven was almost 800°F. We loved what it portended. When it cooled down enough to bake without burning, at about 600°F, the oven injected a smoky quality into the bread that was, like authentic slow-smoked Texas barbecue, inimitable. No home or even professional oven could ever match it. But what can be matched is a fearlessness about baking at high temperatures and a commitment to deep baking— that is, baking a loaf till it fully gelatinizes and caramelizes, roasting the fermented grain till it releases every hidden flavor. This is possible even in a home oven.

Many of the formulas in this book suggest baking at 450°F. This is good and it is safe. However, bearing in mind that an oven loses about 50°F as soon as the door opens—and the temperature drops even further when steam is created (steam is, after all, only 212°F)—a bolder approach would be to turn up the oven as far as it will go, or at least to 550°F. Hearth bread loves the shock of high heat radiating from the deck; it creates internal steam as the moisture in the loaf heats up and engenders a full-scale feeding frenzy by the yeast cells as they madly convert sugar to both alcohol and carbon dioxide in a final act of valor before surrendering to death when the internal dough temperature hits 140°F.

Steam is critical; the longer you can keep the crust soft and pliable, the greater the oven spring. Commercial ovens have powerful steam injectors that provide enough moisture in twenty seconds to last until the oven spring ends. Spray bottles (I call them spritzers), inject a little moisture into a home oven, but every time we open the door the temperature drops. Pouring hot water into a hot sheet pan or cast-iron skillet provides instant steam and a steady stream of vapor (ideally, this water should evaporate within ten minutes so the loaves can finish in a dry oven). A well-intentioned but inefficient home baker's trick has been to toss ice cubes onto a hot pan for this purpose. The reality is that hot water takes far less energy to convert to steam, and steam is what we really want early on, and plenty of it! Once the hot water hits the hot pan, steam is instantly created, but then things settle down to a period of vapor. At this stage a few well-placed shots from a water spritzer on the oven wall (and not on the oven lightbulb, which must be turned off lest it burst and shatter) can create another generation of instant steam. Meanwhile, the oven temperature keeps going down. The ideal temperature for hearth bread is 450° to 460°F. If we bake any higher for very long, the outside bakes far too quickly, so a few minutes after the completion of the steam drama it is important to adjust the dial from 550° back to 450°F. When the bread appears close to being done, lower the temperature even further (or turn the heat off completely), allowing the bread to continue baking without burning the crust. The more dough moisture you bake out, the crisper the crust, to a point, beyond which you risk overbaking and drying out the bread. Using a probe thermometer is the most accurate way to determine doneness, but many people prefer to trust their own feel for the product, relying totally on the thwack test.

Using a cloche comes about the closest to wood-fired brick baking because of the compact space and trapped steam. I have experimented with my cloche, sometimes letting the bottom section heat up with the oven, like a deck, and then sliding my loaf onto it and quickly sealing it closed with the dome. But I have had my best success when I proofed my loaf directly on the cloche bottom (this avoids unnecessary handling), then spritzed the inside of the dome with water, placed it over the loaf, and slid the whole unit into a very hot oven. I turn down the temperature only when I am sure the heat has fully penetrated the cloche.

Here are some other tricks worth trying to capture the spirit of brick-oven baking at home:

❑ Why settle for just one deck when two pizza stones, properly placed, can radiate from above and below, replicating even more accurately a professional deck oven?

❑ Use a cast-iron skillet or pot for generating steam (put it in the oven while preheating to get red-hot); it holds heat longer than a sheet pan.

❑ Get a small wooden or metal peel for sliding your doughs into the oven. It will make you feel like Nicolas Cage playing the baker in *Moonstruck*.

❑ Make a *lame* with a wooden coffee stirrer and a double-edged razor blade (see page 25). Replace the blade when it gets dull. Scoring the tops of the loaves with distinctive cuts will be part of your artistic expression.

❑ Get a few *bannetons* (authentic ones are very expensive), or some tightly woven, nonlacquered bread baskets that can do the same job. Remember to treat them with a mist of cooking spray and then generously dust with flour (a combination of bread flour and rice flour works best) so the dough will slide out easily. Clean them out after each usage to prevent a buildup of flour clumps.

It does not take a lot of time or money to outfit your kitchen for world-class baking. If you bring passion to the process, you will barely notice that you do not have a wood-fired brick oven. As your bread skills develop and you begin turning out bread from your home oven that is good beyond belief, you may, however, find yourself dreaming about your own wood-fired brick oven radiating at 800°F. Such passion is the stuff that dreams are made of. Meanwhile, try some of these advanced tricks on the breads that follow.

MASTER FORMULA:
YEASTED RYE

You do not need a wood-fired oven to make these rye breads, though rye, more than even wheat, seems to evoke the ancient, earthy imagery associated with bread and fire. Rye is a heartier grain than wheat, often grown where wheat does not do well, and so has become known as a bread of the people.

Though rye bread is at its best when made with a sour starter, excellent versions are made with commercial yeast. The following bread uses the pre-fermented sponge method (a variation of the *poolish*) to draw out the most grain flavor and promote digestibility of the rye flour.

While there are many permutations of the rye-wheat ratio, including some breads that are 100 percent rye, I find that very few people, in the United States at least, actually prefer the heavier ryes. For this reason, I use a ratio of three parts wheat to one part rye, though you can experiment with different proportions. I use coarsely ground rye, also called pumpernickel flour or rye meal, rather than fine rye. This gives the loaf better texture and a more open crumb.

Most people in America associate rye with the flavor of the ubiquitous caraway seed, but black onion seed (nigella), anise, and orange zest also complement the sweet, earthy rye tones. Some rye breads are flavored with molasses, but I prefer just a hint of the less obtrusive sugar or malt. This first bread can be made as a free-standing loaf, but I think it works best as a loaf-pan bread for sandwiches.

COMMENTARIES

❏ The rye pre-ferment allows the rye flour a chance to influence the flavor of the bread. It also makes the rye more digestible. The sponge is thick and takes awhile to develop. When it is mature, it will be bubbly and very active.

❏ Caraway seeds are a mixed blessing for rye breads. They complement the flavor wonderfully but also mask the subtleties. You may want to try black onion seed, also called nigella, which has a savory, crackly taste. Or, if you really want to experience the full flavor of the grain, leave the seeds out.

❏ The different coloring agents each add a subtle flavor of their own but are not necessary to good rye bread. Experiment with them until you decide which flavor you prefer. Keep in mind that cocoa and coffee burn easily, so use only a small amount. (Caramel coloring is already burned sugar. You can buy it, liquid or powder, from baking supply stores or ask to buy some from your neighborhood baker.)

❏ In step 1, the falling of the sponge is a sign of full maturity. If your sponge is bubbly but not fallen you may still use it, though it may not be quite as potent.

❏ Mixing time for rye breads is shorter than for straight wheat breads. The rye tends to break down faster than wheat, causing the dough to feel gummy. It is best to catch the dough before this happens.

❏ I bake the hearth version of this bread at a lower temperature than regular hearth breads because of the buttermilk and sugar, which cause the bread to caramelize more quickly. The lower temperature also allows for a more gradual bake.

INGREDIENT (SPONGE)	%
Unbleached bread flour	50
Rye flour	50
Instant yeast	1
Water	89

RYE SPONGE

1 cup (4.5 ounces) unbleached bread flour

1 cup (4.5 ounces) coarse rye flour

1 teaspoon (0.11 ounce) instant yeast

1 cup cool water (65° to 70°)

=*Approximate Weight: 17 ounces*

INGREDIENT (DOUGH)	%
Unbleached bread flour	100
Sugar	5.5
Salt	3.6
Instant yeast	0.7
Caraway seeds	N/A
Caramel coloring	N/A
Buttermilk	22
Rye sponge	189

DOUGH

2 cups (9 ounces) unbleached bread flour

1 tablespoon (0.5 ounce) brown sugar or diastatic malt powder

1¼ teaspoons (0.33 ounce) salt

½ teaspoon (0.06 ounce) instant yeast

1 tablespoon (0.33 ounce) caraway or other seeds (optional)

1 teaspoon caramel coloring, instant coffee, or cocoa powder (optional)

¼ cup (2 ounces) buttermilk

Rye sponge (from above; use all)

Vegetable oil cooking spray

=*Approximate Weight: 30 ounces (1 pound, 14 ounces)*

1. To make the sponge, combine all the sponge ingredients in a mixing bowl and stir to form a smooth, thick paste. Cover the bowl with plastic wrap and allow the sponge to ferment at room temperature for 4 hours. It should rise and fall during this time.

2. If making by hand, combine all the dough ingredients with the sponge in the same bowl, and stir till they form a ball. Turn the dough out onto a floured surface and knead for about 10 minutes. If making by machine, combine the sponge and the dough ingredients in the bowl of an electric mixer with a dough hook; mix on low speed for 1 minute and medium speed for about 8 minutes. The dough should be smooth and stretchy, tacky but not sticky, and neutral to the touch (77° to 80°F). If you are using a coloring ingredient (coffee, cocoa, or caramel coloring), it should be evenly dispersed, not streaky or spotty. The dough should pass the windowpane test (page 29).

3. Place the dough in a clean bowl, cover the bowl with plastic wrap or enclose it in a plastic bag, and allow it to rise at room temperature for 90 minutes, or till double in size.

4. Shape the dough into a pan loaf, free-standing loaf, or rolls, as described on pages 20–21. Mist the top of the dough lightly with cooking spray, cover it loosely with plastic wrap or place it in a plastic bag, and let it rise for 60 to 90 minutes, till the dough is nearly double in size. Pan bread should crest above the pan when risen, doming but not mushrooming over the sides of the pan. The dough should slowly spring back when poked. Score hearth-style loaves just before baking; do not score pan bread.

5. Preheat the oven to 350°F for pan bread, 425°F for hearth bread. Prepare the oven for hearth baking as described on page 25, making sure to put an empty steam pan on the bottom rack. Spritz the loaves and oven walls with water and pour 1 cup of hot water into the steam pan. Close the oven door. After 2 minutes, spritz again. Bake the pan bread for 45 to 55 minutes, hearth bread 35 to 40 minutes. The finished bread should be evenly colored and hollow sounding when thwacked on the bottom. The internal temperature should be 195°F.

6. Move the bread to a cooling rack and allow it to cool thoroughly before slicing, about 90 minutes.

NATURALLY LEAVENED RYE BREAD

The key to the wonderfully complex flavor of this bread is the building process. Allow plenty of time, as you will be making a special rye sponge starter from the basic barm sponge described on page 72. Otherwise, the process is very similar to making *levain* and sourdough breads. Though I love this bread just the way it is, you can make any variations you want by adjusting the percentage of rye, the type of seed, or the choice of coloring agent. The seeds and coloring are optional. I suggest you first make this bread without the extras so you can experience the unadulterated flavor of great rye bread. Then, if you want to accentuate certain flavor tones, add the additional ingredients next time.

COMMENTARIES

❑ This is another version of *pain au méteil,* what the French call rye bread made with more wheat than rye flour. If the rye exceeds the wheat, the bread is called *pain au seigle.* When colored with cocoa or caramel coloring, it can also be called pumpernickel, though this name has lost its specific meaning. (Traditional pumpernickel is made with darkly toasted crumbs from previous batches.)

❑ As with all the wild yeast breads, you need to have ready a refreshed batch of basic barm starter, from page 72, to begin this bread. The rye sponge, which is an additional "build" not included in the other sourdoughs, converts the barm into a rye bread starter and begins the enzyme action that makes the rye more digestible. The rye sponge and subsequent firm starter can both be made on the same day if you start early. If not, you can refrigerate the rye sponge overnight, adding an extra day to the overall process.

❏ Do not use fine rye flour but only coarse, also called *pumpernickel grind* or *rye meal.* This coarse grind gives the bread the proper, opened-crumbed texture.

❏ The firm starter is the intermediate starter, sometimes referred to as the *levain* or *chef.* It is this stage that gives the bread its complex flavor.

❏ The bread is wonderful with or without coloring, but caramel coloring, cocoa powder, and instant coffee each lend their own flavor tones. They tend to burn easily so only a small amount is used, just enough to give the bread an interesting color and hint of flavor.

❏ Seeds are a matter of personal taste in rye breads. There are times when I prefer the flavor burst of caraway or black onion seed (nigella) and times when I want to savor the distinctive but subtle flavor of the rye alone.

❏ Wait till the rye sponge starter is bubbly and clearly alive in step 1 before moving to the next step. Overnighting the sponge allows it to slowly continue developing, but it also adds an extra day to the process.

❏ Refrigerating the firm starter overnight is necessary to get the fullest flavor from the grain.

❏ Rye tends to break down if kneaded too much and then takes on a gummy quality. Mix this dough only until the gluten develops to the windowpane stage, no longer. This means you will have to make any flour or water adjustments early in the mixing cycle to avoid over-mixing it later. This feel for the dough will come after you have made it a few times.

❏ The dough's rising will slow down quickly once refrigerated, so it is important to get it almost fully to size before the retarding cycle. It will grow a little more overnight and should be ready to bake when you take it out of the refrigerator the following day.

❏ If the bread is baked in a loaf pan, follow the pan-bread baking instructions for Yeasted Rye on page 106.

❏ The bread is technically baked when it reaches an internal temperature of 185°F, but the deeper baking to 205°F or higher brings out more complex flavors. A probe thermometer is a valuable tool for determining doneness, but if you do not have one, wait for the loaf to bake as deeply as possible without burning. Using the cool-down technique (turning off the oven while leaving the bread in) extends the oven time to preserve a crackly crust.

❏ Always wait till the loaf has completely cooled if you want to taste the full array of complexity. This bread has many interesting levels of flavor.

MAKES 2 LOAVES

INGREDIENT (SPONGE STARTER)	%
Coarse rye flour	100
Wheat bran	11
Barm sponge starter	178
Water	178

RYE SPONGE STARTER

$^1/_2$ **cup (2.25 ounces) coarse rye flour**

1 tablespoon (0.25 ounce) wheat bran (optional)

$^1/_2$ **cup (4 ounces) barm sponge starter (page 72)**

$^1/_2$ **cup cool water (65° to 70°F)**

=*Approximate Weight: 10.5 ounces*

INGREDIENT (FIRM STARTER)	%
Unbleached bread flour	100
Rye sponge starter	240

FIRM STARTER

1 cup (4.5 ounces) unbleached
bread flour

1¼ cups (10.5 ounces) rye sponge starter
(from above; use all)

=*Approximate Weight: 15 ounces*

INGREDIENT (DOUGH)	%
Unbleached bread flour	75
Coarse rye flour	25
Salt	2.8
Caramel coloring	N/A
Caraway seeds	N/A
Water	67
Firm starter	63

DOUGH

15 ounces firm starter (from above; use all)

4 cups (18 ounces) unbleached
bread flour

1¼ cups (5.75 ounces) coarse rye flour

2½ teaspoons (0.66 ounce) salt

1 to 2 tablespoons caramel coloring,
cocoa powder, or instant coffee

1 to 2 tablespoons (0.33 to 0.66 ounce)
caraway or black onion seeds
(optional)

2 cups cool water (65° to 70°F)

Vegetable oil cooking spray

=*Approximate Weight: 55 ounces*
(3 pounds, 7 ounces)

1. Stir or whisk together all the rye
sponge starter ingredients in a mixing
bowl till the flour is absorbed. Cover
the bowl with plastic wrap and allow
the sponge to ferment for 4 to 5
hours. It should be very bubbly. Proceed to the firm starter or refrigerate
overnight.

2. If the sponge is refrigerated, remove
it from the refrigerator at least 1 hour
before proceeding, to take off the
chill. Stir together the firm starter
ingredients in a mixing bowl till they
form a ball. Add a few drops of water
if necessary. On a lightly floured surface, knead the starter till all the flour
is absorbed. The gluten does not need
to be fully developed. If using an electric mixer, mix only long enough to
make a smooth dough ball. Place this
firm starter in a clean bowl, cover the
bowl with plastic wrap, and allow
the starter to ferment for 3 to 4 hours,
until it has risen somewhat. It does
not have to double, or even grow sig-
nificantly, but it should be showing
signs of life and growth. Refrigerate it
overnight.

3. Remove the firm starter from the refrigerator 1 hour before making the
dough, to take off the chill. Break it
into small pieces.

4. If making the dough by machine,
combine the firm starter and all the
other dough ingredients in the bowl of
an electric mixer with a dough hook.
Mix on low speed for 1 minute and
then on medium speed for 6 to 8 min-

utes. If making by hand, stir the ingredients until they form a ball, and then knead on a lightly floured surface for about 10 minutes. The dough should be smooth, stretchy, and neutral to the touch (77° to 80°F) and should pass the windowpane test (page 29).

5. Return the dough to a clean bowl, cover the bowl with plastic wrap, and allow the dough to rise at room temperature for 3 hours, until it just begins to swell.

6. Divide the dough into 2 equal pieces and round the dough into balls. Cover and allow the doughs to rest for 5 minutes, then shape into round loaves (*boules*) as directed on page 20, or any shape you like.

7. If using baskets or *bannetons,* place the dough, top side down, in the floured baskets. If free-standing, place the loaves on an inverted sheet pan that you have lined with parchment and sprinkled with semolina, cornmeal, or polenta. Lightly mist the exposed part of the dough with cooking spray. Enclose each pan or basket in a plastic bag and let the dough rise at room temperature for 3 to 4 hours, or till it is 1¹/₂ times its original size. Refrigerate overnight.

8. Remove the dough from the refrigerator 1 hour before baking, to take off the chill. Prepare the oven for hearth baking as directed on page 25, making sure to put an empty steam pan on the bottom rack. Preheat to 475°F.

9. Generously dust a baking peel with semolina, cornmeal, or polenta and transfer the dough, 1 loaf at a time, to the peel. Score the dough and slide it onto the baking stone. Spritz the loaves and oven doors with water and pour 1 cup of hot water into the steam pan. Close the oven door. After 2 minutes, spritz the oven again. After 5 minutes, reduce the heat to 450°F.

10. The bread should bake in 25 to 35 minutes, depending on size and shape. When the crust is hard and well caramelized and the loaf makes a hollow sound when thwacked, turn off the oven. Leave the bread in for 5 to 10 additional minutes, until it appears that it can't go a minute longer without burning, and the internal temperature has reached 205° to 210°F.

11. Transfer the bread to a cooling rack, and let it cool for at least 45 minutes before eating.

GERMAN FIVE-KERN BREAD

I am not a huge fan of dense and chewy German-style breads. A few years ago, however, one of our customers, a trader of German imports, brought me a loaf of five-kern bread from one of his frequent trips, and it reminded me so much of the multi-grain bread we had served at the Root One Cafe in Boston in the early seventies that I decided to create my own version.

There are many variations of this bread—three-kern, seven-kern, etc. (*kern* means grain in German)—and you may want to try substituting other grains or using fewer varieties, as described on page 97. Two essential ingredients, though, are the flax seeds and the cooked rice. Flax seeds, from which linseed oil is derived, are very good for digestion. Flax has become a huge cash crop in Canada, and flax seed breads are quite the rage there. They are easier to assimilate into dough if ground slightly. For the top, however, I suggest leaving them whole, as they give a very distinctive look and crunch to the bread. The brown rice helps the bread retain its moistness. Be sure it is thoroughly cooked, not al dente, or it will be hard on the teeth. The rye flour should be a pumpernickel or a similar coarse grind, which may be called rye meal in some markets. Using a finer grind of rye makes the loaf dense and a little gummy.

Using the firm starter method, combined with the rye and other grains, gives this bread a very complex sour flavor that fills the mouth and lingers long afterward. Because of the many low-gluten grains, the loaf cannot support the open-holed crumb of the lighter French and Italian breads. The loaf has very little oven spring, but the trade-off is a moist, flavorful bread perfect with deli foods, mustard dishes, or as a meal unto itself.

COMMENTARIES

❑ Regardless of which firm starter you use, be sure to make it one or two days ahead, and take it out of the refrigerator 1 hour before using. To temper the sourness, you can add 1 tablespoon instant yeast to the dry ingredients before the final mixing. This is called *spiking* the dough. It allows rising to occur more quickly (about 90 minutes). You can then treat it like any other yeasted bread, decreasing the rising periods as indicated below, and baking it on the same day. The texture will be as usual but the flavor will be only mildly sour—somewhere between a leavened and yeasted bread.

❑ High-gluten flour is stronger than regular bread flour (about 14.5 percent versus 12.5 percent gluten). Most natural foods stores carry it. It may also be called *hard spring wheat flour*. The added gluten helps support the high percentage of low-gluten grains.

❑ Flax seed comes from linen plants (flax is also called linseed) and is rich in linoleic enzymes, which are beneficial for digestion. They can be found at specialty food stores and may be ground in a regular household blender. If you cannot find them, ask your local bakery if you can buy some from their stock.

❑ Because of the variety of flour, grain, and seeds in this recipe, I am combining them to total 100 percent. High-gluten flour represents two thirds of the total grain weight, which is at the low end of the proportion scale for multigrain breads. However, in this style of bread the final crumb is intentionally dense.

- If spiked with yeast, the dough will take only about 90 minutes to rise, and the loaf may be baked at that point. It can also be retarded overnight, as described, for a better flavor. If making the bread without spiking, you may also bake the loaf after it has properly risen, but the flavor will be more developed after an overnight retarding.

- The flavors in this bread, especially if made without additional yeast, are very complex and cannot be fully appreciated until the bread has completely cooled. It will be even more flavorful the following day.

INGREDIENT	%
Flour (high gluten and rye)	100
Firm starter	31
Total other grain	31
Salt	2.6
Honey	3
Water	78
Ground flax seeds	8
Whole flax seeds	6

2 cups (8 ounces) firm starter (page 108 or page 82)

4²/₃ cups plus 1 tablespoon (21 ounces) high-gluten flour

1 cup (4.5 ounces) coarse rye flour

1/2 cup (4 ounces) cooked brown rice

1/3 cup (2 ounces) polenta

1/3 cup (2 ounces) rolled oats

1/4 cup (2 ounces) ground flax seeds

2¹/₂ teaspoons (0.66 ounce) salt

1 tablespoon (0.75 ounce) honey

2¹/₂ cups cool water (65° to 70°F)

3 tablespoons (1.5 ounces) whole flax seeds for top

Vegetable oil cooking spray

=Approximate Weight: 66 ounces (4 pounds, 2 ounces)

1. Make the starter 1 or 2 days ahead and remove it from the refrigerator at least 1 hour before proceeding, to take off the chill.

2. Break the starter into small pieces, and combine it with all the other ingredients, except the whole flax seeds, in a mixing bowl or the bowl of an electric mixer with a dough hook. Knead by hand for 15 minutes, or by machine for about 12 minutes (1 minute on low speed, 11 minutes on medium), or till the dough is smooth and elastic, tacky but not sticky. Add more water or flour if necessary. The dough should

pass the windowpane test (page 29) and register between 77° and 80°F on a probe thermometer.

3. Put the dough in a clean bowl, cover with plastic wrap or enclose in a plastic bag, and allow the dough to rise at room temperature for about 3 hours, until it begins to swell noticeably.

4. Divide the dough into 3 equal pieces and shape them into pan or hearth loaves as described on pages 20–21. Brush the tops of the loaves with water or moisten them with a wet towel and roll them in the whole flax seeds. (If using baskets for rising, add the seeds later.) Place the loaves in greased loaf pans, or for hearth bread, on parchment-lined sheet pans. Spray the tops of the loaves with cooking spray and cover with plastic wrap or enclose in a plastic bag. Allow to rise at room temperature for 3 to 4 hours, till nearly doubled. Refrigerate overnight.

5. Remove the dough from the refrigerator 1 hour before baking to take off the chill. Preheat the oven to 475° for hearth bread, 350° for pan bread. If hearth baking, prepare the oven as described on page 25, making sure to put an empty steam pan on the bottom rack.

6. If the loaves have been rising in baskets, turn them out onto a floured peel, brush the tops with water, and sprinkle with whole flax seeds.

7. If baking hearth bread, score the bread, then slide the loaves into the oven on a floured peel. Spritz the loaves and oven walls with water and pour 1 cup of hot water into the steam pan. Close the oven door. After 2 minutes, spritz again. After 5 minutes, reduce the oven temperature to 450°F. Hearth bread will take 30 to 35 minutes to bake. When the loaves appear done—golden brown with a hard crust, and hollow sounding when thwacked on the bottom—turn off the oven and allow 10 additional minutes of baking. Internal temperature should exceed 200°F.

8. Loaf-pan bread will be done in 45 to 55 minutes at 350°F. It should be firm and golden all around and hollow when thwacked. Internal temperature should be approximately 185°F. Remove from the oven when done.

9. Allow the bread to cool on a rack for at least 60 minutes before cutting.

6

ENRICHED DOUGHS: NOT WHAT YOU PUT ON BUT WHAT YOU PUT IN

Master Formula: Brioche; Master Formula: Kugelhopf; Master Formula: Challah;
Master Formula: All-Purpose Holiday Bread; Master Formula: Multipurpose Sweet Dough

I did not consider myself a brioche fan until recently. Lean breads were enough for me, low in fat, high in carbs, full of natural grain flavor; who needed rich, buttery bread?

Looking back, I see the flaw in my logic. As a youth I fell in love with croissants well before I knew what was in them or how they were made. There was just something different about them; they were, well, more buttery than regular rolls. My mother would buy a large bag of small croissants once a month from a bakery at a local farmers' market and put it in the freezer. Every day, while they lasted, I got to choose from among the frozen croissants, frozen Tasty Cake Chocolate TandyTakes, or fresh fruit when I came home from school desperate for a snack. I rotated among these treasures, sometimes doubling up. (What a treat to follow a croissant with a chocolate TandyTake!) When competing on sports teams, I did not get home till dinnertime, so I had to wait till 8 P.M. for my ritual snack break. Life was tough.

After I left home for college and beyond and got involved with natural foods, the only survivor of my snack trilogy was fresh·fruit. I went twenty-five years without a TandyTake, rediscovering them when my wife's Aunt Eileen, in true Philadelphia fashion, sent us a gift box of Tasty Cake products for Christmas. I had practically forgotten about croissants when, after joining a religious order, one of the brothers in our seminary started a holiday custom of making them for Christmas and Easter. Passion rekindled!

Still later, I was thrust into the bread world and took my stand with traditional and neotraditional lean breads, eschewing, except on special occasions, the rich breads that seemed to increase my girth. (I was haunted by the image of a cartoon tacked to the wall at the gym where I worked out: One woman is saying to another, "No more doughnuts for me; they go straight to my thighs," and as you look down at her thighs, you see little doughnut shapes popping out everywhere.)

Then, in 1995, I met Mark Furstenberg, the founder of the Marvelous Market bakery in Washington, D.C. Mark had been flown in for the grand opening of the Culinary Institute of America's Greystone campus in St. Helena, California, to make some of his signature breads, including his renowned brioche. He came up to me with a loaf he had pulled from the oven thirty minutes earlier. "Try this," he said. I wanted to say, "No, I don't do brioche," but there was an urgency about his request. "This is my favorite," he said intensely. He wore the distinctive look of bread passion, the same look I assume when trying to get someone to taste my Struan or wild yeast loaves—a look, dare I say it, of love. And so I tried it. Whoa! Now brioche, but only truly great brioche like Mark's, has been added to my own stable of passions.

Having never made a Parisian pilgrimage like so many of my fellow bread lovers, my passions are homegrown, and I am something of a bread chauvinist. For years I avoided brioche not only because it was laden with butter or because most bakeries make a rather mediocre version of it, but because it is so definitively French. But Mark's bread won me over.

Brioche, like most famous French breads and pastries, did not originate in Paris but in Vienna, seemingly the true headwater of great baking. However, like so many other Viennese delights, brioche found its most passionate following in Paris, where Marie Antoinette, herself a transplanted Viennese royal, went to her death saying, not "Let them eat cake," but rather "Let them eat brioche." There is some debate over whether this was a catty little dig or a last-ditch appeal to the public's love of rich bread, but her head rolled nonetheless. Brioche, however, survived, and from what I can tell, is entering a revival phase as Americans discover how versatile and delectable it is.

If you are going to make brioche, though, you have to do it right, with lots of butter. (In France they make two types: rich man's and poor man's brioche—the difference being the amount of butter.) Technically, brioche can have anywhere from 33 to 75 percent butter (see "Baker's Percentage," page 10), but unless it has more than 50 percent, it will be disappointing. More butter means greater difficulty handling the dough, but it is worth it.

The same could be said of other enriched doughs like croissants, Danish, and kugelhopfs, but usually so much more is going on besides flour and butter in these doughs that the acceptable butter range can vary without noticeable detriment. I have had excellent croissants with only 33 percent butter, though I prefer 50 to 75 percent. Danish can be excellent even with margarine since they are also sweetened and spiced. But brioche requires a commitment to butter.

The scope of this book does not include rolled-in (also called *laminated*) doughs like croissants and Danish, but in this chapter I will give you master formulas for four wonderful enriched breads from which you can make numerous variations. In addition to brioche they are kugelhopf, a yeasted, brioche-like coffee-cake bread; sweet dough, used for cinnamon and sticky buns as well as for sweet tea rolls and breads; and an all-purpose holiday bread dough that can be used, with minor adjustments, for panettone, stollen, hot cross buns, and kulich.

Brioche has many guises. You often find it as a *petite brioche à tête,* a small roll with a topknot; it may be used as a wrap for a terrine or aspic-molded entrée; it can be baked in loaf pans and sliced like any other bread; or it may simply be shaped into torpedo rolls and eaten on the side with foie gras and other rich delights. It makes wonderful French toast and bread pudding. No wonder Marie Antoinette went to her death with brioche on her mind!

Kugelhopf, also known as *gugelhopf,* is not nearly as buttery as brioche but it is nearly as delicious. It is baked in special fluted molds, or coffee-cake rings, coated with sliced almonds, and frosted with a sugar glaze. It is the classic yeasted coffee cake. The same dough can be baked in loaf pans to make the ever-popular babka, which is simply a coffee cake that looks like a bread instead of a cake.

Sweet dough, though not overly rich in itself, is ideal for that ultimate indulgence, the sticky bun (or its tamer cousin, the cinnamon bun). It also makes an excellent version of raisin bread and can be made into a wide array of morning sweet rolls and mock Danish pastry.

The master formula for holiday bread is an excellent representation of the celebratory function of bread. Around the world, religious festivals, which originated as a means for one generation to pass on its wisdom and world view to the next, always include a celebratory bread. Stollen, a German Christmas bread that originated in Dresden, is full of colorful fruits and nuts enfolded in a rich dough. The folds symbolize the swaddling clothes of the baby Jesus, the fruits and nuts the gifts of the magi. Panettone employs the same symbolism in a differently shaped, round loaf. Kulich, the rich Easter bread of Eastern Orthodoxy, is laden with golden fruit to represent the resurrection of Christ and is baked in a tall cylindrical mold so that it crowns above the top. The crown of the loaf is given to the local bishop for sharing with visitors during Bright Week, the days following Easter. The rest of the loaf is eaten with a cheese confection called *paskha* as another form of remembrance.

Our Judeo-Christian heritage is laden with breads that express both the transcultural unity of faith and the local customs of a particular people. I have written elsewhere about the symbolism of Struan, the harvest bread from western Scotland associated with Michaelmas, the harvest festival. Challah, the braided Sabbath bread of Judaism, represents the interweaving of heaven and earth and the twelve tribes of Israel. Britain's hot cross buns are spiced and fruited tea cakes adorned with a cross. There was a time when a baker could be fined or jailed for selling hot cross buns any time but during the week leading up to Easter; now, like many ritual breads, they are available year-round, but retain their special significance during Holy Week.

Every holiday bread has its own story and its own authentic recipe. Some have more eggs, and others are richer in butter. Some use red and green fruit, and others use only golden fruit. Sometimes the story is more interesting than the taste; how many of us, for example, actually enjoy Christmas fruitcakes? (I do, but only certain ones.) Unfortunately, by the time many of us get to taste a folkloric bread, it has been reformulated to make its production machinable and efficient. It is not only taken out of its context, but it is dumbed down.

Whether or not a traditional holiday bread was ever as good as our memory or idealization of it is one issue. That these breads can be resurrected for popular usage by making them wonderfully delicious is another. These are not health-food breads that we eat out of a sense of ecological obligation (though if we expand our understanding of ecology to its deeper meaning, they are very much that kind of bread). They are festive expressions of the goodness of creation, and for that reason they need to taste good. There are times when it is good and right to celebrate. These breads are a celebration waiting to happen.

MASTER FORMULA:
BRIOCHE

The sponge used in this formula is a type of *poolish,* also called *levain levure* (yeast), made with milk; it is thicker than the version on page 35. It has enough yeast so that no additional yeast is required, providing enough leavening push to raise the dough without leaving a yeasty flavor.

Though this is a tender bread product, we need the strength of bread flour rather than all-purpose flour to provide structure and a light crumb. The butter, eggs, and milk all serve to condition the dough, making it tender, even though strong.

The amount of butter in this formula looks like a lot of butter, and it is, but if you factor in the flour from the sponge it represents a 70 percent butter-to-flour ratio rather than the 88 percent indicated. This is well within the usual fat-to-flour ratio for brioche, though definitely on the high ("rich man's brioche") end of the spectrum.

COMMENTARIES

❏ The five-hour minimum for retarding is for flavor development. The dough may, in fact, be cold enough to mold after 2 hours, but it will not taste quite as good. Making the dough in the evening and finishing it the next day is the most efficient method.

❏ You can find true brioche molds at restaurant and bakery supply houses. You may also use fluted tartlet or kugelhopf molds.

❏ Master baker and author Bo Friberg taught me a perfect pan coating with butter: Melt 3 parts butter and stir in 1 part flour (by measure, not weight). Brush this on pans whenever you need a buttery pan release. The flour keeps the butter from burning.

❏ The speed of the final rise will depend on the temperature. Wait till the dough is nearly doubled in size and allow for a 10 percent to 15 percent oven spring.

❏ As with all breads, the flavor is best after the brioche completely cools. If still warm, it will be very tender and almost greasy. When cool, the texture is like satin.

MAKES 3 LOAVES, OR UP TO 4 DOZEN SMALL ROLLS, OR *PETITES BRIOCHES À TÊTES*

INGREDIENT (SPONGE)	%
Instant yeast	2.4
Milk	89
Unbleached bread flour	100

SPONGE

1 teaspoon (0.11 ounce) instant yeast

$^{1}/_{2}$ cup (4 ounces) lukewarm milk (90°F)

1 cup (4.5 ounces) unbleached
  bread flour

  =Approximate Weight: 8.6 ounces

INGREDIENT (DOUGH)	%
Unbleached bread flour	100
Sugar	6.25
Salt	2.1
Eggs	50
Sponge	53
Butter	88

DOUGH

$3^{1}/_{2}$ cups (16 ounces) unbleached
  bread flour

2 tablespoons (1 ounce) sugar

1 teaspoon (0.25 ounce) salt

5 large eggs (8 ounces), cold, plus
  1 large egg for egg wash

$1^{1}/_{2}$ cups sponge (from above; use
  all 8.6 ounces)

$1^{3}/_{4}$ cups (14 ounces) unsalted butter,
  softened

Vegetable oil cooking spray (optional)

Melted butter and flour for the molds
  (optional)

  *=Approximate Weight: 47.85 ounces
  (about 3 pounds)*

1. To make the sponge, stir the yeast into the milk in a mixing bowl. Add the flour and stir till smooth. Cover the bowl with plastic wrap, and allow the sponge to ferment at room temperature for 1 to 2 hours. It will become very bubbly.

2. In a mixing bowl or the bowl of an electric mixer with a paddle attachment, combine the flour, sugar, salt, 5 eggs, and sponge. If making the

dough by machine, mix it on low speed for about 2 minutes, till a smooth dough is formed. Cut the butter into 3 pieces and beat in 1 piece at time at medium-low speed till each is absorbed. Continue beating at the same speed till the dough is smooth, about 6 minutes. It will be very soft and sticky.

3. To make the dough by hand, gradually combine all the ingredients and beat vigorously with a wooden or metal spoon for about 10 minutes, to make a smooth, wet dough.

4. Mist the top of the dough with cooking spray, cover the bowl with plastic wrap, and place the bowl in the refrigerator overnight (or for a minimum of 5 hours). The dough will firm up considerably as it retards.

5. Remove the dough from the refrigerator and shape it, while it is still cold, into loaves, rolls, or molded *petites brioches à têtes,* as illustrated. If making *petites brioches à tête,* grease the molds well with cooking spray or with melted butter and flour.

6. Mist the top of the shaped dough with cooking spray, cover it with plastic wrap or enclose it in a plastic bag, and let rise at room temperature for about 2 hours, or till nearly doubled in size.

7. Position an oven rack in the center of the oven and preheat to 375°F for a large, full-size brioche, 400°F for smaller loaves. Beat the remaining egg till smooth and brush it on the tops of the brioche, taking care not to let it drip down the sides of the molds. Bake 35 to 45 minutes for loaves, 20 to 25 minutes for small rolls or *petites brioches à tête,* until a rich, deep gold.

8. If using molds, remove the rolls 1 or 2 minutes after they come out of the oven, taking care not to tear them (use a small knife to loosen them from the side walls).

9. Cool the brioche on a rack for 20 to 40 minutes, depending on size, before eating.

Petite brioche à tête is formed by rolling premeasured pieces of dough first into rounds. Then, with the edge of the hand, divide the round into a large and small section, connected by a thin strand. The small topknot is then centered on the top of the larger piece while the dough is positioned in special fluted molds (available at most gourmet kitchenware shops).

MASTER FORMULA:

KUGELHOPF (YEASTED COFFEE CAKE BREAD)

This is one of those breads that's great to have around for unexpected visitors. It's more complex and less sweet than baking-powder coffee cakes, which makes it suitable for savory as well as sweet applications. This was originally an Alsatian bread, so it is found in various guises in both German and French bake shops. Kugelhopfs are usually baked in fluted metal or ceramic ring molds. You can also make them in bundt pans or coffee cake ring molds. Though most commonly spelled *kugelhopf,* you may find it masquerading under the name *gugelhupf, koeglof, kugelhupf,* or *kougelhopf.* Regardless of how it is spelled, this is a great bread, not so rich as brioche, but sweeter and ideal for entertaining friends.

COMMENTARIES

❏ This dough is soft, so it must be baked in a ring mold or some other type of mold, such as a loaf pan. When baked as a loaf, it is very similar to a babka, an eastern European coffee bread.

❏ The pre-ferment gives this loaf added flavor. It is the element that distinguishes this formula from more familiar, straight-dough versions. If you want to use it on the same day you make it, let it ferment at room temperature for 5 hours.

❏ The raisins are optional, but they do add sweetness and flavor. Another version of kugelhopf calls for cooked bacon and onions instead, something you might want to consider if serving this as a table bread with hot food or for a picnic.

❏ You may substitute kirsch, Grand Marnier, and other flavored brandies, or even whiskey, for the rum. For a nonalcoholic version of this bread, use orange juice concentrate.

❏ Sliced almonds are characteristic of this bread, adding a very attractive aspect and a complementary flavor.

❏ In steps 3 and 4, I refer to the dough clearing the bowl. This is a baking term that means the dough forms a ball rather than sticking to the walls of the bowl like a batter. It is an indication that hydration has taken place and that the dough is beginning to set up, i.e., the gluten molecules are bonding and the dough is developing structure.

❏ This dough is mixed for a shorter time than most doughs. Since it is more of a pastry bread, longer mixing time is not really needed, as excessive gluten development makes the bread tougher.

❏ The confectioners' sugar is, of course, optional, but it gives the bread a very attractive finish (we do eat first with our eyes!).

INGREDIENT (SPONGE)	%
Unbleached bread flour	100
Instant yeast	0.5
Milk	100

SPONGE

$2/3$ cup (3 ounces) unbleached bread flour

$1/3$ teaspoon instant yeast

6 tablespoons (3 ounces) room
  temperature milk

=*Approximate Weight: 6 ounces*

INGREDIENT (DOUGH)	%
Raisins	50
Rum	12.5
Unbleached all-purpose flour	100
Granulated sugar	19
Salt	1.6
Instant yeast	1
Milk	50
Eggs	50
Sponge	37.5
Butter	50
Almonds	N/A
Confectioners' sugar	N/A

DOUGH

$1^1/2$ cups (8 ounces) raisins
  (packed tightly)

$1/4$ cup (2 ounces) rum

$3^1/2$ cups (16 ounces) unbleached
  all-purpose flour

6 tablespoons (3 ounces) granulated sugar

1 teaspoon (0.25 ounce) salt

1 tablespoon (0.33 ounce) instant yeast

1 cup (8 ounces) cold milk

5 large eggs (8 ounces), cold

6 ounces sponge (from above; use all)

1 cup (8 ounces) unsalted butter,
  softened

2 tablespoons (1 ounce) soft butter
  for the mold

$1/2$ cup sliced almonds for edging

Confectioners' sugar for dusting

Vegetable oil cooking spray

=*Approximate Weight: 60 ounces
(3 pounds, 12 ounces)*

1. The day before making the dough,
    combine the sponge ingredients in a
    mixing bowl and stir till they form a
    smooth batter. Cover and allow the
    sponge to ferment at room tempera-
    ture for 3 hours, till bubbly, then
    refrigerate overnight.

2. Also the day before, immerse the
    raisins in the rum, cover, and let them
    soak at room temperature overnight.

3. The next day, combine the flour, gran-
    ulated sugar, salt, yeast, milk, eggs,
    and sponge in the bowl of an electric
    mixer with a dough hook. Mix on slow
    speed for 1 minute, then on medium
    speed for 4 minutes, or till the dough
    smooths out and clears the sides of the
    bowl. If mixing by hand, combine all
    the dough ingredients and beat vigor-
    ously with a wooden or metal spoon for
    approximately 6 minutes.

4. Cut the unsalted butter into 3 pieces, and add it to the dough 1 piece at a time, waiting till each piece is incorporated before adding the next. Mix for 2 or 3 minutes more, till all the butter is incorporated and the dough again clears the sides of the bowl. It should be smooth and very tacky.

5. Add the raisins with the rum (most of it will be absorbed by the raisins), and mix just till they are evenly dispersed, about 1 minute. The dough temperature should be between 75° and 78°F, or just slightly cool to the touch. The dough will now be sticky.

6. Cover the bowl with plastic wrap, and allow the dough to rise for 1 hour. Knead it by hand for a few seconds to release the gas, reshape the dough into a ball, and return it to the bowl. Cover and let rise for another 45 minutes, till the dough swells noticeably.

7. Meanwhile, grease a 10-inch ring mold (a fluted kugelhopf mold, bundt pan, or coffee-cake ring) with butter and sprinkle it thoroughly with the almonds.

8. Flour your hands, form the sticky dough into a ball, and poke a hole through the center, pulling it out like a bagel. Mist the dough with cooking spray, cover it with plastic wrap, and let it rest on a lightly floured counter for 20 minutes.

9. Enlarge the hole with your thumbs and fingers until it is wide enough to drape over the center and fit into the mold. It should fill the mold a little more than halfway. Mist the dough again with cooking spray, cover it with plastic wrap, and allow the dough to rise at room temperature for 2 hours, or till it just fills the mold.

10. Position an oven rack in the center of the oven, and preheat the oven to 375°.

11. When the dough is ready, bake it for about 35 minutes, until a dark golden brown (rotate it during the bake, if necessary, for even coloring). Turn off the oven and leave the loaf in for an additional 5 minutes. The kugelhopf should be springy to the touch and have an internal temperature of at least 185°F. The exposed dough will be darker than the rest of the loaf when it is unmolded.

12. Remove the loaf from the oven and wait 5 minutes before unmolding it onto a cooling rack; the part in the bottom of the mold will now be the top of the loaf (like an upside-down cake). Let it cool for at least 45 minutes.

13. Just before serving, put some confectioners' sugar in a strainer and hold it above the bread, tapping the side of the strainer to release a light dusting of sugar.

MASTER FORMULA:
CHALLAH

Braided breads are beautiful and make a strong symbolic presence. Challah is one type of braided bread (though it is not always baked in a braid; it makes a perfectly wonderful loaf-pan bread as well, or a coiled loaf for special occasions such as Rosh Hashanah, the Jewish New Year celebration). It is distinctive because of its rich golden color, the result of a fair number of eggs. Challah is best known as the traditional Sabbath bread of the Jewish faith and is sometimes made even more ornately for major celebrations such as weddings and Bar and Bas Mitzvahs.

Challah, like bagels, has evolved from its Jewish roots into a mainstream bread enjoyed by people of all backgrounds. When made properly, it is a stunningly appealing loaf, plump and shiny, its braided strands symbolizing the interweaving of heaven and earth, God and mankind. Whether or not we read deeply into the symbolism of challah, we face the same challenge as with all breads: how to make an excellent loaf.

Challah is not a difficult or complex bread to make. It does not rely on long, slow fermentation, but it does take patience and sensitivity to know when it is ready to bake. Most people rush their challah into the oven too soon and miss out on the dramatic visual effect it can have when it plumps to its fullest size. Though not technically a rich bread in the style of brioche and kugelhopf, it is enriched and conditioned by fat, eggs, and sugar.

COMMENTARIES

❏ You can also use vegetable oil instead of butter, especially if you are observing strict kosher dietary laws and plan to serve meat with your meal (see below). I prefer unsalted butter because it tastes better. Be sure it is at room temperature (or you can melt it and let it cool) so that it disperses evenly.

❏ The milk in this formula gives the bread a more tender crumb, but you may substitute water if you observe kosher laws and plan to serve the bread with meat.

❏ An egg yolk wash creates the most intense shine on a bread, adding drama to its presentation. You can use a whole egg for a less intense shine.

❏ The additional kneading and rising period further develops the dough and helps produce a spectacular final push when it is baked. I learned this trick from a Jewish woman demonstrating her challah on a Sabbath meal video, with host Myra Chanin, also known as "Mother Wonderful." The additional knead really seems to make a difference, since it extends the rising time.

❏ The dough pieces need to be rolled out quickly, with a minimum of handling. The more you play with the strand the more the surface will dry out. This will show up later as stretch marks in the finished loaf. Keep the resting pieces covered while working on the current piece for the same reason.

❏ Challah can also be braided in four strands but the loaf is plumper, and I think, more attractive done with three. The number of strands also affects the symbolism.

❏ Be sure to wait until the bread is fully risen before baking. It will spring in the oven, but since you do not have to score it you can wait a little longer than for hearth breads.

❏ Brushing egg yolk on the braid both before and after the final rise intensifies the sheen. The egg causes the crust to brown quickly, so you must resist the temptation to pull it out of the oven too soon.

INGREDIENT	%
Unbleached bread flour	100
Sugar	12.5
Salt	1.6
Instant yeast	1.4
Butter	6.25
Eggs	21
Egg yolks	8.3
Milk	12.5
Water	25
Poppy seeds	N/A

MAKES 1 LOAF

3¹/₂ cups (16 ounces) unbleached bread flour

¹/₄ cup (2 ounces) sugar

1 teaspoon (0.25 ounce) salt

2 teaspoons (0.22 ounce) instant yeast

2 tablespoons (1 ounce) unsalted butter, softened

2 large eggs (3.33 ounces), beaten

2 large egg yolks (1.33 ounces), beaten, plus 1 yolk for egg wash

¹/₄ cup (2 ounces) milk, at room temperature

¹/₂ cup water, at room temperature

Poppy or sesame seeds for topping (optional)

Vegetable oil cooking spray

=Approximate Weight: 30 ounces (1 pound, 14 ounces)

1. Combine all the dough ingredients (everything except the the poppy seeds and the egg yolk for the wash) in a mixing bowl or the bowl of an electric mixer with a dough hook.

2. If making the dough by hand, stir till it forms a ball. Then turn it out onto a floured counter and knead for 12 to 15 minutes, until the dough is soft, pliable, and neutral to the touch, between 78° and 80°F. It should be slightly tacky (if it is too sticky, add flour) and pass the windowpane test (see page 29). If using a machine, mix on slow speed for 1 minute and then on medium for about 10 minutes.

3. Place the dough in a bowl, mist it with cooking spray, cover it with plastic wrap or enclose it in a plastic bag, and allow it to rise at room temperature for 1 hour, until it noticeably swells.

4. Remove the dough from the bowl and knead it by hand for 5 minutes. Return it to the bowl, cover it, and allow it to rise for another hour, until it again swells.

5. Divide the dough into 3 equal pieces. Round the pieces into balls, mist with cooking spray, cover with plastic wrap, and let them rest for 20 minutes, to relax the gluten.

6. Working quickly to minimize handling the dough, roll each piece into a cigar-shaped strand or log about 8 inches long. It should be a little plumper in the middle than at the ends. Cover each piece as you move to the next.

7. Braid the bread as shown in the illustration. Lay the logs side by side on a lightly floured work surface. I prefer beginning in the middle. Cross the right-hand strand over the center strand, then the left-hand strand over the center, continuing until you reach the end. Tuck the tail of dough under and pinch to seal. Flip the loaf over, and also back to front, and braid the other half in the same way.

8. Place the loaf on a sheet pan lined with baking parchment. Whisk the remaining egg yolk till smooth and brush a coating of it onto the loaf, saving the extra. Mist the loaf with cooking spray, cover it with a towel or plastic wrap, and allow it to rise for about 1 hour, until plump and doubled in size.

9. Position an oven rack in the center of the oven, and preheat the oven to 375°F. Brush the loaf with the remaining egg wash. If using seeds, sprinkle them over the loaf at this time.

10. Place the sheet pan in the oven and bake for about 45 minutes, rotating front to back about halfway through to ensure even browning. The loaf is done when it is golden brown and looks as though it is about to burst at the seams. It should be firm, not squishy, and the internal temperature should be at least 185°F in the center.

11. Transfer the loaf to a rack, and allow it to cool for at least 45 minutes before slicing and eating.

BRAIDING

Regardless of the number of strands of dough, the most important thing to remember is that the number refers to the position, not to any particular strand. Therefore, the strands will go in and out of different numbered positions as they loop through the braiding process. Also remember to make each strand the same weight and length.

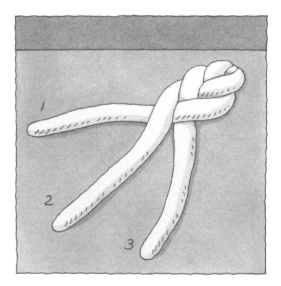

THREE-STRAND

The three-strand braid is the most common, especially for challah. The braiding sequence is as follows: 1 over 2, 3 over 2, 1 over 2, 3 over 2, and repeat till done, pinching and tucking the ends together to prevent them from unraveling.

Note: Some people like to begin this braid from the middle and then work down toward each end (for a tapered effect). If so, after you reach the first end, flip the entire loaf over and repeat the pattern. If you merely rotate it 180° without flipping it over, you will need to change the sequence to 1 under 2, 3 under 2, etc., in order to keep the same pattern.

FOUR-STRAND

This sequence creates a diagonal ridge down the center of the loaf that distinguishes it from the three-strand braid. Fan out the strands and pinch the tips together at the top end. Then proceed, following this braiding sequence: 4 over 2, 1 over 3, 2 over 3 (this internal step creates the central ridge). Then repeat the pattern. When you reach the end pinch and tuck the strands together to prevent unraveling.

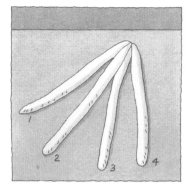 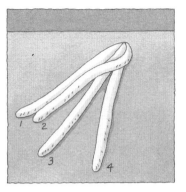

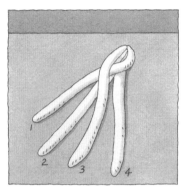 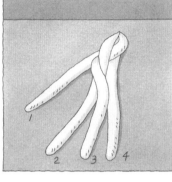 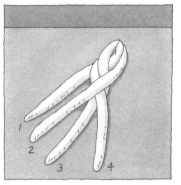

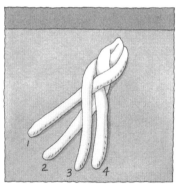 

FIVE-STRAND

This sequence creates a slightly more elaborate pattern, again, like the four-strand, yielding an attractive diagonal ridge down the center. Fan out the strands and pinch them together at the top end and proceed in the following sequence: 1 over 3, 2 over 3, 5 over 2, then repeat the pattern. When you reach the end pinch and tuck the strands together to prevent unraveling.

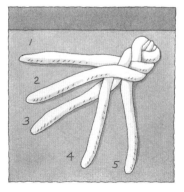

MASTER FORMULA:

ALL-PURPOSE HOLIDAY BREAD

Dresden stollen, Milanese panettone, Russian kulich, and English hot cross buns can all be made from this multipurpose holiday bread master formula. Culturally, they derive from slightly different recipes, but they are so close in concept that the real difference seems to be the way they are shaped and baked (see page 128).

COMMENTARIES

❏ The sponge in this formula is similar to a *poolish,* except made with buttermilk. You may substitute other types of milk, but buttermilk gives the best flavor. After 1 hour of fermentation, you can retard the dough for up to 24 hours.

❏ The additional ingredients are appropriate for different breads, and the amount given is merely a guideline.

MAKES 1 VERY LARGE LOAF, SEVERAL SMALL LOAVES, OR UP TO 24 HOT CROSS BUNS

INGREDIENT (SPONGE)	%
Unbleached bread flour	100
Instant yeast	7
Buttermilk	228.5

SPONGE

3/4 cup (3.5 ounces) unbleached bread flour

2 teaspoons (0.25 ounce) instant yeast

1 cup (8 ounces) buttermilk, at room temperature

=*Approximate Weight: 11.75 ounces*

INGREDIENT (DOUGH)	%
Unbleached bread flour	100
Sugar	11.5
Salt	1.3
Eggs	41
Unsalted butter	20.5
Sponge	60

DOUGH

4 1/3 cups (19.5 ounces) unbleached bread flour

1/3 cup (2.25 ounces) sugar

1 teaspoon (0.25 ounce) salt

5 large eggs (8 ounces), cold

1/2 cup (4 ounces) unsalted butter, softened

11.75 ounces sponge (from above; use all)

=*Approximate Weight: 45.75 ounces (2 pounds, 13.75 ounces)*

ADDITIONAL INGREDIENTS FOR DIFFERENT LOAVES (SEE PAGES 128–129)

1/2 cup chopped dried apricots for kulich

1/2 cup golden raisins

1/2 cup dark raisins (not for kulich)

1/4 cup rum or orange juice concentrate

2 teaspoons vanilla extract

1 cup sliced almonds or walnuts

1/2 tablespoon ground allspice (for hot cross buns)

1/2 cup candied fruit, chopped

$^1/_4$ cup multicolored candy sprinkles (for kulich)

Vegetable oil cooking spray

1 large egg (1.66 ounces) for egg wash (optional)

1. To make the sponge, stir together the flour and yeast in a mixing bowl. Stir in the buttermilk and mix till smooth. Cover the sponge with plastic wrap and allow it to ferment at room temperature for 1 to 2 hours, till very bubbly.

2. If using dried fruit, soak it in rum and/or vanilla in a bowl while the sponge is developing.

3. To make the dough, combine all the other dough ingredients and the sponge in a mixing bowl or the bowl of an electric mixer with a dough hook. (If making hot cross buns, add the allspice now.)

4. Mix the dough on slow speed for 1 minute, then on medium speed for 5 minutes. Add the fruit and nut mixture and mix for an additional 2 minutes, or until the dough is soft and tacky, registers about 80°F on a probe thermometer, and passes the windowpane test (page 29). Add water if the dough is too stiff or flour if it is too sticky. To make by hand, knead the dough on a well-floured counter with floured hands for about 15 minutes, adding the fruit and nuts during the final 3 minutes.

5. Mist the dough with cooking spray, cover it with plastic wrap, and allow it to rise at room temperature for 60 to 90 minutes, till it increases in size by $1^1/_2$ times.

6. Form the dough into the desired holiday bread shape (see pages 128–129). Cover it and allow it to rise at room temperature for 60 to 90 minutes, till the loaves or rolls are nearly double in size.

7. Position one of the oven racks one third of the way up from the bottom of the oven, and preheat the oven to 350°F. Brush the dough with egg wash if so directed on pages 128–129.

8. Bake for the length of time specified for the type of bread. Finished breads will be a deep golden brown, with an internal temperature of 185°F.

9. Remove to a cooling rack. When the loaves are no longer hot but are still warm to the touch, decorate them as directed.

Here is how to make several well-known holiday breads. You can also bake the holiday dough in regular loaf pans, or as a free-standing round, or in long loaves for terrific breakfast toast.

Stollen: In addition to soaking the full amount of raisins, candied fruit, and nuts (almonds are preferred) in the orange juice, rum, or vanilla, soak an equal amount separately to be folded into the dough when shaping.

Use the dough in one large piece or divide it into several smaller pieces. Roll the finished dough into rectangles about 1 inch thick. Spread the second fruit-nut mixture, liqueur and all, over the surface, and fold the dough gently and loosely

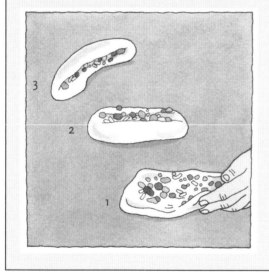

like a business letter. Allow the folds to show (they represent the folds of the swaddling clothes of the baby Jesus). Curve the folded dough into a crescent, with the folds facing inward. Use the pinky edge of your hand to indent a crease around the top of the outer edge of the crescent. This will cause the dough to tighten everywhere, helping the bread retain its shape. Let the dough rise, brush it with egg wash, and bake it for 45 to 60 minutes, depending on the size of the loaf as directed in the master formula. While the loaves are cooling, drizzle streaks of sugar glaze (page 130) across the tops.

Hot Cross Buns: Add the allspice to the dough as in step 3. Some bakers also add a pinch of ground ginger, nutmeg, and/or cinnamon, but allspice is enough for me. Shape the dough into 2-ounce rolls as directed on page 19. Let the dough rise, brush with egg wash, and bake for about 20 minutes.

After the rolls have cooled somewhat, paint crosses on the top with lemon- or orange-flavored sugar glaze (page 132). Or you can pipe crosses onto the buns before baking using a standard pastry cream recipe and a decorating bag; it bakes into the rolls very dramatically.

Panettone: Use up to the full amount of dried and candied fruit and nuts (almonds or walnuts), according to taste. For a single large loaf, grease a 9-inch round cake pan, and line the sides of it with a parchment collar that is about 2 inches taller than the pan. For smaller loaves, use smaller pans or simply make free-standing rounds. Form the finished dough into a ball and press it nearly to the edge of the prepared pan. Let it rise, brush with egg wash, and bake as instructed in the Master Formula for about 60 minutes. When the loaves are baked, you may brush them with a simple syrup made by boiling equal parts sugar and water for 1 minute. This will give the tops a shiny look.

Kulich: This formula makes one large kulich or a number of smaller ones. For each loaf, generously spray the inside of a clean coffee can or other can with cooking spray. To make a large kulich, you will need a 2-pound coffee can; small tuna fish cans make many cute baby ones. Fill each can slightly more than halfway with a ball of dough. Let the dough rise till it comes just above the rim of the can. The dough may take anywhere from 1 to 3 hours to rise enough, depending on the warmth of the room.

Bake the loaf at 325°F till the top begins to brown, 20 to 45 minutes depending on size. The bread will have crowned above the can and mushroomed slightly over the edge. The exposed dough will bake much faster than the rest of the loaf, so cover the top with aluminum foil and continue to bake it for about 15 minutes longer, till the center reaches 185°F. Turn off the oven and allow it to bake another 5 minutes.

Allow the kulich to cool in the can for about 10 minutes. Carefully extract the loaf, taking care not to separate the crown from the base (tap the sides of the can if necessary). Cool on a rack.

Decorate the crown with lemon or orange sugar glaze (page 132), and sprinkle golden raisins, chopped dried apricots, sliced almonds, and/or colorful candy sprinkles into the glaze as it drips down the side of the loaf. Use golden-colored fruit to symbolize Christ's resurrection.

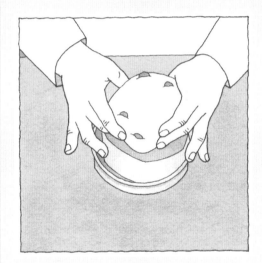

Panettone is often rounded like a *boule* and baked in parchment-lined pans. (You may also use commercially available decorative *panettone* baking papers.) The liner provides higher walls and added structure to prevent the bread from mushrooming over the edge. (Note: Kulich, on the other hand, similarly shaped but without a collar, is supposed to mushroom over the edge of the pan, creating a distinctive crown effect.)

MULTIPURPOSE SWEET DOUGH

This dough can be used for sticky buns, cinnamon buns, raisin bread, and mock Danish pastries. It is tender but still strong enough to hold up to any application, not as rich as brioche, but sweeter. This sweet dough can also be used as an alternative dough for hot cross buns and other tea cakes and sweet rolls. Rich breads take longer to ferment than lean breads because the large amounts of sugar and fat slow down yeast activity. This is a straight-dough formula (direct method), made without a pre-ferment because, as a sweet dough, it is not dependent on strongly fermented dough flavor. It can be made quickly, yet with exceptional results.

COMMENTARIES

❏ A touch of baking soda in this formula sweetens the dough a bit while neutralizing the buttermilk. This process creates carbon dioxide, as in quick breads and pancakes.

❏ Rich doughs like this one often need to be chilled so that the butter firms up enough for easy handling. You can make the dough up to the point of refrigeration in step 3, freeze it, tightly sealed, and save it for another time. Allow 1 hour at room temperature for it to soften enough to be workable.

INGREDIENT	%
Unbleached all-purpose flour	100
Granulated sugar	12.5
Instant yeast	2
Salt	0.75
Baking soda	0.5
Unsalted butter	12.5
Buttermilk	50

**MAKES 9 TO 16 STICKY BUNS
OR SMALL ROLLS, OR 1 LOAF**

3¹/₂ cups (16 ounces) unbleached
  all-purpose flour

¹/₄ cup (2 ounces) granulated sugar

1 tablespoon (0.33 ounce) instant yeast

¹/₂ teaspoon (0.12 ounce) salt

¹/₄ teaspoon (0.08 ounce) baking soda

¹/₄ cup (2 ounces) unsalted butter,
  softened

1 cup (8 ounces) buttermilk, at room
  temperature

5 teaspoons cinnamon sugar
  (1 teaspoon ground cinnamon mixed
  into 4 teaspoons granulated sugar)

Vegetable oil cooking spray

*=Approximate Weight: 28 ounces
  (1 pound, 12 ounces)*

1. Combine all the ingredients, except the cinnamon sugar, in the bowl of an electric mixer with a dough hook or in a mixing bowl.

2. Mix on slow speed for 1 minute, then on medium speed for about 8 minutes. If mixing by hand, stir the ingredients together till they form a ball and knead for 10 to 12 minutes. The dough should be soft, smooth, and a little bit sticky, and should pass the windowpane test (see page 29).

3. Place the dough in a clean bowl, mist it with cooking spray, cover it with plastic wrap, and allow it to rise for 45 minutes. Then put it in the refrigerator for 1 hour. It will firm up as it cools.

4. For sticky or cinnamon buns (see page 132 for other options), lightly dust the counter with flour and roll out the dough into a square about $^1/_4$ inch thick. Sprinkle the top with the cinnamon sugar and roll it up like a jelly roll.

5. Prepare one or more cake or baking pans (at least 1 inch deep) by greasing them with butter (for cinnamon buns) or by covering them with sticky bun slurry (page 132).

6. Cut the rolled dough into 1-inch-wide pieces and place them in the pans so that either of the spiraled sides is facing up. The pieces should be about $^1/_2$ inch apart, yet fill the pans as full as possible.

7. Mist the tops with cooking spray, cover loosely with plastic wrap, and set the buns aside to rise at room temperature for about 1 hour, till the dough swirls thicken and the pieces have grown together.

8. Position a rack in the lower third of the oven, and preheat the oven to 350°F. Place the pans on a sheet pan to catch any overflow. Bake for about 30 minutes, till the tops are deep brown and the buns are firm to the touch. The sticky bun glaze should caramelize to a golden amber color.

9. Remove from the oven and wait 5 minutes before inverting sticky buns onto a clean platter. Cinnamon buns do not need to be inverted. Decorate the cinnamon buns with drizzles of sugar glaze (page 132); serve sticky buns without.

VARIATIONS

For raisin bread: Add 2 cups raisins during the last 2 minutes of kneading. Allow 60 to 90 minutes for rising, till the dough increases about $1^1/_2$ times in size. Roll it into a square, as you would for cinnamon buns, and sprinkle with the cinnamon sugar. Roll up the dough like a jelly roll, pinch the ends and the seam closed, and place the loaf in a greased 5 by 9-inch loaf pan. Mist the top with cooking spray, cover the loaf with plastic, and allow it to rise at room temperature till nearly doubled in size, 60 to 90 minutes. Bake the loaf in a preheated 350°F oven for about 40 minutes, till it is golden brown and makes a hollow sound when thwacked on the bottom. The internal temperature should be about 190°F.

Remove from the pan and brush the top with melted butter. Immediately roll the top in a bed of cinnamon sugar or sprinkle about 2 tablespoons of cinnamon sugar on top. This crust will harden as the loaf cools.

For spice buns: Add $^1/_2$ teaspoon allspice and $^1/_2$ teaspoon ground ginger when first mixing the dough, and add 2 cups currants or raisins during the last 2 minutes of kneading. Let rise for 60 to 90 minutes, till doubled in size. Form the dough into 2-ounce rolls (see page 19), let rise till doubled (60 to 90 minutes) and bake in a preheated 350°F oven for about 20 minutes. For hot cross buns, paint with sugar glaze as directed below. These rolls may also be made with the currants or raisins but without the spices.

STICKY AND CINNAMON BUN GLAZES

Sticky and cinnamon buns have emerged as America's true comfort pastry. Every region in the country claims some version, including Southern pecan rolls, Midwestern cinnamon swirls, and Pennsylvania Dutch raisin-walnut sticky buns. The sweet dough formula provides the basis for any version of these treats. Here are a few hints to make them extra special:

Sticky bun slurry: Beat together 2 cups (1 pound) softened unsalted butter, 3 cups (1$^1/_2$ pounds) granulated sugar, $^2/_3$ cup (9 ounces) corn syrup or honey, 1 teaspoon salt, and 1 teaspoon lemon extract until the mixture is very fluffy. Spread a portion of this on the bottom of the baking dish, about $^1/_4$ inch thick. Save any extra for another time; it will keep indefinitely in the refrigerator. Sprinkle chopped or whole pecans or walnuts over the surface. Add raisins if you like them, and place the cut and rolled dough pieces $^1/_2$ inch apart to fill the pan. The slurry will caramelize during baking, turning a beautiful, translucent, golden brown. Wait 5 minutes before you flip the pan and be careful, as the slurry is very hot.

Sugar glaze: The simplest glaze is made with 1 cup sifted confectioners' sugar and 1$^1/_2$ to 2 tablespoons hot water whisked together into a paste that is thick but still can be drizzled on the pastry. You can jazz this up by adding a few drops of lemon, orange, vanilla, or almond extract. You can also make a thinner sugar glaze that can be brushed on by adding a little corn syrup and a few drops of milk.

Some people like to drizzle the glaze from a fork in streaky little lines. Others prefer to brush it on with a pastry brush to coat the whole piece. Pastry bags are a way to control the design patterns, but few home bakers are comfortable with them. With a little practice, though, you can make designer buns with signature glaze patterns.

7

A TORTILLA BY ANY OTHER NAME: FLATBREADS AROUND THE WORLD

Master Formula: Peppery Polenta Crackerbread; Master Formula: Chapatis and Matzoh;
Master Formula: Pita Bread; Master Formula: Naan; Master Formula: Flour Tortillas
PIZZA AND FOCACCIA (147): Master Formula: Pizza Dough I; Master Formula: Pizza Dough II;
Master Formula: Focaccia

The day before the grand opening of the Culinary Institute of America's Greystone campus in St. Helena, California, I found myself working side by side with Naomi Duguid, coauthor of the beautiful book *Flatbreads and Flavors*. I had been asked to help Naomi make flatbreads for the expected two thousand guests. She has made her breads in many exotic places around the world and for many famous people, including Julia Child, but she had never been asked to make them in this quantity before. It is one thing to sit beside a hot rock in Afghanistan or Pakistan, peeling off wonderful breads one at a time from a hand-kneaded ball of dough for a communal meal; it is quite another to knock them out of a forty-pound dough ball and bake them in a state-of-the-art, steam-injected Bongard deck oven with an automatic conveyor loader.

As we worked, Naomi gave me a crash course in the history of some of the breads, and I gave her suggestions on how they could be produced more quickly and efficiently and what neotraditional sprinkles we could put on them. ("Of course," she said, "we can no longer call it what the Afghans call it, but that's okay; it does taste good!") The most important things I learned are how thinly you have to roll out some flatbreads and how similar many are. Some breads puff and some are like crackers; some are made with wheat, others with corn or cassava flour. Some are cooked on convex stones and others in concave pans. Some are topped with sesame seeds and others with paprika or hot pepper flakes. But chapatis, tortillas, naan, pita, and even pizzas are all variations on a theme.

More than anything, I learned that flatbreads are time capsules of civilization, freeze-framing cultures like the Hubbell telescope captures light rays. Flatbreads are the oldest of all breads; they symbolize mankind's exodus from the bondage of primitiveness and the beginning of the development of human consciousness.

In our Judeo-Christian heritage, no flatbread more perfectly illustrates this transition than matzoh. We are all familiar with the story of Moses and the Hebrews' escape from Egypt, celebrated in the festival of Passover. For thousands of years, on the first night of Passover, the youngest child at the table has asked the family elder, "Why is this night different from all other nights?" And thus begins a ritual meal, the Seder, that not only tells a story but acts it out through symbolic foods. One of the four questions the child asks is, "On all other nights we eat leavened bread; why on this night do we eat unleavened bread?" The elder answers the child's questions by recounting how Moses led the Hebrews out of Egypt and to the gates of the Promised Land.

Here it might be useful to recall something not mentioned during the Passover Seder: Leavened bread was created in Egypt! It represents, on one level, the superiority of this conquering nation, the almost mystical power of enlivening (the root meaning of *leaven*) a lump of dough and transforming it into fermented nourishment. That unleavened bread, matzoh, should play a major role in the story of the escape of the Hebrews is not without ironic significance. A thousand years later, Jesus might have been thinking of this symbolism when he said, "The meek shall inherit the earth."

Unleavened breads represent simplicity, leavened breads complexity. Flatbreads have an aboriginal association, evoking a primitiveness that civilized people try to deny or transcend; leavened breads traditionally symbolize that transcendence. Fortunately, we live in a time when we can draw upon treasures both old and new.

"On all other nights we eat leavened bread; why on this night do we eat unleavened bread?" One way of answering this question might be to say, "We eat unleavened bread once in a while to remind us that while we may have pretensions of godliness, we are simple, primitive humans wondrously created in the image of some all-powerful being we call God." Our potential reveals itself through the symbolism of leavened bread, but we are rooted in an ancient age where unleavened bread ruled and led us humbly to the land of the city of peace.

The following formulas use many of the techniques introduced in earlier chapters, but also a few new concepts. Some of these flatbreads are leavened and some are not, but when making an unleavened bread, the issue of fermentation, so important to leavened bread, is moot. Matzoh, for instance, must be baked within eighteen minutes of mixing to be considered, rabbinically, a kosher unleavened bread (rabbis hover with stopwatches in matzoh bakeries to insure compliance). This is most critical during Passover, when kosher dietary laws are more strictly observed in many Jewish homes. The premise is that, after eighteen minutes, the natural yeast in the air and on the wheat begins to ferment the dough and create leavening. Since

Passover matzoh refers so pointedly to the Hebrews' hasty exit from Egypt, leavened bread would ruin both the story and the symbolism.

Other breads, such as focaccia, pita, and naan, contain leavening but are considered flatbreads because they are baked in flat rather than loaf shapes. *Flat,* then, is a relative term, depending on the culture from which the bread emerged. It may mean a crisp cracker such as matzoh or lavash, a tender soft naan, a savory focaccia, or a tortilla-like wrap.

Other than corn tortillas, most of the flatbreads we Americans eat are wheat-based, but that is not the case in other parts of the world. Cassava (manioc) flour breads, for instance, are common in equatorial climates. Though academic interest in these esoteric, native-style breads is at an all-time high, they are not likely to become widely popular in the United States because of their limited uses and because the ingredients are not native to our climate.

Unleavened breads are relatively simple, and because there is little or no fermentation, fast to make. For the same reason, the flavor depends primarily on the raw ingredients and lacks the complexity of leavened breads. Flatbreads, however, have their own charm. They are a breed apart from leavened breads, and we will treat them as such in the following master formulas.

As I said, Naomi Duguid taught me that while cultures and customs may vary, there really is very little difference among world flatbreads other than their names. So perhaps their most significant symbolism is the way in which they demonstrate the universality of humankind.

MASTER FORMULA:

PEPPERY POLENTA CRACKERBREAD

Here is a master formula for an all-purpose crackerbread similar to lavash, the wonderful Armenian bread used for the Americanized roll-up sandwiches called *arams.* As a crackerbread, this is perfect with dips and sauces; as a snack food, it can easily take the place of tortilla or potato chips. This versatility is possible because the crisp cracker softens when spritzed with water and allowed to sit for five minutes (that's the secret to using it for roll-ups). I like this bread crisp, but recently discovered that it takes on another personality if eaten just after spritzing it with water, before it completely softens—soft and crisp at the same time!

This version is flavored with coarsely ground black pepper and whole fennel seeds, but you can omit either or substitute your own favorite spices. The critical thing is to roll out the flatbreads as thin as possible. Naomi Duguid told me, as she rolled out dozens of lavash, that whenever she thinks they are thin enough, her husband and coauthor, Jeffrey Alford, "insists that I can roll them out even thinner. He tells me to keep going. It's amazing how thin you really can get these things!"

COMMENTARIES

❑ This dough is also wonderful for pizza; the texture and flavor make it seem as though there is Italian sausage in the crust. If you'd like to try it, see pages 153–154 for how to roll out and bake pizza.

❑ Don't substitute regular cornmeal for the polenta. Polenta is a coarser grind and retains its identity in the dough, like small golden nuggets. Cornmeal, on the other hand, disappears into the dough and muddies it.

❑ Be sure to use coarsely ground pepper; table grind is too fine and makes the dough taste overly peppery. You can omit the pepper and fennel altogether or substitute an equal amount of cumin seeds, cayenne, crushed red pepper, dried herbs, chopped onion and/or chives, or other favorite seasonings.

❑ Letting the dough rest for 20 or 30 minutes relaxes the gluten and makes it easier to roll it out into thin crackers. You will be amazed at how thin this dough can be rolled without tearing.

❑ The first baking method makes large sheets of crackerbread that can later be softened with water and used to make roll-up sandwiches. Do not stack the pieces when they first come out of the oven or they will not crisp properly.

❑ The second baking method makes lots of crackers with interesting colors and flavors. For instance, you can sprinkle, side by side, lines of paprika, poppy seeds, sesame seeds, and ground cumin, and then cut strips perpendicular to the lines so that every cracker has a little bit of each topping. (Don't try to cut the crackers after baking or they will shatter.) These are excellent with Middle Eastern and Mediterranean dips and spreads (not bad with guacamole, either!).

INGREDIENT	%
Unbleached bread flour	100
Polenta	10.5
Salt	2.6
Fennel seeds	1.3
Black pepper	0.5
Instant yeast	1.7
Olive oil	10.5
Honey	1
Water	63

4¼ cups (19 ounces) unbleached bread flour

⅓ cup (2 ounces) uncooked polenta

2 teaspoons (0.5 ounce) salt

1 tablespoon (0.25 ounce) whole fennel seeds

¾ teaspoon (0.1 ounce) coarsely ground black pepper

1 tablespoon (0.33 ounce) instant yeast

¼ cup (2 ounces) olive oil

1 teaspoon (0.2 ounces) honey

1½ cups cool water (65° to 70°F)

Vegetable oil cooking spray

=Approximate Weight: 37.5 ounces (2 pounds, 5.5 ounces)

1. Combine all the ingredients in a mixing bowl or in the bowl of an electric mixer with a dough hook. If making the dough by hand, mix till it forms a ball, and turn it out onto a lightly floured surface. Knead the dough for about 15 minutes, till it is soft and smooth, not quite sticky but definitely tacky, and passes the windowpane test (page 29). It should be between 78° and 80°F. In an electric mixer, this will take about 1 minute on low speed and then 11 minutes on medium.

2. Place the dough in a clean bowl, lightly mist with cooking spray, cover with plastic wrap or enclose in a plastic bag, and allow the dough to rise for 90 minutes, until nearly doubled in size.

3. Divide the dough into 6 equal pieces and lightly round them into balls. Mist the tops of the balls with cooking spray, cover them, and let the dough rest for 20 to 30 minutes.

4. Place a baking stone or tiles on the lower rack of your oven, and preheat it to 475°F.

5. Working on a floured surface, roll out each piece of dough as thin as possible without tearing it (you may roll the pieces into either circles or rectangles). They should be paper thin; if a piece of dough resists, move on to another piece and return later.

6. There are two ways to bake this crackerbread:

    For large crackerbread, roll a sheet of dough up onto the rolling pin, transfer the dough to the baking stone, and bake for 2 to 4 minutes, or till the dough bubbles and starts to brown and crisp. With a metal spatula or thin peel, gently transfer the baked crackerbread to a cooling rack.

    For individual cracker strips, transfer the large rolled dough piece to a sheet pan (make only one pan at a time). Lightly mist the top of the dough with a spray of water, sprinkle on spices and/or seeds (paprika, sesame, poppy, caraway, etc.), and cut the dough into cracker-size strips (a pizza cutter works well). Slide the pan into the oven and bake for about 5 minutes, or till the crackers begin to bubble and brown. Remove the crackers from the oven and allow them to cool on the pan. They will crisp as they cool.

MASTER FORMULA:

CHAPATIS AND MATZOH

Chapatis are the most basic of breads: flour, water, and salt. Matzoh is made without salt during Passover and with salt the rest of the year. Chapatis are baked in a skillet or pan; they are soft, not crisp. Matzoh is baked in a hot oven till it crisps. Matzoh is the quintessential noshing cracker; chapatis are great with dal or chutneys, or simply as a flatbread accompaniment to any food. Though chapati is from northern India and matzoh from the Middle East, my guess is that they both predate the era of Babel and were once called by the same name: bread.

COMMENTARIES

❑ Chapatis are customarily made with finely milled whole-wheat flour, though they can also be made with all-purpose flour, or a combination of the two. Matzoh can also be made with either flour, but is more often made with white.

❑ Salt is omitted from Passover matzoh but used the rest of the year (matzoh does taste better with salt). You may even add a little oil (2 to 4 tablespoons) to the dough at times other than Passover, but it is not necessary. Chapatis contain no oil.

❑ If you are using whole-wheat flour, consider the measure for water an approximation. Whole-wheat flour absorbs more water than white flour, so add only enough water to make a soft but not sticky dough.

❑ Like chapati, matzoh may also be rested if you are not concerned with the 18-minute rule (see page 134). Relaxing the gluten by resting the dough does make it easier to roll out.

❑ *Docking* is the term for cutting or poking holes in dough. It keeps the dough from ballooning when it is baked. Flatbread stamps, made with dozens of tiny needles, are commonly used in countries that make a lot of flatbread. They can be decoratively designed with patterns specific to certain villages or areas. A fork will also do the job, but not nearly as efficiently.

❑ With practice, you may be able fry chapatis on two or more skillets at once, greatly increasing your productivity.

❑ Take the chapatis off the heat before they crisp, or the air pocket will not flatten. This ballooning is similar to what occurs in pita bread and flour tortillas and is an indication that the heat has penetrated to the center of the dough.

INGREDIENT	%
Unbleached all-purpose flour	100
Salt	2
Water	62.5

MAKES 7 TO 14 PIECES

3¹/₂ cups (16 ounces) unbleached all-purpose flour or whole-wheat flour

1¹/₄ teaspoons (0.33 ounce) salt (optional)

1¹/₄ cups cool water (65° to 70°F)

Vegetable oil cooking spray (optional)

=*Approximate Weight: 26 ounces*
(1 pound 10 ounces)

MATZOH

1. Combine the dough ingredients in a mixing bowl and stir till they form a ball.

2. Turn the dough out onto a lightly floured counter. Knead for 5 to 7 minutes, till the dough is smooth and stretchy, tacky but not sticky.

3. Place a baking stone or tiles on the lower rack of the oven, and preheat the oven to 450°F.

4. Divide the dough into 7 to 14 equal pieces and lightly roll them into balls. On a lightly floured counter, roll out the pieces into paper-thin circles, with a rolling pin. If the dough resists, work on another piece and come back around to finish. Dust a touch of flour under the rolled-out pieces from time to time to keep them from sticking to the counter.

5. Use a fork or flatbread stamp to dock the flattened dough all over with pin-prick-size holes.

6. Lift the dough from the counter, and gently stretch the dough to widen the holes. Transfer it to the baking stone by hand, on a floured peel, or by wrapping it first around the rolling pin.

7. Bake the dough for 2 to 3 minutes, till it begins to crisp and get brown around the holes. Transfer to a cooling rack; do not stack the matzohs while cooling or they will not stay crisp.

CHAPATIS

1. Combine the dough ingredients in a mixing bowl and stir till they form a ball.

2. Turn the dough out onto a lightly floured counter. Knead for 5 to 7 minutes, till the dough is smooth and stretchy, tacky but not sticky.

3. Place the dough in a clean bowl, mist the dough with cooking spray, cover it with plastic wrap, and refrigerate it for 1 hour.

4. Remove the dough from the refrigerator, cut into 7 to 14 pieces, and roll it out as in step 4 for matzohs, but do not dock the dough with holes. The pieces should be about $1/8$ inch thick—not quite as thin as for matzoh.

5. Heat a heavy cast-iron skillet over medium-high heat. Lightly mist it with cooking spray.

6. Using a metal spatula, place a chapati in the pan. Cook for 10 seconds on one side, then flip the chapati over and cook it for 1 minute, until the starches have gelatinized and the dough begins to develop brown spots.

7. Flip the chapati back to the first side, and cook until it starts to balloon in the center. With a pot holder or oven mitt, press lightly on the bulging dough to flatten it. After a few seconds, when the bottom of the dough is golden brown, remove it from the pan. You may stack the chapatis on top of each other to keep them warm, and wrap them in a clean towel. The ballooning dough will flatten out.

MASTER FORMULA:
PITA BREAD

The first time I had pita bread was in a restaurant in Philadelphia aptly named The Middle East. It was around 1963, and I was eating hummus and baba ghanouj for the first time while belly dancers swirled around our table urging us with their hips to tip freely—a memorable experience for a teenage boy! Jim Tayoun, the owner of the restaurant, came over to demonstrate how to use our pita bread to scoop up the tantalizing garlicky dips. I remember wondering out loud why I had never seen these foods before, and saying how popular I thought they would be if more restaurants served them. My brother, Fred, thought I was being effusive because of the spell cast by the belly dancers. Maybe so, but sure enough, pocket pita bread, like bagels, eventually moved from its ethnic enclave into the mainstream. Pita sandwiches, both Middle Eastern–style gyros and souvlakia and healthful deli sandwiches with bursts of alfalfa sprouts are everywhere these days.

Twenty years after my introduction to pita bread, I made it to Israel and renewed my love affair with Middle Eastern foods. I practically inhaled the olive oil–drenched tabbouleh, hummus, and baba ghanouj we encountered at every meal. I was just beginning my bread-baking pursuits and came home determined to learn how to make a decent pita bread, one that did not fall apart as soon as I tried to stuff it.

The following master formula represents the fruit of my pita labors. The key to pita bread, as it is for so many breads, is to get both the oven and the stone very hot. Another trick is to spray the baking stone with water just before putting the flatbreads on it, to keep the dough from developing a wrinkled skin.

There is a drama to the full ballooning of a pita bread on the hearth; it almost seems like magic. It is easy to imagine peasants gathered around a hot village hearth, waiting for the baker to toss his circles of dough onto the deck, where they pop open, and a few minutes later, become the centerpiece for a family meal—without alfalfa sprouts!

COMMENTARIES

❏ Whole-wheat pitas are more traditional than white-flour pitas, but also more fragile, because the bran cuts the gluten, weakening the structure. A blend of the two flours is a good compromise. I prefer to use $2/3$ bread flour and $1/3$ whole wheat, but any combination is acceptable.

❏ Some people claim to be able to use their doughs for up to seven days, but I would not count on that much longevity; I find that the dough begins to break down from the third day on.

❏ When baking, the pitas really do pop. The outer edge of the circle becomes like the seam of the ball. Make sure there is enough headroom in the oven to accommodate the dough's expansion. If it hits a shelf or the ceiling of the oven, the dough will burn. If the dough does not balloon, a piece may be sticking to itself or the oven may not be hot enough. These so-called failed pitas can still be used as flatbreads, like a naan (page 142), perfect for scooping up dips or serving with a meal.

INGREDIENT	%
Unbleached bread flour	100
Salt	1.6
Instant yeast	1.4
Olive oil	6.25
Water	62.5

MAKES 4 TO 8 BREADS

3¹/₂ cups (16 ounces) unbleached bread flour or whole-wheat flour

1 teaspoon (0.25 ounce) salt

2 teaspoons (0.22 ounce) instant yeast

2 tablespoons (1 ounce) olive oil

1¹/₄ cups cool water (65° to 70°F)

Vegetable oil cooking spray

=Approximate Weight: 27.47 ounces (1 pound, 11.5 ounces)

1. Combine the dough ingredients in a mixing bowl or in the bowl of an electric mixer with a dough hook.

2. If kneading by hand, mix till the ingredients form a ball, then turn the ball out onto a lightly floured counter and knead it for 12 to 15 minutes. In a mixer, mix the ingredients for about 1 minute on slow speed and 10 minutes on medium. The dough should be soft and pliable, similar in texture to baguette dough. It should pass the windowpane test (page 29) and be between 78° and 80°F. (If using all whole-wheat flour, you may need to increase the water by 2 or 4 tablespoons to achieve this consistency.)

3. Place the dough in a clean bowl, mist with cooking spray, cover with plastic wrap, and allow it to rise for about 90 minutes, till double in size.

4. Place a baking stone or tiles on the bottom rack of the oven, and preheat the oven to 475°F.

5. Divide the dough into 4 to 8 pieces (remember that each pita can be halved to yield 2 sandwiches). Lightly round each piece into a ball and flatten it into a disk. Cover the dough with plastic wrap and allow it to rest for 20 minutes, or refrigerate it for up to 2 days.

6. Roll out each piece of dough with a rolling pin into a circle about ¹/₄ inch thick (the circles will be 6 to 12 inches in diameter, depending upon the number). If the dough resists, move on to the next piece and return in a few minutes. When all the pieces are rolled out, allow them to rest, uncovered, for 10 minutes before baking.

7. Spritz the baking stone lightly with water and place as many pitas on it as will fit without overlapping. Lower the oven temperature to 450°F and bake the pitas for about 3 minutes, or till they balloon.

8. When the pitas have fully expanded, remove them from the oven and set them on a rack to cool. Do not wait for them to brown or darken, or they will get too crisp. Or to serve pitas warm, stack them and wrap them in a clean towel or napkin. Bake the remaining dough in the same manner.

NAAN BREAD

A tandoor is a clay baking kiln that heats up to 800° or 900°F, the ultimate barbecue pit for cooking Indian-style tandoori chicken, seafood, and meats. You can also cook naan in a tandoor in a matter of moments. *Naan* is the generic name for dozens of different breads made in India, Pakistan, Afghanistan, Tibet, and other countries of Asia. As Naomi Duguid and Jeffrey Alford point out in *Flatbreads and Flavors,* there are many ways to make naan, but a tandoor is one of the keys to great naan. We can only approximate the naan served hot from the kiln at Indian restaurants.

A home oven can get hot enough to bake great naan, if the dough is properly made, using good fermentation techniques. With an understanding of how long, slow fermentation conditions the dough, we can recreate the essence, if not the actuality, of traditional breads.

Real naan is slapped onto the inside wall of a tandoor by a baker whose hand is protected by a special mitt. As the bread quickly bakes, it peels off the oven wall; it is fished out before it falls into the glowing coals below. The naan is then brushed with butter, folded, and covered with a towel to keep it hot, soft, and moist. As the bread cools it gets stiffer and more brittle.

Naan dough is soft and pliable, and spreads out quickly in the hands of the tandoor master. It picks up a smoky flavor from the coals that cannot be duplicated in a home oven. However, the following master formula will produce naan that is true to the spirit of tandoori naan.

FLATBREAD TOPPING TO DIE FOR

When a pita bread does not balloon, or pop, it is not all that different from a naan and actually makes an excellent basic flatbread. You can even intentionally dock, or prick, the center of an unbaked pita bread to keep it from popping when it is baked. When docking the bread, you may want to baste it with a flavorful topping.

A few summers ago, I was hired as a consultant for a Washington, D.C., restaurant group called Clyde's. The company makes its own breads, and Tom Meyer, the corporate chef, brought me in to help with some new formulas. We made flatbreads together one afternoon, and Tom blew the roof off my mouth with this incredible pepper-and-garlic topping.

It will keep indefinitely in the refrigerator, so you can make a large supply (double or triple the recipe below). You can use this topping on any number of breads, but I think it works best on naan or docked pita. Be forewarned: This is one spicy and addictive topping.

$1/2$ cup crushed red pepper

1 tablespoon Tabasco or other hot pepper sauce

$1/2$ cup olive oil

24 garlic cloves, minced

$1^1/2$ cups grated Parmesan or Romano cheese (finally, a good use for the powdery boxed stuff!)

Mix all the ingredients together till they make a paste. Place a heaping tablespoon on the center of each naan or docked pita before baking, spread it a little, and bake as usual. Then, watch out!

COMMENTARIES

❑ Milk, buttermilk, or yogurt softens the texture of naan, adds flavor, and promotes browning. You may, however, substitute water.

❑ As with all of the pre-ferments, you need to make the *poolish* for this formula ahead of time, preferably the day before. If it is refrigerated, take it out 1 hour before using.

❑ Along with the butter or garlic butter, you may also use small amounts of chopped green onions or chives, cracked black peppercorns, or herb and spice mixtures, adding them directly to the dough or brushing them on after the bake.

❑ This dough responds well to a slightly longer kneading time and a slightly warmer mixing temperature than regular hearth breads. This way the yeast goes to work a little faster and the dough is ready for baking in a timely manner without losing quality.

❑ I like to line my pans with parchment because it keeps the pans clean and also protects the dough from picking up any oxidation or rust from the pans. Once you start working with parchment, it is hard to work without it.

❑ My method for forming the naan is a variation of the toss-and-spin method used for pizza doughs (see page 153). The dough will have thin and thick spots, and may even tear a little; this is okay. Just patch it together and continue flicking till you have a size you like. The edges should be thicker than the center, like a pizza dough. You may also shape oblong, snowshoe-shaped naan by flicking from only one end rather than turning the dough. This is an interesting way to serve the bread, and conveys a more rustic quality. Or you may roll the dough with a rolling pin, or press it out with wet or floured hands, as described in step 7 on page 151 for pizza.

❑ The bake time depends upon the thickness of the dough. Naturally, the thinner you make the dough the faster it will bake. Do not let it get too dark or it will crisp up (you want it soft).

INGREDIENT	%
Unbleached bread flour	100
Salt	3.1
Instant yeast	0.7
Olive oil	12.5
Buttermilk	25
Poolish	100
Water	N/A
Butter	N/A

MAKES 6 TO 8 BREADS

3¹/₂ cups (16 ounces) unbleached bread flour

2 teaspoons (0.5 ounce) salt

1 teaspoon (0.11 ounce) instant yeast

4 tablespoons (2 ounces) olive or vegetable oil

¹/₂ cup (4 ounces) buttermilk or yogurt

2 cups (16 ounces) *poolish*-style sponge (page 35)

Cool water (65° to 70°F), as needed

Vegetable oil cooking spray

¹/₂ cup (4 ounces) melted butter or garlic butter (optional)

=*Approximate Weight: 38.61 ounces (2 pounds, 6.61 ounces)*

1. Combine the flour, salt, yeast, oil, buttermilk, and *poolish* in a mixing bowl or in the bowl of an electric mixer with a dough hook.

2. If making the dough by hand, mix till it forms into a ball. Turn it out onto a well-floured counter and knead it for 12 to 15 minutes, working in

additional flour as needed to keep the dough from sticking. It should be soft, pliable, and a little sticky (slightly wetter than French-bread dough). Add water if the dough is too stiff. The temperature should be about 80°F, and the dough should pass the windowpane test (page 29). By machine, mix for about 1 minute on slow speed, then 10 to 12 minutes on medium.

3. Place the dough in a clean bowl, mist with cooking spray, cover with plastic wrap or enclose in a plastic bag, and allow the dough to rise at room temperature for 1 hour, until it swells noticeably.

4. Meanwhile, line a sheet pan with parchment. Mist the parchment with cooking spray and dust it with flour.

5. Turn the dough out onto a lightly floured surface and divide it into 6 to 8 equal pieces. Loosely round each piece into a ball and place it on the prepared pan. Mist the dough lightly with cooking spray, slip the pan into a large plastic bag, and refrigerate the dough for 1 hour.

6. Place a baking stone or tiles on the bottom rack of the oven and preheat the oven to 550°F or as high as it will go.

7. To shape the dough, you will need to either dampen or flour your hands frequently (keep a bowl of cold water or flour nearby). Flatten each dough ball into a disk. Hold one edge of the disk with both hands and flick your wrists, snapping the far edge of the dough down toward the floured counter. Give the dough a quarter turn and repeat. Continue rotating and flicking the dough, dampening or flouring your hands as you go, until it is extended as far it can go without tearing apart.

8. Either drop the dough directly onto the hot stone or slide it into the oven on a semolina- or cornmeal-dusted peel, baking as many pieces at a time as will fit on the stone without overlapping. Bake for 3 to 5 minutes, or till the bread just begins to develop brown spots.

9. Remove the breads from the oven with a peel or metal spatula and brush the tops with melted butter or garlic butter, if desired. Serve immediately, or wrap the finished pieces in a clean towel to keep them warm and soft as you continue baking.

FLOUR TORTILLAS

Though the concept has been around for thousands of years, one of the hottest trends these days is wrapped food. Restaurants with names like *World Wraps* and *Wrap and Roll* are springing up almost as frequently as juice bars and coffeehouses. Wraps are simply internationalized burritos. When made by someone who really knows how, wraps can be an exceptional treat filled with smoked meats, jambalaya, chutneys, seasoned vegetables, or spicy sauces. If you want to make your own wrap sandwiches, make the tortillas at least ten to twelve inches across. Many wrap restaurants offer a choice of flavored tortillas, a major trend in baked goods that adds spice and color to a once-simple staple. Following the master formula are suggestions for creating your own flavored tortillas, though I advise you to first make the basic version to develop your technique. If made without fat, tortillas tend to be rubbery. Most commercial flour tortillas are made with lard or vegetable oil, but I use butter for the best possible flavor.

COMMENTARIES

❑ Butter tastes best for tortillas, but you may substitute an equal amount of canola, corn, olive, or other oil for lower cholesterol, or you can use the traditional tortilla fat, lard, or vegetable shortening.

❑ It is not necessary to work the gluten in tortilla dough too hard. Tortillas should be tender, not tough, but strong enough to stand up to filling without tearing.

❑ Tortillas can be made any size. For eating out of hand or as a side bread, I prefer small ones, but for wraps or burritos, you need larger tortillas.

❑ It is also possible to bake tortillas on the stove top in a hot skillet, like chapatis (see page 139), but I prefer the oven-baked version.

INGREDIENT	%
Unbleached bread flour	100
Salt	1.1
Butter	25
Water	50

MAKES 8 TO 16 TORTILLAS

3¹/₂ cups (16 ounces) unbleached bread flour

³/₄ teaspoon (0.17 ounce) salt

¹/₂ cup (4 ounces) butter, room temperature

1 cup lukewarm water (80°F)

Vegetable oil cooking spray

=*Approximate Weight: 28 ounces*

1. Combine all the ingredients in a mixing bowl and stir till they form a ball (add a few drops of extra water if needed).

2. Turn the dough out onto a floured counter and knead for 3 or 4 minutes, just till a smooth, soft dough is formed. The dough should not be sticky, but like French-bread dough, soft, pliable, and a bit tacky.

3. Divide the dough into 8 to 16 equal pieces. Round them into balls and then flatten them into disks. Mist the pieces

with cooking spray, cover the dough with plastic wrap or a large plastic bag, and let it rest for 20 to 30 minutes.

4. Place a baking stone or tiles on the bottom rack of the oven and preheat the oven to 500°F.

5. On a lightly floured surface, roll out the dough into very thin rounds, about $1/8$ inch or less (the dough circles will be about 6 to 12 inches across, depending on the number you are making). If the dough resists, move on to another piece and return in a few minutes, after the gluten has relaxed. As you roll the dough, cover the tortillas with a towel to keep them from drying out. (You can stack the rounds six high if you lightly dust each layer with flour.)

6. Spritz the baking stone with water to prevent the tortillas from wrinkling and use a floured peel, or your hands (taking care not to touch the hot stone), to place as many tortillas on the stone as will fit without overlapping. Bake the tortillas for 1 minute. Then gently lift them and flip them over with a metal spatula. Bake them for 45 seconds more. They will puff and develop a few speckled brown spots but should not be allowed to crisp up. Use a metal spatula to transfer the baked tortillas to a clean towel. Keep them wrapped if you want to serve them warm. Repeat this process (including spritzing the stone) for the remaining tortillas.

7. Let the tortillas cool thoroughly and store them, well wrapped, in the refrigerator or freezer. Warm them up quickly in a hot skillet or on a hot baking stone.

FLAVORED TORTILLAS

The simplest way to make a flavored tortilla is to add powdered spices to the dough. Paprika is perfect because it adds color and a pleasant flavor but is not hot. Chile powder, which is made of a blend of ground hot chiles, cumin, garlic powder, and salt, is another easy addition if you want something a little picante. Use about 1 tablespoon of spice for every 16 ounces of flour, or season to your taste.

Another, more complex way to flavor tortillas is with a flavorful purée or infusion. For instance, sundried tomatoes can be soaked in warm water, then puréed and added to the dough in place of an equal amount of water. Fresh, leafy herbs like basil, coriander, and parsley can also be puréed in the water and added to the dough.

Flavored tortillas are like flavored pasta—anything is possible. Lemon pepper, dried mushroom powder, chives, carrot or beet juice, or any combination thereof are among the options. Herbal and flavor concentrates available at supermarkets can also be used instead of fresh herbs. Concentrates pack a lot of flavor into just a few drops, making it easy to incorporate them into the formula without major modifications.

PIZZA AND FOCACCIA

Many of us grew up believing that some foods from our hometown are the best of their kind in the world, especially if we grew up in Paris, New York, or... Philadelphia. Eventually, you meet people from other regions who dispute your chauvinistic claims. I am talking about pizza here, not cheese steaks or hoagies, for which I, as a native Philadelphian, could make a compelling argument. I once did, however, contend that the world's best pizza also comes from my hometown. I now admit, after visiting many cities over the past twenty-five years, that both great and lousy pizza exists everywhere.

I have never been to Italy where, Carol Field, the author of the wonderful *The Italian Baker,* tells us, many types of pizza exist under different names. I understand, however, that pizza really is a simple affair: flatbread and toppings, a pie made with a bread-dough crust, and savory ingredients. I also understand, thanks to Ms. Field, that what I grew up with and understand to be true pizza is merely one version, a southern Italian, Neapolitan-style pizza. Over the years, I have tasted Sicilian, Greek, Spanish, and French versions of the pizza. This last one, from the Niçoise region, is called *pissaladière,* and consists of an olive oil–rich crust covered with anchovies and chopped fresh tomatoes. I have savored regional variations such as focaccia, schiacciata, stromboli, and calzone. I once flirted with Chicago deep-dish pizza, but it never captured my heart like the thin, crisp, flat pies. I have

gone restaurant hopping in northern California's wine country in search of new and excellent models, getting pies right out of wood-burning ovens, off mesquite grills, covered with Tuscan sausage, creamy goat cheese, and freshly picked figs. I am, as you can see, pizza-obsessive.

As a kid I did not think lousy pizza was possible, till I tasted the quickly made versions sold out of trucks at fairs and carnivals—you know, the cardboard crusts with tomato paste, grated pseudo-Parmesan, and a sprinkle of old, faded oregano. Then, I had supermarket frozen pizzas and understood that you really can screw up anything if you put your mind to it. It made me appreciate even more the wonderful pies from Mama's, Pagano's, and the other pizza parlors of my youth. As I met people from New York, Washington, D.C., New Haven, Chicago—and even Lincoln, Nebraska, and Raleigh, North Carolina—and learned that they felt the same about their favorite hometown pizzas, I began to relinquish my assertion that nobody outside of Philadelphia knew good pizza. It was a wise decision. World-class pizza, like world-class bread, can exist anywhere there is a commitment to doing it right.

Then, along came Alice Waters and Wolfgang Puck, and the whole discussion was taken to a new level. In 1995, I wrote an article for a wine country magazine on the new wave of gourmet pizzas showing up in fine restaurants, thanks to the neopizza revival spawned at Chez Panisse and Spago. Doing the research for that article was one of the better homework assignments I have ever had, and it brought into focus the simple elements that constitute a great pizza:

the sauce, the cheese and toppings, and most important, the crust. I will say only a few things about the sauce and toppings; I will have much to say about the crust.

Do not use too thick a sauce, as most home pizza cooks do, because it turns to paste when baked. Make the sauce thin, well seasoned, and a touch acidic, with a good wine vinegar, as the sauce will sweeten as it bakes. Use fresh tomatoes and basil when they are in season instead of sauce.

For the toppings, use the best ingredients you can find—freshly grated real Parmesan or Romano cheese, for example. Mix these cheeses with good melters like whole-milk mozzarella, Monterey Jack, or even aged Cheddar or Gruyère. Fresh herbs and some toppings should be buried under the cheese so they do not burn. Sausage and most other meats can go on top, as they taste best when crisped. Experiment with exotic toppings like fresh figs and Gorgonzola cheese, but remember, it will all be for nought if your crust is not superb. I have had some unbelievably wonderful pizzas with caramelized onion confits, goat and feta cheeses, roasted garlic, andouille and other sausages, and fresh figs. (Yes, I have mentioned figs three times, but once you have tried them on pizza you will understand why!) You can get the recipes for these from the dozens of pizza books already on the shelves. (James McNair's *Pizza* is a particularly good one.)

What I really and urgently want to convey, though, is how to make a great pizza crust. This is the foundation of world-class pizza, and even after all the designer toppings, the most memorable aspect of the pizza. The same alchemy that sets bread apart from other foods is at work; the taste memories from great crust go deep into our psyches. The various pizza styles—Sicilian, Neapolitan, Roman, Greek, etc.—generally refer to the type of crust. And the guiding principles for crust are the same as for bread; only the ingredient proportions and roll-out methods are different. There are many ways to make pizza dough, just as there are many ways to make French bread, but as you have observed, I like to push the limits of dough possibilities. Why make a good pizza crust when you can make a world-class crust, something to stop conversation, to plant those fond, deep memories?

A national organic frozen food company recently asked me to develop a pizza dough. The people who run the company wanted something that would distinguish their product from the frozen pizzas already on the shelves. Coming up with the formula was fairly easy. To build flavor and longer shelf life, we used the *poolish*-style pre-ferment. To give the dough tenderness even when crisped, we hydrated it beyond normal levels, treating it almost like a *ciabatta* dough. Our first test batch was so well received that I thought my work was over. The difficulty, we discovered, was not in making the dough but in rolling it out fast enough to make it commercially cost-efficient. It was too springy and sticky to simply run through the standard rolling equipment; it needed special handling. Ultimately, we had to customize existing machinery, but we finally got the product to the market, where it is doing quite well. Frankly, I have not tasted any frozen pizza like it; I think it's about as good as it gets.

The following formulas are similar to the one I developed for commercial production, and they are unlike any I have seen in print. They will take your pizza making to another level. To get there, you will need a pizza stone, a peel, parchment paper; a two-day head start for the pre-ferments; a good sauce, cheese, and toppings; and a really hot oven. Most home ovens do not get as hot as professional pizza ovens or wood-fired ovens, but they will get hot enough to make these formulas work. As with bread, the rest is dough technique, based on many of the same principles applied to hearth breads.

I also assume, as I have throughout this book, a certain kinship of passion and commitment. I have come to realize that, with so many styles of pizza, there is no way to say, "This is the world's greatest." However, I do think it is possible to say, "This is my favorite." My goal is to give you a method and a product you have never had before, to set a new standard, to kindle a passion for excellence that will serve as guidepost. Memorable pizza is merely a means to that end—and what a delectable means it is.

MASTER FORMULA:
PIZZA DOUGH I

When pressing out the dough in this recipe, you can be aggressive, using your hands like a rolling pin to squeeze out the bubbles and push the dough outward. With the wet-hands method, the dough will slide right off your fingers and you can control exactly where you want it to go. You may, instead, use a floured-hands method, dipping them into flour instead of water. The flour will keep the surface dry, facilitating handling. With enough dusting flour you may even use a rolling pin to help shape your dough. Try making pizza both ways—and with the alternatives described on page 153—and use the method that works best for you. Of course, if you have enough confidence in your skills, you can always use the toss-and-spin pizza parlor method. Just watch out for the ceiling!

COMMENTARIES

❏ You may substitute up to 1 cup of whole-wheat flour or 1/4 cup of wheat bran for an equal amount of bread flour to achieve a more textured, peasant-style dough. The crust will not be quite as light and bubbly, but will still be wonderful.

❏ You can substitute an equal amount of sugar for the honey in this formula.

❏ The *poolish* should be made at least 5 hours before mixing the dough, preferably the day before. If refrigerated, take it out 1 hour before using.

❏ Because of the high percentage of liquid in this dough, the flour takes a while to fully absorb it, so do not worry about overmixing.

❏ Every time you add an inch to the diameter

of a pizza you greatly increase the surface area. So, 4 ounces of dough makes a 6-inch pizza; 7 ounces, a 9-inch; 10 ounces, a 10-inch; and 12.5 ounces, a 12-inch.

❑ You can make a pizza crust without the parchment by using lots of flour on the counter, but the paper is a much better method for easy handling, especially with this particularly wet dough. See also Other Methods of Rolling Out Pizza Dough on page 153.

❑ When you dress the pizza, the weight of the toppings will make the center thinner and the edges thicker yet.

INGREDIENT	%
Unbleached bread flour	100
Salt	3.1
Instant yeast	0.2
Honey	9.5
Olive oil	25
Water	40
Poolish	62.5

MAKES 3 TO 8 PIZZAS

3¹/₂ cups (16 ounces) unbleached bread flour

2 teaspoons (0.5 ounce) salt

¹/₄ teaspoon (0.03 ounce) instant yeast

2 tablespoons (1.5 ounces) honey

¹/₂ cup (4 ounces) olive oil (any grade)

³/₄ cup plus 1 tablespoon cool water (65° to 70°F)

1¹/₄ cup (10 ounces) *poolish*-style sponge (page 35)

Vegetable oil cooking spray

―――――――――――――――――
=*Approximate Weight: 38.5 ounces (2 pounds, 6.5 ounces)*

1. Combine all the ingredients in the bowl of an electric mixer with a paddle attachment (not a dough hook) or a mixing bowl. If mixing by machine, mix on slow speed for 1 minute; increase to medium speed and mix for about 12 minutes, till the dough is smooth and creamy. The dough will be very wet, like a thick pancake batter. If mixing by hand, beat with a whisk or spoon for 15 minutes.

2. Cover the bowl with plastic wrap and allow the dough to rise at room temperature for 3 hours, till bubbly. Refrigerate overnight; it will thicken as it cools.

3. Turn the dough out onto a heavily floured work surface and use a knife or pastry blade to cut it into 3 to 8 pieces. (You can make three 12-inch pizzas, eight 6-inch pizzas, or any number in between.)

4. Toss the pieces, one at a time, in the flour, gently round them into loose balls, and place them on the prepared pan. Mist the tops of the dough with cooking spray and cover with a plastic bag or plastic wrap. Let the dough rise for at least 30 minutes before proceeding. You can hold it up to 2 days in the refrigerator, tightly covered, if necessary.

5. Preheat the oven to 550°F or as high as it will go. Prepare the oven for hearth baking as described on page 25 and have your sauce and toppings ready (see page 154). Line an inverted sheet pan with parchment and mist it with cooking spray. Set out a bowl of cold water to dip your hands in, as needed, to keep the dough from sticking to you.

6. Spread a piece of parchment on the counter or on the back of a sheet pan and give it a light misting with cooking spray. Have the bowl of cold water ready.

7. Dip your hands in the water and place 1 piece of dough in the center of the parchment. Dip your hands again and press the dough into a circle as far as it will go. When it begins to spring back, stop pressing and let it relax for a few minutes while you work on another piece or simply wait. Dip your hands and press again, forcefully, spreading the dough as thin as possible (about $1/4$ inch) without tearing it and leaving a thicker lip around the edges.

8. Dress the pizza with the sauce and toppings, leaving at least $1/2$ inch of uncovered border around the edge.

9. Cut away most of the paper, leaving just enough for gripping, and lift the parchment onto an oven peel, or use the sheet pan as a peel. Press gently down on the center of the pizza, directly on the toppings, giving it one final spread (this is optional, but recommended). Then slide it, paper and all, onto the hot baking stone.

10. Bake for 10 to 12 minutes, or till the edge is golden brown and the cheese is bubbly and golden. Lift up the edge of the pizza with a metal spatula or the peel to check that the underside is golden brown, a good sign of crispness (if it is not browned, the crust will be soft and soggy as it cools). If the crust needs more time but the cheese is browning, cover it with aluminum foil or a piece of parchment to buy some time.

11. Remove the pizza from the oven with a spatula or peel, remove the parchment, and slice and serve.

MASTER FORMULA:

PIZZA DOUGH II

This is a drier, easier-to-handle dough with
different characteristics than the previous
rustic pizza crust. It does not bubble as
much and is slightly chewier, though the
buttermilk tenderizes the dough and gives
it a pleasant flavor. The *poolish* sponge provides more flavor than if simply made as a
straight yeasted dough.

COMMENTARIES

❑ Make the *poolish* the day before, or at least
5 hours ahead. If it is refrigerated, take it out
1 hour before using.

❑ An 8-ounce piece of dough makes an 8- to
10-inch pizza. Smaller pieces are easier to handle, so you might want to make individual-size
pizzas using 4 to 6 ounces of dough for each.

❑ You may freeze the dough for up to 3 weeks,
defrosting and using it as needed. After that, it
will begin to break down and lose its "push."

INGREDIENT	%
Unbleached bread flour	100
Salt	2
Instant yeast	2
Honey	5
Olive oil	6.25
Buttermilk	37.5
Poolish	50

3^1/2 cups (16 ounces) unbleached
bread flour

1^1/2 teaspoons (0.33 ounce) salt

1 tablespoon (0.33 ounce) instant yeast

1 tablespoon (0.75 ounce) honey

2 tablespoons (1 ounce) olive oil

3/4 cup buttermilk, at room temperature

1 cup (8 ounces) *poolish*-style sponge
(page 35)

Vegetable oil cooking spray

=*Approximate Weight: 32 ounces
(2 pounds)*

1. Combine all the dough ingredients
in the bowl of an electric mixer or a
mixing bowl. If mixing by machine,
mix with a dough hook on low speed
for 1 minute, then on medium speed
for 10 to 12 minutes. If mixing by
hand, stir the ingredients together
till they form a ball and knead the
dough on a lightly floured surface for
12 to 15 minutes. The dough is ready
when it windowpanes (page 29) and
feels neutral to the touch, 78° to 80°F.
It should be soft, stretchy, and tacky,
somewhat like baguette dough. Adjust
with additional flour or water, if necessary, while mixing.

2. Place the dough in a clean bowl, cover
the bowl with plastic wrap, and allow
the dough to rise at room temperature
for 1 hour, till it swells noticeably.

3. On a floured counter, divide the dough
into individual pieces. Roll the pieces

into balls and place them on a sheet pan that has been lined with parchment and lightly floured. Spray the tops with cooking spray, cover with plastic wrap or enclose in a plastic bag, and refrigerate for at least 1 hour. The dough can be held in the refrigerator for up to 48 hours.

4. Preheat the oven to 550°F or as high as it goes. Prepare the oven for hearth baking as described on page 25.

5. On a floured surface, roll each piece of dough into a circle $1/8$ to $1/4$ inch thick (thicker for Sicilian-style pizza). Transfer the dough to a peel that has been sprinkled liberally with flour, semolina, cornmeal, or polenta. Crimp the outer edge into a small lip.

OTHER WAYS TO ROLL OUT PIZZA DOUGH

The method described in the first pizza dough formula is an easy and convenient way to roll out a pizza, especially with a slack, sticky dough like ours. Here are two other techniques that work well once you master them. They give slightly different textures and qualities to the finished pizza. No matter what method you use, it takes practice. Try different approaches till you find the one that works best for you. Like every aspect of pizza, the crust is a very personal matter.

The classic toss and spin: Because the dough is very soft and sticky, to use this method you will need to roll the dough in flour, and as it spreads, continue to dip it in flour to keep it from sticking to your hands. The knuckles are an important tool in this method. Each time you toss and spin the dough, catching it on your fists, you must gently stretch the dough into a wider circle. The trick is keeping the dough in a circle; it may try to oblong itself or wobble as you toss. This method allows you to make a thin inner crust while still retaining a nice, bready edge, or lip.

The fling technique: I am becoming increasingly fond of this method, but again, it requires practice and patience to master. With floured hands, press the dough out into a circle. Pick it up by one edge with both hands and hold it between your fingers. Then flick your wrists as if shaking out a wet towel. Give the dough a quarter turn and repeat the motion. Continue turning and flicking the dough until it reaches the desired size. The dough will stretch out much as it would with the toss-and-spin method, again leaving a thicker edge. It takes practice to determine just the right amount of force for flicking; the dough will tear if flicked too forcefully. By emphasizing one edge or direction you can also make oblong, Roman-style pizzas, which are very attractive and actually easier to handle than circles.

Here are a few additional pointers:

❏ Rolling pins also work, but the gluten in the dough fights against being rolled, so you have to rest it for a few minutes between rollings. This method works best with drier, less sticky doughs, or heavily floured wet doughs.

❏ Regardless of the method, keep a bit of a lip on the edge. It puffs up nicely, surrounding the filled center with a beautiful border.

❏ You can prevent bubbling in the center by docking, or piercing, the center of the rolled-out dough with a fork or a flatbread stamper (a tool with many nail-like pricking points) before topping. This helps keep the center thin and crisp.

6. Top the dough with pizza sauce and fixings as described below.

7. Slide the pizza onto the baking stone. Bake for about 8 to 12 minutes, or till the dough is crisp and golden and the cheese is bubbly and golden.

8. Remove the pizza from the oven with a spatula or peel. Slice and serve.

PREPARING TO BAKE A PIZZA

When making pizza you need to move quickly, so here are important preparatory steps to follow:

❑ The pizza stone should be put into place and preheated along with the oven. If you do not have a stone, substitute an inverted sheet pan.

❑ The oven should be preheated to its highest heat—the hotter the better. Allow at least 30 to 40 minutes for it to heat fully.

❑ Have your baking peel, wooden or metal, at the ready. You can improvise by using the back of a sheet pan and baking parchment, but a peel works better.

❑ The pizza sauce needs to be fairly thin since it will thicken under the high oven heat. If you are using pasta sauce, thin it down with water and a splash of wine vinegar.

❑ Have your topping ingredients sliced, chopped, or grated and ready to go.

❑ When layering the toppings, put most of them under the grated cheese to protect them from burning. I spread sauce on first (not too heavily), then fresh herbs, garlic, mushrooms, etc., then the cheese. Fatty meats like sausage and pepperoni can go on top for crisping, but lean cuts like precooked chicken or duck should go under the cheese.

❑ For the cheese layer, I mix the standard mozzarella with freshly grated Parmesan, Romano, Asiago, or dry Jack. Don't use pregrated box cheese, which is really made from scrap shavings and does not melt.

❑ Cheeseless pizzas can be made with caramelized onions and sautéed mushrooms (not raw mushrooms, which tend to burn), as well as other veggie favorites such as roasted eggplant, red bell peppers, marinated artichoke hearts, and cooked spinach. Puréed fresh basil without cheese (cheeseless pesto!) can also be used, along with other fresh, puréed herbs. Lightly precooking the veggies and marinating them in a flavorful olive oil dressing will prevent them from burning when baked.

MASTER FORMULA:

FOCACCIA

What the Tuscans call *schiacciata,* their Genoese neighbors to the north call *focaccia.* Those to the south, in Naples and Rome, favor the word *pizza.* Through the centuries, the pie has been called *piadinia, laganum,* and even *placenta.* Stuffed versions are called *panzarotti, calzone,* and *stromboli* (see page 158). Whatever the name, topped or stuffed flatbreads are wonderful, and their popularity continues to grow as Americans become aware of the many varieties.

COMMENTARIES

❏ This sticky dough is much more manageable when made in a mixer with a dough hook, but with perseverance, hand kneading is possible.

❏ This formula makes enough dough for one full-size, commercial sheet pan (16 by 24 inches), but most home ovens cannot hold a full pan, so you will probably have to divide it into 2 or 3 smaller units. Do not put too much dough in the pans. Focaccia is best when the finished product is about 1 inch thick rather than the 2 to 3 inches that many people make. To achieve this, press the dough only to about $1/2$ inch thick in the pans prior to the rise.

❏ Strong flour is necessary to sustain the long fermentation and oven spring. The beauty of this version of focaccia is the cell structure, which is like such rustic breads as *ciabatta* (see page 47). The gluten really stretches, leaving long and irregular pockets. When this stretch takes place properly, the dough is very soft and spongy because it is full of air.

❏ Make the *poolish* at least 5 hours ahead of time— preferably at least 1 day ahead—and if it is refrigerated, take it out at least 1 hour before using. There is a lot of pre-ferment in this dough but very little yeast. This allows for a long fermentation and maximum flavor and structure development.

❏ The cold-water method of forming the dough is my favorite because the dough does not stick as long as your hands are wet. If you prefer, you can flour your hands instead. Whichever method you choose, you will be adding extra water or flour to the dough; to keep things in balance, you may want to switch halfway, beginning with the wet-hands method and finishing up with the floured-hands method.

❏ Dimpling helps break up any major air pockets that could turn into large tunnels during the bake. The dimples also serve as pockets for the olive oil, turning those spots into flavor centers during the bake.

❏ The overnight retarding allows the dough to continue developing flavor and texture. The focaccia could be baked without this step, as most recipes instruct, but the additional fermentation vastly improves the final results.

❏ Pizza-style focaccia is really a pizza variation, made popular by many bakeries that sell it as designer focaccia.

❏ Cooling the focaccia before serving allows the dough to finish cooking and the flavors to come through fully. Remember, sheet-pan focaccia is more like a flatbread than a pizza.

INGREDIENT	%
Unbleached bread flour	100
Salt	2.5
Instant yeast	0.2
Olive oil	12.5
Honey	5
Poolish	100
Water	12.5

MAKES 1 LARGE SHEET PAN, 2 SMALL PANS,
OR UP TO 8 INDIVIDUAL FOCACCIAS

7 cups (32 ounces) unbleached
   bread flour

1 tablespoon (0.75 ounce) salt

1/2 teaspoon (0.06 ounce) instant yeast

1/2 cup (4 ounces) olive oil, or more as
   needed

2 tablespoons (1.5 ounces) honey

4 cups (32 ounces) *poolish*-style
   sponge (page 35)

1/2 cup cool water (65° to 70°F)

Raisins, herbs, additional olive oil, and
   toppings (see page 157)

=*Approximate Weight: 74 ounces
(4 pounds 10 ounces)*

1. Combine all the ingredients, except
    the toppings, in the bowl of an elec-
    tric mixer with a dough hook or in a
    mixing bowl. If mixing by machine,
    mix on low speed for 1 minute, then
    on medium for about 12 minutes. The
    dough will be sticky, but it should
    clear the sides of the bowl. It should
    be smooth and soft, and feel neutral to
    the touch (between 78° and 80°F) and
    pass the windowpane test (page 29).
    If mixing by hand, stir the ingredients
    till they form a ball, then turn the
    dough out onto a well-floured counter.
    Dip your hands into cold water and
    knead the dough until it begins stick-
    ing to your hand and the counter.
    With a spoon, sprinkle more flour on
    the counter, dip your hands again in
    cold water, and begin another round
    of kneading. Use a pastry blade or

metal spatula to scrape off the dough
that sticks to the counter, and discard
it. Keep this up for about 15 minutes,
until the dough achieves the state
described above.

2. Rub the inside of a large, clean bowl
    with olive oil, and place the dough
    in it. Mist the top of the dough with
    cooking spray, cover the bowl with
    plastic wrap or enclose it in a plastic
    bag, and allow it to rise at room tem-
    perature for about 3 hours, until it
    swells considerably (it will not double).

3. If making a sheet-pan focaccia, brush
    the pans with olive oil. If using a gar-
    lic, herb, or raisin mixture, add it to
    the dough, and work it in with your
    hands until it is well distributed,
    reserving some for the top or inside.
    If making more than 1 pan, divide the
    dough accordingly.

4. Place the dough on the prepared pan
    or pans and let it rest for 20 minutes.

5. Press and stretch the dough to fill the
    pan evenly; it should be about 1/2 inch
    thick. If it resists or springs back, let
    it rest for 3 to 10 minutes and press
    again; it may take a few cycles to
    press it all the way out.

6. Rub the top of the dough generously
    with more olive oil and dimple the
    dough all over by pressing your fin-
    gertips into it. Place the sheet pans
    inside large plastic bags and allow the
    dough to rise for about 1 hour, till it
    just begins to show signs of rising.
    Then place it in the refrigerator
    overnight (without toppings). If mak-

ing pizza-style focaccia, press out the rounds on parchment as described for pizza in step 6 on page 151. Place toppings on the dough, cover loosely with plastic wrap or place in a plastic bag, and immediately refrigerate. Do not proof first.

7. Remove the pans from the refrigerator 2 hours before baking. Preheat the oven to 550°F or as high as it will go. Spread with any remaining herb mixture, or sprinkle with any other toppings. Grated cheeses should be added halfway through the bake, to avoid burning or overcrisping.

8. Place the pans in the oven. After 5 minutes, turn the heat down to 425°F and bake the focaccia for 25 to 30 minutes, or till the top is golden brown and springy. The dough should spring, or rise, about 25 percent in the oven. (If making pizza-style focaccia, follow the instructions for baking pizza on page 154.)

9. Let the focaccia cool in the pan for 5 minutes. Then, using spatulas and oven mitts or pot holders, transfer the focaccia to a cutting board. Allow it to cool an additional 5 minutes before slicing and serving.

FOCACCIA TIPS AND TOPPINGS

As a rule, I prefer to work larger items like raisins or onions into the dough, where they can anchor themselves and not burn, saving the top for smaller treats like herbs and spices (protected by olive oil) or coarse sugar or salt. If you plan to top a focaccia with dry items like nuts, vegetables, fruit, or herbs, cook or dampen them first with olive oil or water to hold them in place. It is very frustrating to create a beautiful focaccia and have all the goodies slide off when you cut it. (Melted cheese, of course, will hold toppings on, but not all focaccias use cheese.)

Here are two of my favorite toppings, plus additional suggestions:

Raisins: I love focaccia with raisins better than any style of focaccia. Use lots of raisins, 6 cups for the full batch of dough, 3 cups for a half batch. The raisins should be plumped in hot water for about 10 minutes, then thoroughly drained, and they need to be distributed through-

out the dough. You may, if you like, sprinkle a little kosher salt in with the raisins. It contrasts nicely with the sweetness. I have also had raisin focaccia made with a sprinkle of fresh rosemary, but a little rosemary goes a long way. If you have a sweet tooth, you can sprinkle coarse sugar on the raisins to accentuate the sweetness. When you press the dough into the pan, pick out any raisins on the surface and press them deeper into the dough so they are not exposed. The ones that stay on the surface will burn during baking. You may substitute seedless grapes for the raisins; this makes for a juicier and very delicious focaccia. You may also fold grapes or raisins into a dough so that they are between a top and bottom layer, like a pie filling between two crusts.

Herb/Oil: For classic focaccia, dimple the dough just before baking and brush on olive oil and fresh herbs such as rosemary, basil, oregano, or marjoram. You can infuse the oil with the herbs by steeping them together for a few hours, or up to a

(continued)

---

few days. Use the oil as liberally as your conscience and waistline allow, up to about $^1/_2$ cup for the full recipe.

Other classic toppings and variations:

4 cups Gorgonzola or any rich blue cheese with walnuts and caramelized onions (a truly amazing topping)

$^1/_2$ cup garlic-infused olive oil

2 cups chopped, roasted red bell peppers and garlic

2 cups pesto, grated cheese, roasted whole shallots, and whole pine nuts

1 tablespoon cracked black pepper, 2 to 6 tablespoons garlic (fresh or roasted), 1 to 2 cups tomato sauce, and/or a sprinkling (1 to 2 cups) of cheese such as Cheddar, Swiss, Muenster, teleme, or Gouda (or your favorite)

STROMBOLI AND CALZONE: VARIATIONS ON A THEME

Stromboli starts out looking like pizza—a flattened piece of dough topped with cheese and such—but then it is rolled up into a large loaf and baked like a bread. The fillings spiral through the bread, gushing out when the hot stromboli is sliced. Calzone (the word means "pants leg") is likewise a stuffed pizza, but shaped more like a turnover. The English might call it a cheese pasty.

Here is how to savor these delights:

Use Pizza Dough II (page 152); the first dough is too wet and sticky for this purpose.

For individual calzone, roll out 4- to 6-ounce pieces of dough into circles about 6 inches in diameter. Fill the centers of the calzones with the goodies (sauce, grated or creamy cheese, onions, garlic, etc.), brush some egg wash around the edges, and fold them into half moons, matching the edges evenly and crimping them shut with a fork or your fingers. They will look like turnovers. Brush some olive oil over the top. Bake on a sheet pan at 400°F for 15 to 20 minutes, or till the dough is crisp and golden.

A stromboli is made by rolling out a piece of dough, from 8 to 48 ounces, into a square or rectangle about $^1/_4$ inch thick. Cover the stromboli as you would a "loaded" pizza (sauce is optional) and then roll it up like a jelly roll, lengthwise, sealing the ends and edges well to hold in the filling. You can bake it immediately for a thin crust, or let it rise first, for 1 hour, for a more bready texture. Bake the stromboli on a parchment-lined sheet pan at 375°F till done. Large stromboli can take up to an hour, but smaller ones will be finished in about 35 minutes. They should be very crisp and firm on the outside; the crust will soften as it cools.

You can also slice an unbaked stromboli into 1-inch-thick pieces and bake them face up (like a sticky bun) on a sheet pan for about 15 or 20 minutes. I call these *strombolini*. They make wonderful snacks.

8

THE BANANA BREAD REVOLUTION: BREADS FROM OTHER LEAVENS

QUICK BREADS

The first bread I ever made was what I now know as a quick bread. I fell under the spell of banana bread during the early seventies and made it, along with a wonderful carrot bread, to sell in Boston's Haymarket Square during the first open farmers' markets there. This enterprise led to the opening of the Root One Cafe, a vegetarian restaurant that supported a small commune for three years, eventually leading me to a religious vocation that came full circle back to breads twenty years later.

Banana bread was one of the harbingers of the bread revolution, moving quickly from an alternative, hippie-style product into the mainstream. It is now universally popular, associated more with the American heartland—from where it was appropriated in the first place—than with radical politics and back-to-the-land lifestyles (proof positive that the bread revolution has indeed been won, or at least, mainstreamed).

Quick breads, along with their first cousins, muffins, are technically batter breads, usually leavened chemically by baking soda, baking powder, or a combination of the two. In the previous chapters leavening was viewed as a natural fermentation process initiated by either tamed or wild yeast. The difference between yeasted and chemically leavened breads is similar to the difference between natural carbonation of beer versus CO_2 injection in sodas.

Chemically leavened breads have some very distinct characteristics that differentiate them from yeasted breads. The flavors are generated strictly by ingredients, rather than by fermentation; they are usually, though not always, sweet; they are tender rather than chewy (lower gluten content and development); they rise about 50 percent, rather than 100 percent as does yeasted bread, and as a result, are denser and moister; they are almost always enriched with fat (either butter or vegetable oil) and with eggs or egg replacers; and they are usually made from poured batter doughs rather than stiff, moldable doughs.

What made the banana and carrot breads at the Root One Cafe so popular was that they followed the three rules of good quick breads: moist, moist, and moist. The keys to preserving flavorful moistness (as opposed to just plain wet moistness) are to use plenty of fruit or vegetables, the proper amount of fat and liquid, and enough sweetness to satisfy the palate. Using hydroscopic (water-holding) sweeteners such as honey and corn syrup creates moister breads than does regular sugar, though I have made wonderfully moist breads with plain sugar, adjusting the other ingredients to compensate.

Savory quick breads using vegetables, spices, herbs, and cheese follow the same principles. Corn bread, in its many guises, is probably the most popular bread of this category. As with many regional foods, there is ongoing debate over what constitutes authentic corn bread—sweet versus savory, dry versus moist, thin versus thick. These issues will rage for as long as there are northern and southern states and regional cuisines. My favorite formula will give you what I think is the best corn bread you will ever taste, but I have learned that taste in these matters is sacred ground. There are unofficial clubs-of-one, consisting of people who think they have the world's greatest recipe for barbecue sauce, chili, coleslaw, corn bread, and so forth, and there is no arguing with them. I am a member of each of the aforementioned clubs and am constantly amazed at how much company I have.

Quick breads, especially, seem to spawn family favorite, heirloom-type recipes. This is partly because quick breads are both easier to make, and because of their high fat and sugar contents, easier to keep than yeasted breads. They are great vehicles for sour, clabbered, and butter milks, which all neutralize with baking soda, creating CO_2. Quick breads condense the bread-making process to a few consecutive steps, producing a finished product within an hour. There is no rising, resting, and proofing.

In addition to muffins, spoon breads, biscuits, scones, and even pancakes and waffles fall into the quick-bread category. We could stretch even farther and throw in cobblers, crisps, bettys, and pandowdies. Together, they represent a vast expanse of American iconography: pioneerism, wholesomeness, harvest, and heartland. They evoke childhood; they pique the essence of food memories.

Quick breads and community are intrinsically linked in my memory. For a number of years, I lived under a vow of poverty in a semicloistered Christian community where the members held everything in common. Since no one had any money, we became very inventive when it came to holiday gift giving. One Christmas I received a zucchini bread, a nut bread, two banana breads, and a carrot bread, as well as jars of hand-picked blackberry jam, plum jam, strawberry jam, fruit conserve, and a box of candied orange peels. I believe that was the year I began giving out a bread I called Gilhooley's Revenge, based on a funny little English music hall song called "Miss Fogarty's Christmas Cake":

As I sat in me window last evening, the letterman brought it to me,

a little gilt- edged invitation, saying Gilhooley come over for tea;

Well, I knew that Miss Fogarty'd sent it, so I went just for old friendship's sake,

and the first thing they gave me to tackle, was a slice of Miss Fogarty's cake.

There were plums and prunes and cherries, citrons and raisins and cinnamon too;

there was nutmeg, fruits, and berries, and a crust that was nailed on with glue.

There were caraway seeds in abundance, sure t'would work up a fine stomachache;

ah, t'would kill a man twice after eating a slice of Miss Fogarty's Christmas cake.

The song ends: "Maloney was took by the colic, O'Donald a pain in his head;/ McNulty lay down on the sofa, and he swore that he wish'd he was dead./ Miss Simmons went into hysterics, and there she did shiver and shake;/ and everyone swore they was poisoned ... from eatin' Miss Fogarty's cake!"

The Gilhooley bread was my antidote for Miss Fogarty's cake: a light, cinnamon-raisin nut bread perfect for toasting and serving with the many jams and jellies everyone had received.

Living in a spiritual community and sharing communal meals brought all of us into the kitchen often. Sister Susan was the community cook, in charge of the kitchen. I was a frequent volunteer, trading my help for the chance to experiment on my latest version of Holy Smoke Barbecue Sauce or Abbey Jack cheese. I made ginger and herbal tonics, tofu hot dogs (legendary!), and bread, lots of bread. All of us became proficient at making pancakes, coffee cakes, Christmas cakes, and zucchini breads. I proposed marriage to Susan in the walk-in cooler, surrounded by my molding cheeses. Shortly thereafter we opened Brother Juniper's Cafe and Bakery, putting our cloistered community experience into neighborhood practice. The first things we baked for the public were muffins.

The master formulas that follow are the result of an ongoing search for the best of these heartland recipes. These are the rally-round-the-table products that bring families together and link generations to each other. I think of them as "soul" foods because they seem so intertwined with the soulful aspects of our lives.

This is a small list of quick bread formulas from which many variations can be devised. There are dozens of ways to make quick breads, muffins, biscuits, and pancakes, but we need to know one way in which to make them memorable. I hope these formulas fulfill that promise.

Note: Because quick breads do not follow the baker's percentage system (page 10), percentages are not listed in these formulas.

MASTER FORMULA:
BANANA BREAD

Banana bread is the standard by which quick-bread artists are judged. The criteria for great quick breads are simple: They must be moist; they must be delicious. The way to accomplish this is by using plenty of ripe fruit (for fruited breads) and the proper proportion of supporting ingredients. Tenderness is produced by fat, which means butter, though canola, corn, and other oils can be substituted if cholesterol is a concern. The rest is just flavor blending, the eternal balancing act among sugar, fat, and starch.

This banana bread formula is a template for many types of quick breads and muffins. Replace the bananas with other fruits or vegetables, adjust the complementary ingredients accordingly, and you can make numerous quick breads and muffins with whatever happens to be in season.

Quick breads come out like cake if made by the creaming method because it incorporates more air into the batter, allowing it to bake up lighter and evener. They can also be made with the simpler batter method, which is sometimes called the *muffin* or *dump method* because everything is mixed in one or two steps. If you are using oil instead of butter, margarine, or solid shortening, you will have to use the batter method; the results will be very good regardless of the fat chosen. The following master formula describes both methods.

COMMENTARIES

❏ This batter also makes wonderful banana muffins; one batch yields 18 to 24, depending on the size of the muffin cups. Bake them as directed in the muffin formula on page 164. You can replace the bananas with an equal amount (or combination) of grated zucchini or carrots, raisins, blueberries, or other fruits and nuts to make an unlimited number of breads. Adjust the sugar and spices according to taste. (See page 167 for other variation ideas.)

❏ All-purpose flour is ideal for quick breads and muffins, providing just enough structure to hold the leavened size while retaining tenderness.

❏ Butter provides the best flavor for quick breads, but margarine or solid shortening like Crisco will work as well for the creaming method. For the batter method, corn oil is surprisingly good, while canola has a more neutral flavor and is considered a heart-healthy oil. The main purpose of the fat is to tenderize the crumb by shortening the gluten strands, which any of the above will accomplish.

❏ This banana bread is the perfect solution for the ripe banana problem. As long as the bananas have not fermented, they will work. Ideally, the skins should be covered with brown or black spots. An all-yellow banana won't lend enough flavor to the bread. You may freeze ripe bananas in a freezer bag, out of the peel, and save them for a bake day. Just be sure to strain off and discard any liquid that separates from the pulp when it thaws.

❏ Walnuts, chopped or broken into large pieces, add a lot to banana bread, marrying extremely well with the banana flavor. You may omit them, though, or substitute other nuts, such as macadamia, pecans, or almonds. Some people like to replace the nuts with chocolate chips or use a combination of the two.

❏ Always add the nuts after the dry ingredients have been incorporated and hydrated. Otherwise, flour will lodge in the crevices of the nuts and show up as white spots in the bread.

- ❏ Coating the pan with a butter and flour mixture gives your breads a pleasant buttery flavor without burning, because the flour protects the butter. Do not grease and then flour the pans; this results in flour spots on the bread.

- ❏ The batter will rise approximately 50 percent when baked, just cresting over the top of the pan. If you fill the pan any fuller, the batter will run over the sides.

- ❏ The loaves will shrink a little while cooling; this is fine and a sign of good, moist bread. Don't let them cool completely in the pan or you may have trouble getting them out.

MAKES 2 LARGE OR 3 SMALL LOAVES

3¹/₂ cups (16 ounces) unbleached all-purpose flour

1 tablespoon (0.5 ounce) baking powder

¹/₂ tablespoon (0.64 ounce) baking soda

1 teaspoon (0.25 ounce) salt

1 cup (8 ounces) unsalted butter, shortening, or oil, at room temperature

2¹/₂ cups (20 ounces) brown sugar, packed

4 large eggs (6.65 ounces)

2 teaspoons (0.2 ounce) vanilla extract

1 cup (8 ounces) buttermilk

2¹/₂ cups (20 ounces) mashed ripe bananas (3 or 4 bananas)

1¹/₂ cups (9 ounces) coarsely chopped walnuts (optional)

Vegetable oil cooking spray

=Approximate Weight: 89 ounces (5 pounds, 9 ounces)

CREAMING METHOD

1. Sift the flour, baking powder, baking soda, and salt together into a mixing bowl, and set aside.

2. Using an electric mixer (with a paddle attachment if you have one), cream the butter and brown sugar together on medium speed till smooth and creamy, about 2 minutes.

3. Mix in the eggs, one by one, waiting for each to be incorporated before adding the next. Mix in the vanilla. Continue beating for 2 to 3 minutes, till the mixture is light and fluffy.

4. Mix in one third of the flour mixture, then one third of the buttermilk, then one third of the bananas, repeating till all the ingredients have been added. Mix just till the flour is absorbed and the batter is smooth. Stir in the walnuts if using, just till they are evenly dispersed.

5. Preheat the oven to 350°F. Grease two 4 by 8¹/₂-inch loaf pans, or whatever pans you intend to use. (You can mist them with cooking spray, or brush on a mixture of 3 tablespoons melted butter and 1 tablespoon flour.) Fill the pans two-thirds full with the batter.

6. Bake for about 45 minutes, then reduce the heat to 325°F and bake an additional 15 minutes, or till the loaves are springy to the touch at the center and a rich deep golden brown. The internal temperature should register between 180° and 185°F at the center, and a skewer poked in the center of the loaf should come out clean.

7. Let the loaves cool in the pan for 10 to

15 minutes, then turn them out onto a rack and let them cool for at least 1 hour before slicing.

BATTER METHOD

1. Sift the flour, baking powder, baking soda, and salt together into a mixing bowl, and set aside.

2. Stir the brown sugar into the flour mixture.

3. In a mixer, beat the eggs with the oil (or melted and cooled butter), vanilla, buttermilk, and mashed bananas.

4. Gradually add the flour mixture to the wet ingredients, beating just till it is absorbed. Then stir in the walnuts.

5. Preheat the oven to 350°F. Grease two 4 by 8 $1/2$-inch loaf pans, or whatever pans you intend to use. (You can mist them with cooking spray, or brush on a mixture of 3 tablespoons melted butter and 1 tablespoon flour.) Fill the pans two-thirds full with the batter.

6. Bake for about 45 minutes, then reduce the heat to 325°F and bake an additional 15 minutes, or till the loaves are springy to the touch at the center and a rich deep golden brown. A skewer poked in the center of the loaf should come out clean.

7. Let the loaves cool in the pan for 10 to 15 minutes, then turn them out onto a rack and let them cool for at least 1 hour before slicing.

MUFFINS OF A THOUSAND FACES

Here is a master formula from which you can make many muffins (or quick breads, if you bake them in a loaf pan). I call it Muffins of a Thousand Faces in tribute to Lon Chaney, the great silent screen actor famous for taking on many different appearances.

Muffins have progressed from what master baker and author Nick Malgieri calls "a scone but with more liquid in the dough" to what I think of as a quick bread baked in smaller tins. Nick is right that for many decades muffins were more like biscuits with fillings. They were fairly lean, which explains why they dried out so easily. Then home and professional bakers alike discovered ways to make them more interesting and enjoyable, tenderizing them with fruit, sweeteners, and fat.

Some of my baker friends, like Kathleen Stewart of the popular Downtown Bakery and Creamery in Healdsburg, California, report that during the past few years customers have been moving away from regular muffins but still buy low-fat varieties. Many bakers have formulated low-fat muffin recipes to meet this interest, but still, the feeling in the air is that the passion for muffins is waning. Like so much else in life, these things move in cycles. Muffins are sure to rebound, and when they do, it may be because of formulas like this one. It's definitely not low fat, but it's so good I think it could overcome the most intractable case of muffin inertia.

COMMENTARIES

❑ This batter holds up amazingly well and can be refrigerated for up to 3 days or frozen for up to 1 month before baking.

❑ This formula will also make two large quick breads or up to two dozen mini muffins. The yield will vary, though, depending on which add-ins you choose. Some, like blueberries, fill up a lot of space while others, like poppy seeds, take less.

❑ Hand stirring protects the add-ins from getting chewed up by the mixer. Small and sturdy items, like poppy seeds, can be mixed in by machine.

❑ The easiest way to grease a muffin tin is with cooking spray, but if you prefer the flavor of butter, use the same mixture recommended previously: 3 tablespoons melted butter and 1 tablespoon flour. I like to mist muffin papers with cooking spray because it makes it easier to peel them off the finished muffins. Hold the can well above the muffin tin; if you get too close, the force of the spray blows out the muffin papers.

❑ Blueberry muffins must cool longer because blueberries and other fruit are soft and mushy while still hot, but they firm up as they cool; the muffins need time to set up in the pan before you pull them out. Don't wait till they completely cool, though, or they will stick.

3¹/₂ cups (16 ounces) unbleached all-purpose flour

1¹/₂ teaspoons (0.25 ounce) baking powder

¹/₄ teaspoon (0.08 ounce) baking soda

³/₄ teaspoon (0.17 ounce) salt

²/₃ cup (5.33 ounces) unsalted butter, room temperature

1¹/₂ cups (12 ounces) brown sugar, packed

2 large eggs (3.33 ounces)

2 teaspoons (0.33 ounces) vanilla extract

1¹/₄ cups (10 ounces) buttermilk

Additional ingredients (see page 167)

Vegetable oil cooking spray

=Approximate Weight: About 48 ounces (3 pounds), plus the weight of the additional ingredients

CREAMING METHOD

1. Sift the flour, baking powder, baking soda, and salt together into a mixing bowl and set aside.

2. Using an electric mixer (with a paddle attachment if you have one), cream the butter and brown sugar together on medium speed till smooth and creamy, about 2 minutes.

3. Mix in the eggs, one by one, waiting for each one to be incorporated before adding the next. Then mix in the vanilla. The mixture should be light and fluffy.

4. Mix in one third of the flour mixture, then one third of the buttermilk, repeating until all the ingredients have been added. Mix just until the flour is absorbed and the batter is smooth. Stir in the add-ins, just till they are evenly dispersed.

5. Preheat the oven to 350°F. Grease a muffin tin. Or if using muffin papers, place them in the tin and mist them with cooking spray.

6. Scoop the batter into the prepared tin (an ice cream scoop works great). It should mound slightly over the tops of the cups. Place the muffin tin on a sheet pan to catch any drips, and transfer to the oven.

7. Bake the muffins for 30 to 40 minutes, rotating the pan, front to back, halfway through to insure even browning. The muffins are done when they are golden brown and springy to the touch, with no sign of doughiness.

8. Let the muffins cool in the pan for about 15 minutes (20 to 30 minutes for blueberry muffins) and then remove them. Serve them warm if possible.

BATTER METHOD

1. Sift the flour, baking powder, baking soda, and salt together into a mixing bowl and set aside.

2. Stir the brown sugar into the flour mixture.

3. In a mixer, beat the eggs with the oil (or melted and cooled butter), vanilla, and buttermilk.

4. Gradually add the flour mixture to the wet ingredients, beating just until it is absorbed. Then stir in the add-ins.

5. Preheat the oven to 350°F. Grease a muffin tin. Or if using muffin papers, place them in the tin and mist them with cooking spray.

6. Scoop the batter into the prepared tin (an ice cream scoop works great). It should mound slightly over the tops of the cups. Place the muffin tin on a sheet pan to catch any drips, and transfer to the oven.

7. Bake the muffins for 30 to 40 minutes, rotating the pan, front to back, halfway through to insure even browning. The muffins are done when they are golden brown and springy to the touch, with no sign of doughiness.

8. Let the muffins cool in the pan for about 15 minutes (20 to 30 minutes for blueberry muffins) and then remove them. Serve them warm if possible.

MUFFIN VARIATIONS

Okay. So now you have your basic muffin batter. How do we turn it into the Muffins of a Thousand Faces? I will give you a few ideas, but you will have to come up with your own variations to reach a thousand. Just follow these guidelines. I suggest you begin with the blueberry muffins to get a feel for the batter. After that, let your imagination run wild.

Blueberry Muffins: Blueberry muffins are the supreme choice and standard by which all other muffins are measured. Add 3¹/₂ cups of blueberries to the batter at the very end. If using frozen berries, leave them in the freezer till just before you add them so the juice does not bleed and turn the batter blue.

Cranberry Muffins: Add 3 cups chopped cranberries and replace ¹/₂ cup of the buttermilk with an equal amount of orange juice concentrate.

Poppy Seed Muffins: Add 1 tablespoon lemon extract or ¹/₈ teaspoon lemon oil and ¹/₂ cup poppy seeds (or more, if you like poppy seeds as much as I do).

Chocolate Chip Muffins: Add 3 cups of chocolate chips or mini chips.

Chocolate Cherry Muffins: Add 2 cups of pitted pie cherries and 1¹/₂ cups of chocolate chips.

Bran Muffins: Replace 1 cup of the flour with an equal amount of wheat bran, a combination of wheat bran and wheat germ, or oat bran. Add 3 cups of raisins, chopped apples, or a combination of the two. If adding raisins, increase the buttermilk by 2 tablespoons per cup of raisins.

Honey Muffins: Replace all or part of the brown sugar using this ratio: for every ¹/₃ cup of sugar you are replacing, add ¹/₂ cup of honey and reduce the buttermilk by 3 ounces (6 tablespoons).

Carrot Cake Muffins: Add 1 teaspoon of cinnamon (with the dry ingredients), 1 cup of raisins, 3 cups of grated carrots, and 1 additional egg.

SWEET AND MOIST CORN BREAD

Corn bread, like so many American foods, is claimed by contending regions of the country. There are New England or Yankee, as well as Southern, Midwestern, and Southwestern versions. It is difficult to remain neutral about corn bread. Should it be sweet or savory, thick or thin, crisped with bacon fat or tenderized with butter? The issues go on and on. The following version will probably rankle those of you who have equally strong feelings about corn bread, but I will try to convert you.

The best thing about corn bread is that it is made with corn, my favorite grain. Betty Fussell, among others, has written extensively about the history of corn in the Americas, its role in our culture, the fertility symbolism of the kernel-studded ear. I like the fact that corn is indigenous, deeply rooted in our native soil—more deeply than those of us whose American roots go back only a few generations. You do not have to be Native American, though, to feel its attraction. The memories evoked by corn, especially freshly picked summer corn served on the cob, swirled in butter, and eaten typewriter fashion, embed themselves in our souls the way the kernels embed themselves in our teeth.

Growing up in suburban Philadelphia, I came late to the corn bread debate. We ate it only occasionally, and it was invariably dry; it gave me the hiccups and seemed useful only as an ingredient in turkey dressing, where it could be moistened with gravy and fat and rendered palatable. When I had to start making corn bread as part of a menu I prepared while cooking in a seminary, I discovered a few tricks that gradually moved it up the line. Only later did I learn that a similar corn bread renaissance was occurring in other parts of the country. The *Zeitgeist* had swept me, unknowingly, along with it again.

As with all quick breads, the key to success is moistness. One sure way (other than underbaking) to make corn bread moist is to use fresh corn as an ingredient. Cornmeal is milled from dried corn. It has to be hydrated to be digestible, and by its very nature it sucks up moisture. Fresh kernels, on the other hand, hold on ferociously to their sweet moistness. Corn-on-corn is the best way to amplify the inherent qualities of both dried and fresh corn, delivering moist flavor bursts from the fresh corn while providing starch and structure from the ground cornmeal.

The following formula contains what I consider the best components of the many regional styles popular throughout the country. Its success can be gauged by your response to it: Does it trigger fond food memories? Does it, as good food must, feed your fascination with life? Most important, do you like it enough to make it for your friends and family? I'd like to know.

COMMENTARIES

❏ This batter also can be baked in muffin cups, baked or grilled into pancake-size disks, or thickened with extra flour and fried as hush puppies.

❏ I prefer polenta over regular-grind cornmeal because it retains its identity and adds texture to the bread. If you choose to substitute cornmeal, you do not need to soak it overnight.

❏ It may seem like there is a lot of baking powder in this formula, but it is necessary to give the lift that this heavy batter requires. Baking powder contains its own combination of alkaline and acid, which neutralize themselves when moistened and heated, creating carbon dioxide. The baking soda is neutralized by the buttermilk and provides additional leavening.

❏ When fresh corn is available it is, of course, preferable. However, frozen or canned kernels work well and are available year-round. You may fancy things up a bit by fire-roasting the corn or grilling it over coals (leave the corn whole, in the husks, but pull out the silks) before cutting and adding it to the batter.

❏ Bacon fat has its pros and cons. The pro side is that it tastes great and adds wonderful flavor to the edges of the bread. The con side is cholesterolly self-evident. The choice is yours.

1¼ cups (8 ounces) polenta or coarse cornmeal

1½ cups (12 ounces) buttermilk

1¾ cups (8 ounces) unbleached all-purpose flour

1½ tablespoons (0.75 ounce) baking powder

¼ teaspoon (0.08 ounce) baking soda

1 teaspoon (0.25 ounce) salt

½ cup (4 ounces) brown sugar, packed

2 tablespoons (1.5 ounces) honey

2 tablespoons (1 ounce) unsalted butter, melted

2 large eggs (3.33 ounces)

1¼ cups (6 ounces) fresh or frozen corn kernels

2 tablespoons (1 ounce) bacon fat (optional)

=*Approximate Weight: 45 ounces (2 pounds, 13 ounces)*

1. The night before making the corn bread, soak the polenta in 1¼ cups of the buttermilk. Cover and refrigerate overnight. Remove from the refrigerator 1 hour before proceeding.

2. The next day, sift the flour, baking powder, baking soda, and salt together into a mixing bowl. Stir in the soaked polenta and the brown sugar.

3. In another bowl, dissolve the honey in the melted butter. In a third bowl, whisk the eggs lightly with the remaining ¼ cup buttermilk.

4. Add the honey and egg mixtures to the flour mixture, and stir just until smooth. Stir in the corn kernels just until they are evenly dispersed. Add more buttermilk if the batter is thicker than pancake batter. (It should be pourable.)

5. Preheat the oven to 350°F. Grease a 9-inch round cake pan or an 8-inch square baking dish with butter, vegetable oil, or melted bacon fat. If using the bacon fat, put the greased pan in the hot oven for 10 minutes, or till it just starts smoking.

6. Pour the batter into the pan and bake for 30 to 45 minutes (the 8-inch square pan will take longer) or till the center is springy and a toothpick or skewer comes out clean.

7. Allow the bread to cool in the pan for 20 minutes before serving.

MASTER FORMULA:

BLITZ BUTTERMILK BISCUITS

There are many ways to make great biscuits but this formula is, I think, unique. To understand why, it's necessary to identify just exactly what a biscuit is, why we make them, and what contributes to the qualities that endear them to us.

The qualities are simply stated: tenderness, lightness, flakiness, and creaminess. So are the means for achieving them: fat and proper technique. Making a good biscuit is much like making a flaky, tender pie crust. Unlike bread, which requires full gluten development, a flaky biscuit requires minimum gluten presence, just enough to hold it together. The presence of fat, whether it be as cream, butter, or shortening, provides tenderness by literally shortening the gluten strands. The trick is to keep the fat and flour separate, maximizing the shortening of the gluten and promoting flakiness. The following formula employs a technique culled from the realm of puff pastry called *blitz dough.* Blitz puff dough is really a very flaky pie dough. The pieces of fat, in this case butter, are chopped but still fairly large—larger than for a regular pie dough. By folding, or laminating, the dough over itself, the butter is dispersed while hundreds of microthin layers of dough are formed. This dough is called *blitz dough* because it is much faster to make than traditional puff dough, which is made with a whole layer of butter or fat that is carefully folded over and over, with frequent resting periods. When this concept is applied to biscuits, the butter is cut into slightly bigger pieces than usual and then the dough is laminated a few times to simulate the puff effect. The result is a tall, flaky, buttery biscuit.

Getting back to the "why" of biscuits, we need to confront an American, if not human, condition: We love flaky, creamy, tender, and buttery sensations in food. Even in the face of alarming arterial evidence, we are willing to risk much to experience those wonderful sensations on our palates. Many meal traditions incorporate the biscuit as a central or supporting player, and a cook's baking reputation often rests on his or her ability to deliver the flaky, creamy, tender, and buttery goods.

The Southern custom of biscuits and gravy is frightening to a Northerner who, in turn, thinks nothing of slathering gobs of cream cheese on a bagel or spreading even more butter on an already buttery croissant. Our rich habits follow us from region to region, product to product. A flaky pie crust, which is, after all, simply a type of biscuit, is as American as…well, you know the rest.

There was a time in the United States when eating fat-laden doughs was an economic necessity, a way of fueling the body with affordable calories, as it still is in many impoverished cultures. It was and still is also a way for poor people to find a measure of equity with their so-called betters. A good biscuit is a great leveler, something that rich and poor both love and both can make. It is comfort food on many levels. In a world that promotes and rewards status and other illusory differences, the biscuit—especially the light, creamy, flaky, buttery biscuit—will simply not be denied.

COMMENTARIES

❑ Unbleached flour is more flavorful than bleached (see page 13). Many Southern biscuit recipes call for self-rising flour, which contains its own leavening agent and salt. I prefer to add my own, but if you decide to use self-rising, omit the baking powder and salt. Leave in the baking soda, however; it is neutralized by the buttermilk and gives added lift.

❑ Unsalted butter is better than salted butter for baking because you have more control over the amount of salt in your product. For biscuits, as with pie dough, the butter should be cold and hard. This allows it to retain its identity when mixed with the flour, resulting in flakier biscuits.

❑ The liquid should also be cold to keep the butter hard. Buttermilk gives the biscuits a delicious tangy flavor, and in conjunction with the baking soda, creates added leavening and a lighter biscuit. However, for a richer tasting biscuit you can substitute cream for the buttermilk and omit the baking soda. This is the ultimate in creamy biscuits, but is considerably higher in calories and fat. Caveat emptor!

❑ The folding process is called *laminating* and is done exactly as for croissants, Danish, and puff pastry. It creates dozens of thin layers that enhance the flakiness of the biscuits.

❑ Cutting the biscuits with a knife, in triangular cuts, is more efficient than a cookie cutter because there are no leftover scraps. Cookie cutters leave trimmings that can be reshaped into biscuits, but because of the extra handling, they are never as good as the first cut. If using cutters, try to cut straight down and do not twist, which causes the layers of the biscuits to stick, diminishing the rise and flakiness.

❑ Chilling the cut biscuits relaxes the gluten, assuring a better and more even rise. The final 20-minute resting period is a good idea for pie crust, puff pastry, scones, or any other flaky dough.

❑ Biscuits, unlike yeasted breads, are best eaten still warm from the oven, while the buttery flakiness is at its peak.

3¹/₂ cups (16 ounces) unbleached
all-purpose flour

1 teaspoon (0.25 ounce) salt

2 teaspoons (0.33 ounce) baking powder

¹/₄ teaspoon (0.08 ounce) baking soda

1¹/₂ cups (12 ounces) unsalted butter,
cold

1¹/₂ cups (12 ounces) buttermilk, cold

*=Approximate Weight: 40 ounces
(2 pounds 8 ounces)*

1. Sift the flour, salt, baking powder, and baking soda together into a mixing bowl.

2. Use a knife or pastry cutter to chop the butter into pieces about the diameter of a quarter. Toss them into the flour and mix with your hands, lightly rubbing the flour and butter into each other between your fingers (do not let your fingertips rub against each other or the friction will melt the butter). Work the dough just until the butter pieces are down to the diameter of dimes and are coated by the flour mixture.

3. Stir the buttermilk into the flour mixture just until all the ingredients are gathered and form a dough ball.

4. Line a sheet pan with parchment paper. Lightly dust the work surface with flour, and roll the dough in it. Dust the counter again and roll out the dough with a rolling pin into a rectangle that is ³/₄ inch thick. Using a pastry cutter or scraper, peel the dough up from the counter and fold it, like a letter, into thirds. Give it a one-quarter turn. Flour the counter and the top of the dough, and roll it out again ³/₄ inch thick. Peel it up again and fold it into thirds.

5. Transfer the dough to the prepared pan. Cover it with plastic wrap or enclose the pan in a plastic bag, and refrigerate for 20 minutes.

6. Remove the dough and roll it out again ³/₄ inch thick. Fold it in thirds, give it a one-quarter turn, and roll it out one final time, again ³/₄ inch thick.

7. Use a knife to cut the dough into 2 by 2 by 2-inch triangular pieces, or use a cookie or biscuit cutter and cut the dough into rounds.

8. Place the cut biscuits about 1 inch apart on the parchment-lined sheet pan. Cover them and refrigerate them for at least 20 minutes.

9. Preheat the oven to 500°F. Brush the tops of the biscuits with melted butter or buttermilk. Place them in the oven and reduce the heat to 375°F.

10. Bake the biscuits for 12 to 15 minutes, or till they are lightly browned and golden all around (not white or creamy, or the inside will be doughy). Allow them to cool for 5 minutes, and serve while still warm.

SCONES

The scone (pronounced *SKAHN* in some parts of England and Scotland) is a popular tea biscuit in the British Isles. As sweetened biscuits, scones are best made following the same principles as Southern-style biscuits, cutting the cold butter into the flour to keep them flaky. A second type, called *cream scones*, derive their fat from cream rather than butter. They are tender and moist, without being flaky, and hold up quite well when transported.

Both types of scones are delicious when made well, but for some reason there seems to be a dearth of good scones on the market; they often seem dry or overbaked. The first few times I had a scone, I wondered what all the fuss was about. Then, when I finally had a good one, I understood.

The following master formulas show you how to make both types.

MASTER FORMULA:
BISCUIT SCONES

COMMENTARIES

❑ Currants are a traditional scone fruit. You may substitute not only raisins but chopped dried or candied fruit, such as apricots, citron, or zest, or leave the fruit out altogether.

❑ Buttermilk gives scones the best flavor, but you may also use yogurt or milk, either low-fat or regular. If using milk, eliminate the baking soda.

❑ Double-A (AA) coarse sugar and crystallized ginger are two of the more popular toppings for scones, though they are perfectly delicious plain. Scones are usually served with tea or coffee, so any toppings should be chosen with the occasion and beverage in mind. I would use ginger, for instance, with tea, but not with coffee.

❑ Look for AA coarse sugar in the bakery section of your supermarket, or ask to buy some from your local bakery.

❑ If using your fingers to cut in the butter, do not let them rub against each other or the heat from the friction will melt the butter, diminishing the flakiness of the finished product.

❑ For shorter, fatter scones, divide the dough into two 1-inch-thick disks and cut each disk into 3 or 4 wedges. You can, of course, vary the size and number, but I don't recommend making fewer than 6 scones from this recipe, or they will be too large and unwieldy. And remember, the smaller the scones, the faster they will bake.

❑ The resting period before baking relaxes the gluten and makes for a more tender scone. You can hold the unbaked dough for up to 24 hours in the refrigerator.

4 cups (18 ounces) unbleached
all-purpose flour

2 teaspoons (0.33 ounce) baking powder

1/4 teaspoon (0.08 ounce) baking soda

3/4 teaspoon (0.17 ounce) salt

2 cups (16 ounces) brown sugar, packed

1 1/2 cups (8 ounces) currants or raisins
(optional)

1 1/2 cups (12 ounces) unsalted butter,
cold

1/2 cup (4 ounces) buttermilk, cold

1 large egg for egg wash

3 tablespoons (1 ounce) coarse sugar
and/or crystallized ginger (optional)

*=Approximate Weight: 58 ounces
(3 pounds, 10 ounces)*

1. Sift the flour, baking powder, baking
   soda, and salt together into a mixing
   bowl. Stir in the brown sugar and
   currants, if using, till they are evenly
   dispersed.

2. Cut the butter into quarter-size
   pieces, and add it to the flour mixture.
   Cut the butter in with a pastry cutter,
   2 forks, or your fingers until the mixture has the texture of coarse cornmeal.

3. Stir in the buttermilk just until the
   ingredients gather and form a ball of
   dough, using more buttermilk, if
   needed.

4. Line a sheet pan with parchment paper
   and lightly dust the work surface with
   flour. Turn the dough out and press
   it into a disk about 1 inch thick and
   6 inches in diameter. Cut the disk into
   6 to 8 wedges and place them on the
   prepared pan. (You may also use a
   biscuit cutter and cut out circles.)

5. Enclose the pan in a plastic bag, and
   refrigerate for at least 20 minutes.
   Meanwhile, position an oven rack in
   the center of the oven and preheat the
   oven to 425°F.

6. Remove the dough from the refrigerator. Beat the egg thoroughly and
   brush it on the top of each scone.
   Lightly dust with coarse sugar and/or
   minced crystallized ginger if desired.

7. Bake the scones for 10 minutes, and
   then lower the heat to 375°F. Rotate
   the pan front to back, to ensure even
   browning, and bake the scones for
   about 10 minutes more, or till they
   are golden brown.

8. Transfer the scones to a rack, and allow them to cool for about 10 minutes before serving.

MASTER FORMULA:
CREAM SCONES

COMMENTARIES

❏ This is my version of an incredibly popular
cream scone recipe developed by chef Reg El-
gin, who has been teaching baking and pastry
classes at the California Culinary Academy for
nearly a decade.

❏ Use any combination of candied dried fruit,
such as citron, apricots, raisins, cherries, or
cranberries, for these scones.

❏ The richer the cream the richer the scone, so
buy the heaviest cream you can find. Manufacturing cream (usually available only to commercial bakers) is the heaviest, followed by
heavy cream and then whipping cream.

❏ Sugar or ginger are optional but do add a nice
flavor contrast.

❏ When both stirring and shaping the dough,
handle it as little as possible to insure maximum tenderness.

MAKES 6 TO 8 SCONES

4 cups (18 ounces) unbleached
   all-purpose flour

4 teaspoons (0.66 ounce) baking powder

3/4 teaspoon (0.17 ounce) salt

1 cup (8 ounces) brown sugar, packed

1 1/2 cups (8 ounces) currants or other
   dried fruit

1 cup (8 ounces) heavy cream

1 large egg for egg wash (beat until foamy)

3 tablespoons (1 ounce) coarse sugar or
   crystallized ginger (optional)

=*Approximate Weight: 44 ounces*
  (2 pounds, 12 ounces)

1. Sift the flour, baking powder, and salt
   together into a mixing bowl. Stir in
   the brown sugar and currants till they
   are evenly dispersed.

2. Pour in the cream and stir just until
   the ingredients form a soft dough.

3. Turn out the dough out onto a lightly
   floured counter and shape the dough
   into a disk about 1 inch thick. Cut the
   disk into 6 to 8 wedges and transfer
   them to a parchment-lined sheet pan.

4. Position an oven rack in the center of
   the oven and preheat the oven to
   425°F. Brush the scones with egg
   wash and sprinkle them with sugar or
   minced crystallized ginger if desired.

5. Bake the scones for 10 minutes. Rotate the pan, front to back, reduce the
   temperature to 375°F, and bake the
   scones for about 10 minutes more, or
   till they are medium brown in color
   and are firm to the touch.

6. Allow the scones to cool for about
   20 minutes on a rack and serve them
   while they are still warm.

PANCAKES

There are so many pancake houses, with so many ways to make decent pancakes, that most of us take these eateries for granted. Once in awhile we find a special place with a particularly great pancake, like the amazing Dutch apple pancakes at the Original Pancake House in Portland, Oregon (and the few Original spin-offs scattered around the country). In San Francisco we have Sears Fine Foods and their silver-dollar Swedish pancakes. I had some fantastic sourdough pancakes once at Jeremiah's in Jackson Hole, Wyoming, and International House of Pancakes actually does a pretty good job on a nationwide basis.

Pancakes, though, had never excited me the way bread does until recently when, thanks to Marion Cunningham, I discovered an entirely new way to make them. She said she had the best recipe for pancakes in the world, and I believe she is right. When Marion speaks about good recipes, people listen. She has spent years searching for the best of the best, dating back to her days as a protégé of James Beard and as the author of the revised *Fanny Farmer* cookbooks.

I am part of a group of Bay Area bakers who have been working closely with Marion to assemble a book of baking wisdom culled from the members of the Bakers Dozen, an informal guild that she, Flo Braker, Amy Pressman, and a few others started a few years ago. Our meetings are spent going over chapter material and then, more enjoyably, listening to Marion talk about favorite recipes. When she mentioned her pancake recipe, I wrote it down and tried it out on my wife, Susan, the next day. I could not believe how much better Marion's pancakes were than anything I had ever had in a restaurant.

The difference is that these pancakes are made from a thick batter and have an almost custardlike interior. They are cakey and creamy at the same time, and they soak up maple syrup like a sponge. Marion insists that they only come out right when made in small batches. "If you try to make this in any larger quantity," she says, "the added mixing necessary to combine all the ingredients will toughen the gluten." I don't know if this actually happens, though—I'm afraid to try. Marion said not to make the batches any bigger, and that's good enough for me.

The second formula, for sourdough pancakes, is quite different. It produces a thin, sour pancake, the kind a gold miner or a lonesome mountain man might look forward to, to get the day off to a good start. The flavor is so deep and complex that you will taste them, as with any good sourdough, for hours after you eat them.

BUTTERMILK PANCAKES

Many pancake batters are mixed ahead and then rested. This one is griddled immediately, so it must be handled tenderly to prevent the gluten from toughening. The lumps disappear in the frying pan, so mix only till all the flour is wet and assimilated.

The larger the pancake the more unevenly it will cook, with the center being slow to finish. This is great if you like the same custardy style I do. If you prefer your pancakes well done, make two or three small ones in the same pan (or keep two pans going).

COMMENTARIES

❏ This formula does not lend itself to multiplying, so the measures are given only as volume and not weight.

❏ All-purpose flour provides both the structure and tenderness pancakes require. As always, unbleached flour is preferred but bleached flour will also do.

MAKES 4 TO 6 PANCAKES

1 cup unbleached all-purpose flour

1/2 teaspoon baking soda

1/4 teaspoon salt

1 large egg

1 cup buttermilk

2 tablespoons melted unsalted butter

1 tablespoon butter or oil for the pan

1. Sift the flour, baking soda, and salt together into a mixing bowl.

2. Crack open the egg and pour it whole into the center of the flour mixture. Pour the buttermilk over the egg.

3. With a fork or large whisk, stir the ingredients together just till a lumpy batter forms and all the flour is absorbed. Pour in the melted butter and quickly mix the batter just till the butter is dispersed.

4. Heat a heavy skillet over medium-high heat. When it is hot, add a teaspoon of butter or oil and swirl it around to coat the pan.

5. Ladle or pour the batter into the pan to the desired size and tilt the pan to spread the batter (it is thick so it will not spread very much).

6. When bubbles begin to appear on the top of the pancakes, flip them and continue cooking them for about 1 minute. They should be brown on both sides but tender in the middle.

7. Keep the pancakes warm in a 200°F oven, or on a plate under a clean towel, while making the rest. Serve with hot maple syrup or your favorite fruit preserves.

MASTER FORMULA:
SOURDOUGH PANCAKES

These pancakes are easy to make if you have a barm sponge starter on hand. They will fill your palate with many complex flavors and you will enjoy them for hours after you eat them. Special thanks to Catherine Baker-Fayal, one of my sterling students at the California Culinary Academy, for applying her pancake passion to fine-tuning this formula.

COMMENTARIES

❏ This batter lends itself to plate-size pancakes, swimming in maple syrup. However, you can make lots of silver dollar pancakes quickly, which may be fun for family meals. You may want to keep two or more skillets going if you can handle the pace.

❏ This base is similar to a sourdough bread sponge. The milk lends a strong lactic, almost buttery quality to the batter as it leavens overnight.

❏ I like my pancakes really sour, but many people want them slightly less so. The baking soda neutralizes the acidity of the sponge, sweetening it a bit. It also adds lift to the batter, giving it a more pancakelike texture. If you omit the soda, the pancakes will be thin and more like crepes. Try both methods and see which one you prefer.

❏ A basic rule of pancakes: the less handling, the more tender the pancake. Any lumps will disappear when the pancakes are made.

BASE

$2^1/_2$ cups barm sponge starter (page 72)

2 cups unbleached all-purpose flour

1 cup milk, room temperature (70°F)

1 cup water (70°F)

BATTER

1 teaspoon salt

2 large eggs

2 tablespoons honey

1 tablespoon melted unsalted butter or vegetable oil cooking spray

1 teaspoon baking soda (optional)

1. Make the base the night before: In a mixing bowl, combine the barm, flour, milk, and water and mix till smooth. Cover the base and leave it at room temperature overnight.

2. The next morning, whisk together the batter ingredients in a separate bowl. Add the base and stir just until the ingredients are blended; don't worry if there are a few lumps. The batter will be thinner than buttermilk pancake batter but thicker than crepe batter, about the consistency of cream of potato soup. Cover the batter and set it aside at room temperature for 30 minutes.

3. Heat a skillet over medium-high heat. Grease the pan with a teaspoon of butter or a little cooking spray. Pour in enough batter to make 1 large or a few small pancakes. Tilt the pan with a circular motion to spread the batter. When the tops of the pancakes begin to bubble, flip them over and cook them for about 45 seconds more, till the bottoms are lightly browned.

4. Keep the pancakes warm by covering them with a clean towel or putting them on a platter in a 200°F oven while you finish cooking the batter. Serve them hot with warm maple syrup.

9

THE BREAD BAKERS GUILD OF AMERICA

Master Formula: Team USA Baguettes; Master Formula: Team USA Sunflower Rye Bread;
Master Formula: Team USA *Ciabatta*; Master Formula: Team USA Corn Bread;
Master Formula: Team USA Beer Bread

In 1992 I was attending a meeting of a local bakers' group called the Bakers Dozen, when Marion Cunningham, one of our founders and a wonderful mentor to many of us, mentioned she had just heard about a new organization called the Bread Bakers Guild of America.

"I don't know much about it but it seems very interesting," she said. "This fellow, Tom McMahon, is committed to real bread and to putting bread bakers in touch with each other." She passed out applications and encouraged us to join. I did, and it was probably the best decision I made that year. The Bread Bakers Guild of America changed my perception of bread forever.

One of the first benefits of membership was the opportunity to participate in a seminar with Professor Raymond Calvel, an eighty-year-old master baker and cereal chemist from France who is one of the leading experts on the classic French baguette and other traditional breads. The seminar was held at Berkeley's fabled Acme Bread Company and was attended by some of the best and brightest of the bread-baking world. For three intensive days, Professor Calvel taught us the art and science of French breads, including techniques I have modified for this book. My horizons, not to mention my bread consciousness, were greatly expanded.

Under the leadership of its founder and first executive director, Tom McMahon, the guild has succeeded in connecting artisan bread bakers to each other and to the tradition from which they sprang. Tom and his wife, Melinda, donated four years of their lives to launching the guild, building it to more than six hundred members. Some are ingredient and equipment suppliers, some serious home bakers, but most are professional bakers with small village-style bakeries (or in cases such as Nancy Silverton's La Brea Bakery of Los Angeles, large and incredibly successful artisan bakeries). As a reward for his efforts, Tom was appointed the first executive director of the National Baking Center at the Dunwoody Institute of Baking, in Minneapolis, where he revitalized the bread program for a whole new generation of bakers. (In the spring of 1998, Greg Tompkins, my former colleague at the California Culinary Academy, succeeded Tom as executive director.)

Tom's successor at the helm of the guild is Greg Mistell, founder of Delphina's Neighborhood Baking Company in Portland, Oregon. (Greg's is the only bakery other than the original Brother Juniper's licensed to produce and sell Brother Juniper's breads, which he does throughout northern Oregon, donating a percentage of the proceeds to Raphael House of Portland.) Greg was a member of the first American Coupe du Monde, or Bread Olympics, baking team in 1994, and the manager of the 1996 team.

Both teams were made possible through the sponsorship of The Bread Bakers Guild of America and a number of supportive equipment and supply companies. In 1994 the goal was merely to place in the top six and thereby win an automatic invitation to return in 1996. The team members—Greg Mistell, Rick Kirkby of Berkeley's Acme Bread Company, and Mary Ellen Hatch, then the head baker at Philadelphia's Baker Street Breads—succeeded in that goal, and brought home valuable, hard-won lessons about competing in the international arena. Though because of the rules, they could not compete a second time, they served as coaches to the 1996 team: Craig Ponsford of Artisan Breads in Sonoma, California; Glenn Mitchell, founder of Grace Baking Company in Berkeley, California; and Jeffrey Hamelman, owner of Hamelman's Bakery in Brattleboro, Vermont.

Craig Ponsford is a friend of mine and a truly masterful baker. After graduating from the California Culinary Academy's chef program, he trained under future teammate Glenn Mitchell at Grace Baking before striking out on his own in the historic town of Sonoma. There he quickly established a reputation for exceptional European-style breads. At the 1996 Coupe du Monde, he stunned the bread world by winning first place in the bread division and helping to lead Team USA to a second-place finish overall.

The victory was a result of long practice sessions under the guidance of Tom McMahon, Rick Kirkby, Greg Mistell, and other bread experts, most notably Didier Rosada, lead instructor at the National Baking Center. Didier carefully designed and adjusted the final formulas with Craig. The baguette, for instance, utilizes the preferment principle, but in a different way than Professor Calvel taught, using a sponge or *poolish* method rather than the *pâte fermentée*, or old dough method (the *poolish* method is required of all baguettes in the Coupe du Monde). Also, knowing that the European judges were not fond of the sour flavors loved by Americans, the team needed to tone down the acidity of their natural *levain* breads without sacrificing flavor. Craig also had to modify his rustic *ciabatta* recipe to work with the very different European flour. With Didier and the other coaches, he also developed a corn bread and a beer bread to round out his repertoire.

When judging the practice breads, the coaches analyzed the full aspect of the loaves. Were they uniform in appearance? Was the smell of yeast too noticeable? Did the crumb have the requisite appearance and mouthfeel? Every flaw was dealt with in the formulation, until the breads measured up to the stiffest criteria.

The team spent their final week before the competition in Lille (northern France), training under Dominique Homo of the Saf Yeast Company. They learned to make adjustments for the French flours they would be required to use. For instance, the baguettes had too much of a bow before Dominique helped Craig modify the formula to create a straighter loaf, by introducing the autolyse technique described on page 45. Then it was up to Craig to bake his breads in the foreign environment of a Paris convention center. He and his teammates competed using unfamiliar equipment and ingredients, under the gaze of the international judges and thousands of spectators, many of them participants in the concurrent Europain baking exposition. In other words, our team was on view to the bread-baking world, many of whose members assumed the United States was no contender in the world of "real" bread.

"Actually, I think now the rest of the world is beginning to look to the United States for new direction," Craig told me when he returned victorious from Paris.

"They're even beginning to get interested in American-style sourdough."

Craig, who has lectured to my classes at the California Culinary Academy and now teaches occasionally at the Culinary Institute of America at Greystone, also made the following point: "Europeans have had a very rigid and narrow view of what constitutes good bread. They were, to an extent, bound by their customs while we in America have been free to explore many styles and flavors. We've had to learn from them the best techniques, but they've also learned from us about variety." He went on to say that from what he saw at the Europain show in Paris, "the best overall bread in the world may now be coming from America, though there are still some individual bakers in Europe who make the best bread I've ever tasted."

The Bread Bakers Guild of America represents a turning point in the American bread revolution, bringing together serious artisan bakers in both fellowship and training. The competition for business is a fact of life in every profession, but the guild has allowed competitors to be colleagues as well, helping raise interest and awareness. This has been good for everyone. As the many bread bakeries in the Bay Area have shown, there is enough business to go around when the product is world class. Add to this momentum the young bakers now training in culinary schools, learning traditional and neotraditional techniques, and you can see that the public is just beginning to glimpse what lies ahead.

The following are versions of Craig's championship formulas that I have adapted and scaled down for home bakers. As you will see, they employ many of the methods previously discussed, demonstrating that there is always room for creativity within the structure of classic technique.

MASTER FORMULA:

TEAM USA BAGUETTES

The baguette developed by Craig Ponsford and his coaches for the Bread Olympics adds yet another option for anyone wanting to explore comparative methods (see pages 41–45). In our classes at the California Culinary Academy, I have my students make all three baguettes described in this book, as well as others, to see how different, and how similar, the product can turn out. This version utilizes the *poolish* method rather than the *pâte fermentée* technique of Professor Calvel.

At the competition, the breads are judged not only on taste and appearance but on subtle qualities such as whether the cut marks on each loaf are consistent, whether the baguettes are straight or bowed (deduction), and whether there is any smell of yeast (another deduction). The *poolish* method is required for all baguettes in the Coupe du Monde.

If you make all three baguette formulas in this book, I think you will see that, while they come out with different aspects, if you retard them in the refrigerator overnight the differences tend to diminish. The longer fermentation period appears to be a great equalizer. However, for same-day baking, this formula is hard to beat.

COMMENTARIES

❏ Craig's *poolish* is somewhat different than mine, but I have modified the formula to work with the one in this book.

❏ Craig uses fresh yeast in this dough, but you can substitute instant yeast, as listed, and get comparable results.

❏ *Lively* is Craig's term for the ineffable, springy feel of his dough. Most bread bakers know exactly what he means.

❏ The Team USA formulas use the method of "turning" described in step 3 in almost every dough. Similar to what some authors call punching down, turning strengthens the gluten and revitalizes the fermentation.

❏ This dough could be used for many other shapes, including dinner rolls (called *ballons* in France), or even basket-raised breads.

INGREDIENT	%
Unbleached bread flour	100
Water	50
Poolish	40
Fresh yeast	2.5
Salt	2.5

MAKES 2 OR 3 BAGUETTES

4¹/₂ cups (20 ounces) unbleached bread flour

1¹/₄ cups cool water (65° to 70°F)

1 cup (8 ounces) *poolish*-style pre-ferment (page 35)

1 tablespoon (0.5 ounce) fresh yeast, or 1 teaspoon (0.11 ounce) instant yeast

2 teaspoons (0.5 ounce) salt

Vegetable oil cooking spray

=*Approximate Weight: 39 ounces (2 pounds, 7 ounces)*

1. Combine the flour, water, and *poolish* in the bowl of an electric mixer with a dough hook, or in a mixing bowl.

2. If mixing by machine, mix on slow speed till incorporated, about 1 minute. Add the yeast and then the salt and mix for an additional 3 minutes on slow speed, or until the dough comes away from the sides of the bowl. Beat the dough for about 2 more minutes on medium speed. If making the dough by hand, stir the ingredients together till they form a ball and knead it on a floured surface for about 12 minutes. The dough should be smooth, shiny, lively, and somewhat soft. It should pass the windowpane test (see page 29) and register between 77° and 80°F on a probe thermometer.

3. Cover the bowl with plastic wrap and allow the dough to rise for 2 hours, kneading it for a few seconds and re-shaping it into a ball after the first hour. At the end of this rise, the dough should be about 1 1/2 times its original size.

4. Divide the dough into 2 or 3 equal pieces. Shape them into stubby cylinders on a lightly floured counter or sheet pan. Mist them lightly with cooking spray and cover them with plastic wrap or enclose them in a plastic bag and let the dough rest for 30 minutes. Line the backs of 2 sheet pans with parchment, mist the parchment with cooking spray, and lightly dust it with semolina or cornmeal.

5. Shape the dough into baguettes as described on page 21 and transfer them to the prepared pans. Mist the loaves again with cooking spray, cover them with plastic wrap or enclose them in a plastic bag, and allow them to rise for 2 hours at room temperature, or till nearly doubled in size (or proof them in a warmer spot for less time).

6. Prepare the oven for hearth baking, as described on page 25, making sure to place the empty steam pan on a lower rack. Preheat the oven to 475°F. Score the baguettes (see page 24). Pour 1 cup of hot water into the steam pan. Immediately transfer the loaves onto the baking stones, sliding them on, parchment and all, and steam again by spritzing the loaves and the oven walls. Close the oven door. Repeat the spraying after 2 minutes.

7. Bake the loaves for 20 to 25 minutes, or till they are golden brown. Turn the oven off and leave the bread in the oven for an additional 5 to 10 minutes, until it looks as though it can't go a minute longer.

8. Transfer the loaves to racks and allow them to cool for at least 30 minutes before eating.

TEAM USA SWISS SUNFLOWER RYE BREAD

This bread employs a "soaker," a method used in many European breads to presoften coarse grains, preventing them from drawing moisture from the dough. The bread was added to the Team USA's repertoire to show versatility and to pay respect to bread styles of northern Europe. The ringed shape is similar to breads from the farmlands of Switzerland, where they are hung on rafters. Of all the competition breads tested at Craig's bakery, this one was the most popular with his customers. He now makes it regularly, selling it from a wooden dowel on the wall. Like the other Team USA formulas, this one is modified to work on a small scale in home kitchens.

COMMENTARIES

❏ Rye meal is the coarsest of all rye grinds. It includes the bran and germ. Another grind, almost as coarse, is pumpernickel flour. Either of these will work for the soaker. You should be able to find them at natural foods markets.

❏ Use a regular-grind, light rye for the dough (dark rye produces too heavy a loaf). Using both light rye and the coarse meal described above provides two levels of texture and produces a tighter hole structure.

❏ You will need to make the firm starter the day before. The barm starter is not the same as Craig's *levain*, but will produce similar results.

❏ Though Craig does not stipulate it, I prefer to lightly toast the sunflower seeds before adding them to the dough, either in a dry, hot skillet or in the oven. This intensifies the flavor.

❏ Rye flour will become gummy if kneaded for too long, thus the shorter than usual mixing time, which results in a slightly lower temperature than usual.

❏ The "turn" in step 3 assures that the yeast remains in contact with its nutrients and continues to feed and ferment the dough at a steady pace. It also helps strengthen the dough structure.

❏ Many bakers use their elbows to make the hole in the bread, though fingers work just as well.

❏ This bread was designed for basket rising in specially designed *bannetons* with center spindles (like a tube pan, only for bread). It works fine if raised free-form on a sheet pan or on baking canvas, though it tends to spread a bit. If you want to replicate the basket raising, use a 10-inch tube or bundt pan that has been lined with plastic wrap or cloth napkins, misted with cooking spray, and dusted with flour.

❏ In step 7, do not wait till the loaves double in size or they may fall when scored. You want to catch them on the upswing, while still full of "push," so they will spring about 10 percent in the oven.

❏ If the bread is not thoroughly baked, it will become soggy as it cools. Leaving the bread in the warm oven helps dry it out.

INGREDIENT (SOAKER)	%
Rye meal	100
Water	100

SOAKER

1 cup (5 ounces) plus two tablespoons coarse rye meal

10 tablespoons cool water (65° to 70°F)

=*Approximate Weight: 10 ounces*

INGREDIENT (DOUGH)	%
Unbleached bread flour	84
Rye flour	16
Firm starter	100
Salt	3
Instant yeast	0.7
Soaker	62.5
Water	50
Sunflower seeds	16

DOUGH

4 cups (16 ounces) firm starter (page 77)

3 cups (13.5 ounces) unbleached bread flour

2/3 cup (2.5 ounces) light rye flour

2 teaspoons (0.5 ounce) salt

1 teaspoon (0.11 ounce) instant yeast

1 1/2 cups (10 ounces) soaker (from above; use all)

1 cup cool water (65° to 70°F)

1/2 cup (2.5 ounces) sunflower seeds

Vegetable oil cooking spray

=*Approximate Weight: 53 ounces
(3 pounds, 5 ounces)*

1. Make the soaker the evening before making the dough: In a mixing bowl, stir the rye meal into the water until well incorporated. Cover the bowl and let the soaker sit at room temperature till the next day. The water will all be absorbed.

2. Break the firm starter into small pieces and combine it with all the dough ingredients, except the sunflower seeds, in the bowl of an electric mixer with a dough hook or in a mixing bowl. If using a machine, mix on slow speed for 1 minute, then on medium speed for about 6 minutes. If mixing by hand, stir the ingredients together till they form a ball, then turn it out onto a floured counter and knead for 8 minutes. With either method, add the sunflower seeds during the last minute, mixing or kneading just till evenly dispersed. The dough is ready when it is tacky but not sticky, passes the windowpane test (page 29), and registers 75° to 77°F on a probe thermometer.

3. Place the dough in a clean bowl and lightly mist the dough with cooking spray, cover it with plastic wrap, and allow it to rise for 1 hour. Knead it for a few seconds, reshape it into a ball, and return it to the bowl. Re-cover the bowl, and allow the dough to rise for an additional 2 hours, until it increases in size by at least 1 1/2 times.

4. Divide the dough into 3 equal pieces and round each into a ball. Mist the pieces with cooking spray, cover them with plastic wrap or enclose them in a plastic bag, and let the dough rest on a lightly floured counter or sheet pan for 20 to 25 minutes. Use your fingers to poke a hole in the center of each piece and let it rest for 5 additional minutes.

5 Prepare a baking canvas (*couche*) or flour-dusted cloth napkins, or line an inverted sheet pan with parchment and dust it with flour.

6. Working with 1 piece of dough at a time, place both thumbs in the hole and hold the dough in the space between each thumb and forefinger. Rotate the dough with a circular motion, gently stretching it as you do so to enlarge the hole. Your goal is to form an even ring of dough with a center hole that is 4 to 5 inches across (this is something like forming bagels on a large scale).

7. Place the dough rings on the prepared *couche*, napkins, or sheet pan. Mist the rings lightly with cooking spray, cover them loosely with plastic wrap, and let them rise at room temperature for $1^1/_2$ to 2 hours, till they have increased in size by a little more than $1^1/_2$ times.

8. Prepare the oven for hearth baking as described on page 25, making sure to place the empty steam pan on a lower rack. Preheat the oven to 450°F.

9. Transfer the loaves to a floured peel (or cut the parchment between the loaves and use the sheet pan as a peel). Score the loaves with a razor or serrated knife. You can make 1 continuous cut around the middle of the top, or make a series of 4 or 5 straight cuts. Make the cuts about $1/_2$ inch deep at a 45-degree angle for the fullest bloom.

10. Transfer the bread to the oven and pour 1 cup of hot water into the steam pan. Spritz the loaves and oven walls. Close the oven door. After 2 minutes, repeat the spritzing. After about 25 minutes, when the loaves begin to darken, turn off the oven, open the oven door, and let the bread bake for an additional 10 minutes. (Or if you will be baking again, reduce the heat 425°F, open the oven door, and bake for an additional 15 minutes.) The internal dough temperature should be above 200°F, and the crust should be hard and richly colored (the crust will soften as it cools).

11. Cool the loaves on a rack for at least 1 hour before cutting.

TEAM USA CIABATTA

Here is another version of this classic Italian rustic bread (see page 47). Craig has been making a *pugliese* variation of this bread for years that is the best-seller at his bakery, but he reformulated it for the Coupe du Monde competition to conform with European expectations. This is an adaptation of his competition formula. It was difficult to reduce for home baking; I have modified a few of the steps and proportions in order to make it comparable to the Team USA version, but the methodology is essentially the same.

COMMENTARIES

❏ Craig uses fresh yeast, rather than instant yeast; if you would like to do so, substitute ¹/₂ teaspoon crumbled fresh yeast. Instant yeast, however, produces comparable results.

❏ Remember to make the *poolish* the day before. Craig has a slightly different method from the one in this book, using the tiniest pinch of yeast in a thicker sponge (equal parts water and flour) and then leaving the *poolish* at room temperature for fifteen hours rather than retarding it.

❏ There is some debate among bakers regarding the length of mixing time for this bread. Some people feel that longer more fully hydrates the gluten, but I believe that long fermentation compensates for a shorter mixing time in many instances. And after all, Craig did win the world championship using this shorter method.

❏ Turning the dough, as described in step 2, strengthens the gluten and allows the yeast to stay in contact with the nutrients. You will notice a change in texture with each turn.

❏ The dough is very tender and must be handled gently. When you stretch the pieces, you do not want to de-gas them, but encourage large, irregular holes. The dough does not need to be covered in step 4, since it will not be held overnight. The proofing time depends greatly on the room temperature. On a warm day the dough should be ready in 1 hour; on a cooler day it may take 90 minutes or longer. If the room is very cool, below 65°F, it may take 2 hours or longer.

❏ The loaves will take on a light gold, not a dark brown crust. Since the bread is not scored it will have interesting cracks on the surface, which is part of the charm of *ciabatta.*

❏ Leaving the loaves in the warm, open oven not only finishes baking the interior of the loaves but allows the oven to remain hot for subsequent bakes. If this is the last bake of the day, you can leave the oven door closed and turn off the heat, letting the loaves remain in the oven for 15 minutes before removing them.

❏ You will need an electric mixer with a paddle attachment to make this bread

INGREDIENT	%
Unbleached bread flour	100
Instant yeast	N/A
Poolish	87
Water	66
Salt	2.5

MAKES THREE 1-POUND LOAVES

4 cups plus one tablespoon (18.25 ounces) unbleached bread flour

¹/₈ teaspoon instant yeast

2 cups (16 ounces) *poolish*-style pre-ferment (page 35)

1¹/₂ cups cool water (65° to 70°F)

2 teaspoons (0.5 ounce) salt

Vegetable oil cooking spray

=Approximate Weight: 46.5 ounces (2 pounds, 14.5 ounces)

1. In the bowl of a mixer with a paddle attachment, combine the flour, yeast, *poolish*, and water. Mix on slow speed till all the flour is incorporated, about 2 minutes. Add the salt and continue mixing for 4 minutes on slow, then 4 minutes on medium speed. The dough will be very soft and sticky. It should be 75° to 77°F.

2. Cover the bowl with plastic wrap and allow the dough to rise for 3 hours. Once every hour, "turn" (punch down) the dough by either mixing with the paddle for a few seconds or stirring it with a large spoon. The dough will swell a little prior to each "turn."

3. Line the backs of 3 inverted sheet pans with parchment, mist the parchment with cooking spray, and dust it with flour.

4. Turn the dough out onto a well-floured counter and toss it in the flour to coat. With floured hands, form the dough into a rectangle about 1 1/2 inches thick and cut it into 3 equal pieces. Transfer the dough to the prepared pans, gently stretching each piece lengthwise to about 12 inches. Allow the dough to rise, uncovered, for 1 to 1 1/2 hours at room temperature, or until doubled.

5. Prepare the oven for hearth baking as described on page 25, making sure to place the empty steam pan on a lower rack. Preheat the oven to 500°F. Pour 1 cup of hot water into the steam pan, slide the loaves, parchment and all, onto the baking stone, and then spritz the oven walls to create additional steam. Close the oven door. After 2 minutes, spritz the loaves again. If your oven cannot accommodate all three loaves, cut the parchment between the loaves and bake them one or two at a time. The additional rising time will not hurt the unbaked loaves. (You can also refrigerate and hold those loaves till the next day by misting them with cooking spray and enclosing them in a plastic bag.)

6. Bake the loaves for 10 minutes, then decrease the temperature to 470°F. After 15 to 17 minutes, the loaves should be just browning. Open the oven door and continue to bake the loaves an additional 10 to 15 minutes, till the bread is golden brown and the internal temperature is 205° to 210°F.

7. Remove the loaves to a cooling rack and allow them to cool for 1 hour before eating.

MASTER FORMULA:
TEAM USA CORN BREAD

Every team that entered the Coupe Du Monde was expected to make one bread that might be considered an indigenous or cultural representative of its country. Team USA decided to make a corn bread because of the strong association of corn with the American harvest and with the pioneer spirit of the early settlers. The team members also felt it honored the pioneers from all countries who settled in America, as well as the original native Americans. This adaptation of the Team USA formula challenges us to use many of the techniques discussed throughout the book. The formula uses two types of pre-ferment, a *poolish* and an old dough (*pâte fermentée*). It also uses two types of ground corn: a finely milled corn flour and a coarsely ground flour, such as polenta, slightly precooked to soften it. If you use the polenta, pre-cook it by pouring 1/4 cup boiling water over it. Allow to sit for 15 minutes before using. It was difficult to scale down and modify the formula for home use, but the results are wonderful.

COMMENTARIES

❏ Corn flour is even finer than cornmeal; look for it in natural food stores. If you can't find it, substitute finely ground cornmeal.

❏ Our *poolish* is not as thick as Craig's (equal parts water and flour and a pinch of yeast, fermented for fifteen hours), but I have adapted the formula to suit it.

❏ Craig has his corn specially ground so that it is even coarser, but polenta is easy to find and is the best available substitute. If you can obtain a coarser grind of corn, boil it in water for 3 or 4 minutes, drain, and cool before using.

❏ This bread has an unusual shape and aspect, quite unlike other breads. Proofing time varies according to room temperature, so be patient.

❏ This bread is not scored but instead has a rustic-looking exterior and a deep golden color.

INGREDIENT	%
Unbleached bread flour	25
Corn flour	75
Poolish	73
Ground corn	18
Salt	4.5
Instant yeast	1
Butter	4.5
Water	36.5
Old dough pre-ferment	145

MAKES 3 LOAVES

1 cup (8 ounces) *poolish*-style
 pre-ferment (page 35)

4 cups (16 ounces) old dough
 pre-ferment (*pâte fermentée,* page 38)

2/3 cup (3 ounces) unbleached
 bread flour

2 cups (8 ounces) corn flour

1/4 cup (2 ounces) coarsely ground
 corn or polenta

2 teaspoons (0.5 ounce) salt

1 teaspoon (0.11 ounce) instant yeast

1 tablespoon (0.5 ounce) butter, room
 temperature

1/2 cup cool water (65° to 70°F)

Vegetable oil cooking spray

---

*=Approximate Weight: 42 ounces
 (2 pounds, 10 ounces)*

1. Make both pre-ferments the day before and take them out of the refrigerator 1 hour before using.

2. In a mixing bowl or the bowl of an electric mixer with a dough hook, combine all the ingredients except the old-dough pre-ferment. If using a machine, mix on slow speed for 4 minutes, or till all the ingredients are incorporated. If making by hand, stir and then knead the ingredients till they reach this stage. Break the old dough pre-ferment into small pieces and add. Mix on medium speed (or knead) an additional 4 to 6 minutes, or till the dough passes the windowpane test (page 29), and the temperature is between 75° and 77°F. The dough will be soft and tacky.

3. Cover the bowl with plastic wrap and let the dough rise at room temperature for 1 hour. Knead it for a few seconds, re-form it into a ball, and re-cover it. Let it rise for an additional hour, or until it increases in size about 1½ times.

4. Lightly dust the counter with flour. Divide the dough into 3 equal pieces and lightly round each one and dust it with flour. Cover the dough with plastic wrap, and let it rest for 20 to 25 minutes.

5. Cover an inverted sheet pan with parchment and dust it with corn flour. Shape each of the dough pieces into a triangle about 4 inches long and 1 inch thick. Place the dough on the prepared pan, mist it with cooking spray, cover it with plastic wrap, and allow it to rise at room temperature for 90 minutes, or till nearly doubled in size.

6. Prepare the oven for hearth baking as described on page 25, making sure to place the empty steam pan on a lower rack. Preheat the oven to 475°F. Pour 1 cup of hot water into the steam pan, and immediately slide the loaves onto the baking stone. After 2 minutes, spritz again.

7. After 15 to 20 minutes, when the loaves have just begun to brown, turn off the oven and allow them to bake an additional 10 minutes, or till the crust is golden brown. The internal temperature should be about 195° to 200°F; be sure the bread is cooked thoroughly or it will become soggy.

8. Remove to a cooling rack and wait at least 40 minutes before slicing and eating.

MASTER FORMULA:
TEAM USA BEER BREAD

I have been skeptical of beer breads ever since I tried making an Irish stout bread with Guinness and discovered how much easier it is to simply make it with dark roasted malt and ferment it in the bowl. Beer is often called liquid bread, and we know that beer and bread were developed together at the foot of the pyramids in ancient Egypt, outgrowths of the same process (see page 65). I figured beer bread was a redundant term.

Craig Ponsford, on the other hand, has tasted many international beer breads and decided, with his coaches, to develop one of his own for the Coupe du Monde competition. This is a very creative formula, utilizing two pre-ferments as well as amber ale (a third pre-ferment, if you think about it). The dough includes roasted barley to accentuate the beer-flavored, bitter (hoppy) tones. Needless to say, this bread is great with sausage, ham, or cheese.

In adapting and scaling down Craig's formula for home use, I have had to change some of the proportions, but the results are comparable.

COMMENTARIES

❏ One of my colleagues at the California Culinary Academy, Chef Brian Mattingly, drilled into me the saying "*Mise en place* is your friend!" By this he means always have everything in place before starting; plan ahead. In the case of this bread, that means making pre-ferments well in advance and taking them out of the refrigerator 1 hour before you begin mixing your dough

❏ The main reason for using beer is to impart its distinctive qualities, one of which is the bitter taste of hops. Craig prefers amber ale for its hoppiness. If you do not like this flavor, use a milder beer, such as lager.

❏ If you are keeping a barm sponge refreshed and in the refrigerator, you can make the firm starter for this bread the day before. Other firm *levain* starters will also work.

❏ If you are keeping old dough in the freezer, you can, of course, use it as a starter, but remember to defrost it thoroughly.

❏ Malted barley is also called malt, malt powder or crystal, or malt syrup. It is made by soaking barley in water to begin sprouting, and then roasting the sweetened, sprouted grain. The best malt to use in this bread is dark-roasted powder or crystal, called *nondiastatic* malt (the diastase enzymes have been cooked in the roasting and will not affect fermentation). You can find it at a wine- or beer-making supply house. Or you can roast light malt powder in a 400°F oven for 10 to 20 minutes, till it darkens.

❏ Turning the dough, as in step 3, strengthens it and promotes fermentation. Make sure the dough shows signs of active fermentation before moving to the next step. On warm days it may ferment more quickly, in which case you can slow it down by refrigerating.

❏ You do not have to score and bake all the loaves at once, but can retard them for up to a day, baking off fresh loaves at another time.

INGREDIENT	%
Unbleached bread flour	66.6
Whole-wheat flour	20.9
Rye flour	12.5
Beer	50
Instant yeast	0.1
Salt	2
Firm starter	25
Pâte fermentée	66
Ground malted barley	8
Water	17

MAKES 4 LOAVES

3$^{1}/_{2}$ cups (16 ounces) unbleached bread flour

1$^{1}/_{8}$ cup (5 ounces) whole-wheat flour

$^{2}/_{3}$ cup (3 ounces) rye flour (coarse or fine)

1$^{1}/_{2}$ cups (12 ounces) beer, at room temperature

$^{1}/_{4}$ teaspoon (0.03 ounce) instant yeast

2 teaspoons (0.5 ounce) salt

1$^{1}/_{2}$ cups (6 ounces) firm starter (page 77)

4 cups (16 ounces) *pâte fermentée* (page 38)

$^{1}/_{4}$ cup (2 ounces) ground malted barley

$^{1}/_{2}$ cup cool water (65° to 70°F)

Vegetable oil cooking spray

=Approximate Weight: 66.5 ounces (4 pounds, 2.5 ounces)

1. Combine the flours, beer, yeast, salt, and firm starter (broken into small pieces) in the bowl of an electric mixer with a dough hook.

2. Mix on low speed until the dough forms into a smooth ball, about 4 minutes. Add the water as needed. Break the *pâte fermentée* into small pieces, add it to the dough, and mix on low speed just until it is incorporated. Increase the speed to medium for 1 minute, then add the malted barley and mix for another 3 minutes on medium. The barley should disperse and the dough feel soft and tacky. It should pass the windowpane test (page 29) and register 75° to 77°F on a probe thermometer. You may also knead this dough by hand by first combining all the ingredients in a bowl and then kneading on the counter until it reaches this stage.

3. Cover the bowl with plastic wrap and allow the dough to rise at room temperature for 1 hour. Knead it for a few seconds, re-form it into a ball, and return it to the bowl. Cover the bowl, and let the dough rise for an additional hour, until it nearly doubles in size.

4. Divide the dough into 4 equal pieces. Gently round them into balls and lightly dust them with flour. Leave them on the counter, covered with plastic wrap, to rest for 25 minutes.

5. Shape the dough as instructed on pages 20–21 (*bâtards* and *boules* are the preferred shapes, but other shapes will

work fine). Place the shaped dough into rising baskets or let them stand free-form on an inverted, parchment-lined sheet pan that has been sprinkled with cornmeal or semolina.

6. Lightly mist the loaves with cooking spray, cover them with plastic wrap, and allow the loaves to rise at room temperature for 1½ to 2 hours, or till nearly doubled in size.

7. Prepare the oven for hearth baking as described on page 25, making sure to place the steam pan on a lower rack. Preheat the oven to 475°F. Transfer the loaves to a floured peel and score them with any pattern you prefer.

8. Pour 1 cup of hot water into then steam pan and immediately transfer the loaves to the stone. Spritz the loaves and the oven walls. Close the oven door. After 2 minutes, spritz again. Bake the loaves for about 15 minutes, until they are just beginning to brown.

9. Lower the temperature to 450°F, and bake for 15 to 20 more minutes, until the loaves are a deep golden brown.

10. Turn the oven off and leave the loaves in for another 5 to 10 minutes, until the internal dough temperature is about 200°F, the bread sounds hollow when thwacked on the bottom, and the crust is very hard (it will soften as it cools).

11. Transfer to a cooling rack and cool for at least 1 hour before slicing and eating.

RESOURCES

The revolution of crust and crumb is close to being won, but we are now in an important, though less-dramatic phase than the ferment of the past few years. Franchises and multilocation operations, upgraded supermarket bakeries, improved training and apprentice programs, and the public's hunger for real bread are all signs of victory, but new bakeries are now replicating the breakthroughs already made by others. Home bakers and bread enthusiasts who have fueled this renaissance have high expectations that are actually being met on all fronts. New artisan-quality bakeries, whether independent or franchises, are appearing almost daily in cities and small communities throughout the country. At the same time, exciting new books, tools, and ingredients continue to become available to enhance our skills.

This section offers a small list of resources to help you achieve your baking goals. It is impossible to keep up with the constant growth in the bread world, so there may be unavoidable omissions, but there is enough here to get you started. With these leads, my hope is that the next wave in the bread revolution will find us well-armed and prepared to lead and inspire future generations. When it is the children who lead the charge, then we can say that the bread revolution has truly been won.

Happy baking!

HIGHLY RECOMMENDED BOOKS

The Book of Bread by Jerome Assire (New York: Abbeville [distributing for Flammarion], 1996)

Probably the most beautiful bread book ever published. Translated from the French edition, this is not a recipe book, but it is lush with pictures, profiles, and bread history that illustrate the central role of bread in all societies.

Bread: A Baker's Book of Techniques and Recipes by Jeffrey Hamelman (Hoboken, NJ: Wiley, 2004)

An excellent compilation of sound baking science, classic formulas that make beautiful breads, and the voice of an authentic American baking master.

Bread Alone by Daniel Leader and Judith Blahnik (New York: Morrow, 1993)

One of the best bread books, primarily because of Daniel's easy-to-follow, step-by-step instructions. The side stories recounting his quest for quality are very informative and inspirational.

Breads from the La Brea Bakery by Nancy Silverton (New York: Villard, 1996)

Nancy is the unchallenged queen of breads in Los Angeles and around the country. This book conveys her philosophy, commitment to details, and wonderful, complex recipes.

Special and Decorative Breads Volume I by Roland Bilheux, Alain Escoffier, Daniel Hervé, and Jean-Marie Pouradier (New York: Van Nostrand Reinhold, 1987)

Special and Decorative Breads Volume II by Alain Couet and Eric Kayser (New York: Van Nostrand Reinhold, 1987)

I can't decide which book I like better. Both cover similiar ground in slightly different ways, and both are spectacular, illustrating with great photography the full range of techniques for making every kind of European bread, as well as how to make bread sculptures and artistic showpieces. Every time these books get reprinted, the price goes up ($65 each, as of 1997), but whatever the price, these are must-haves.

The Village Baker by Joe Ortiz (Berkeley: Ten Speed Press, 1993)

This is the book that really explained traditional European methods to a new generation of bakers. Joe's passion, synthesis of information, and storytelling are wonderful.

OTHER RECOMMENDED BOOKS

Amy's Bread by Amy Scherber and Toy Kim Dupee (New York: Morrow, 1996)

Wonderful recipes and easy-to-follow techniques from one of New York City's most popular bakeries.

Artisan Baking Across America (2000) and *A Blessing of Bread* (2004) both by Maggie Glezer (New York: Artisan)

One of our best writers on bread has written two beautiful and useful books. The first tells the stories of some of the bakers who helped forge the American bread renaissance, and the more recent book is a personal exploration of traditional celebration breads, especially challah. Both books have wonderful recipes.

Baking with Julia by Dorie Greenspan
(New York: Morrow, 1996)

> The bread section is fabulous, as is the entire book. It includes recipes from bread luminaries like Steve Sullivan (Acme Bread Company, Berkeley, California), Joe Ortiz, Nancy Silverton, and others.

The Baker's Trade by Zachary Y. Schat
(Ukiah, CA.: Acton Circle, 1998)

> A new book by a successful bakery owner, with detailed instructions for how to open your own bakery.

The Best Bread Ever by Charles Van Over
(New York: Broadway Books, 1997)

> Charles Van Over has nailed down the correct technique for food processor mixing, and he has an intuitive sense of working with cool doughs and slow rise fermentations. While the title may be overly self-congratulatory, his breads are, for sure, pretty darned good.

Beth's Basic Bread Book by Beth Hensberger
(San Francisco: Chronicle Books, 1996)

> Beth seems to come out with a new bread book nearly every year, each more beautiful than the last. I also like her *Bread for All Seasons*.

The Book of Bread by Judith and Evan Jones
(New York: HarperCollins, 1986)

> An oldie but goodie, loaded with recipes, lovingly collected, of breads from around the world.

Boulangerie by Paul Rimbali (New York: Macmillan, 1995)

> An affectionate portrait of a society in love with their bread, Rambali profiles some of the best *boulangers* (bakers) of France. The recipes are sketchy and questionable, but the stories will fan your own bread passion.

Bread by Gail Duff (Oklahoma City, OK: Maxwell MacMillan International, 1993)

> A lovely recipe collection full of international bread recipes, folklore, and pictures.

The Bread Bible by Rose Levy Berenbaum
(New York: W. W. Norton, 2003)

> As in all of Rose's books, which are clearly labors of love, the recipes are very detailed and the book also has wonderful anecdotes.

Breads from Betsy's Kitchen by Betsy Oppenneer
(TBI Press, 1998)

> Betsy Oppenneer has long been one of America's favorite baking teachers. This is her latest book and includes some of the best recipes from previous volumes as well as great tips for substitutions and variety flavored breads.

Bread Machine Baking, Perfect Every Time, Vols. I and II by Lora Brody and Millie Apter
(New York: Morrow, 1993)

> Everything you need to know, and then some, for fully utilizing your bread machine.

The Breads of France by Bernard Clayton, Jr.
(Indianapolis: Bobbs-Merrill, 1978)

> Clayton is more famous for his *Complete Book of Breads,* but this one takes a focused look at some of the great bakers, as well the great breads throughout France. His instructions are also very good.

Brother Juniper's Bread Book: Slow Rise as Method and Metaphor by Peter Reinhart
(Reading, MA: Addison-Wesley, 1993)

> Well, I like it. The title says it all.

CookWise by Shirley O. Corriher (New York: William Morrow, 1997)

> Shirley is a nationally–known food chemist and beloved "answer lady" for many recipe writers and cooks. She spends over a hundred pages explaining the science of bread, illustrating her points with many wonderful recipes, including her famous "Touch-of-Grace Biscuits."

English Bread and Yeast Cookery by Elizabeth David (Newton Highlands, MA: Biscuit Books, 1994)

> An instant classic when it appeared, this book has been instrumental in the revival of quality bread and a wonderful history lesson to boot.

Flatbreads and Flavors by Jeffrey Alford and Naomi Duguid (New York: Morrow, 1995)

> A beautiful and informative book. The recipes are authentic yet simple, but the real gift is the glimpse into ancient and diverse cultures, as if viewing the world through a time capsule.

The Flavor of Bread by Raymond Calvel (New York: Chapman and Hall, 1997)

> This is the life's work of the great master teacher and baker, Raymond Calvel. More technical than most people want, but a must for the serious student. See The Bread Bakers Guild of America listing for the Calvel Video series that consolidates much of his knowledge.

Flavored Breads by Mark Miller and Andrew MacLauchlan (Berkeley: Ten Speed Press, 1996)

> Creative, neotraditional breads from the Coyote Cafe. Bold flavors, beautifully presented.

Great Breads by Martha Rose Shulman (Shelburne, VT: Chapters, 1995)

> Another great collection of international breads, with excellent introductions.

Guide de l'amateur de pain by Lionel Poilane (Paris: Robert Laffont Publishing, 1981)

> The great French master's book for home baking, including designs for his wood-burning oven. In French only.

The Italian Baker by Carol Field (New York: Harper & Row, 1985)

> All of Carol Field's books are a delight. This is the best collection of Italian breads and stories ever assembled for American readers.

The Laurel's Kitchen Bread Book by Laurel Robertson, Carol Flinders, and Bronwen Godfrew (New York: Random House, 1985)

> One of the best whole-grain bread books, full of gentle wisdom and excellent recipes.

Look and Cook: Classic Breads by Anne Willan (New York: DK Publishing, 1995)

> Anne Willan is one of the great cooking instructors in the world. This book, loaded with pictures, is especially helpful for novice bakers because of the step-by-step illustrated guide.

Rustic European Breads from Your Bread Machine by Linda West Eckhardt and Diana Collingwood Butts (New York: Doubleday, 1995)

> Amazingly good recipes, many of them traditional formulas adapted to bread-machine technology. The authors also wrote the award-winning *Bread in Half the Time,* but this one provides lots of background information on European breads, useful with or without the machines.

The Tassajara Bread Book by Ed Espe Brown (Boulder, CO: Shambhala, 1970)

> One of the seminal books of the first wave of the bread revolution. Reprinted many times, it is still a wonderful read, with many excellent recipes.

World Sourdoughs from Antiquity by Ed Wood (Berkeley: Ten Speed Press, 1996)

> This book has a few basic sourdough recipes, but its real charm is Ed's retelling of his trip to Egypt with *National Geographic* to reproduce breads identical to those made 4,000 years ago in the shadow of the pyramids. This is really about a passionate bread fanatic and his love affair with wild yeast.

Whole Grain Breads by Hand and Machine by Beatrice Ojakangas (New York: Macmillan, 1998)

> Beatrice has written many fine books on baking and regional specialties. This new work concentrates on helping the reader make one perfect loaf at a time.

CATALOGS, INGREDIENTS, STORES, AND RESOURCES

For inspiration—and something to drool over:

Alton-Spiller (Monica Spiller),
PO Box 696, Los Altos, CA 94023-0696, barmbaker@aol.com www.barmbaker.com

The foremost authority on barm, Monica Spiller has written her own self-published book that explains her method for making naturally leavened whole-grain breads and starters. She also sells a barm kit with dried lactobacillus culture to help you get started.

The Baker's Catalogue, King Arthur Flour,
PO Box 1010, Norwich, VT 05055, (800) 827-6836 www.kingarthurflour.com

If you are not already on their mailing list, call them as soon as possible. Not only do they have nearly every tool a home baker needs and some of the best flour in America, but every edition of the catalog is full of recipes and stories.

The Bread Bakers Guild of America,
3203 Maryland Ave., North Versailles, PA 15137, (412) 823-2080 www.bbga.org

Membership dues are reasonable and on a sliding scale. The newsletter alone is worth the membership, chock-full of ingredient information, technical reports, seminar and educational trips, and job opportunities. The guild is easily the best network for serious bread bakers. It is also the producer and source for the finest video series ever made on bread baking: *Bread & Baker: From the Source* with Professor Raymond Calvel (3 half-hour tapes, usually $250, but only $150 to guild members).

The Bread Bakers List,
www.bread-bakers.com

Reggie Dwork maintains a community bread conversation through e-mail. Anyone can join the conversation, where recipes are swapped and questions are thrown up for grabs. Just write to her to get on the list.

Chef's Catalog, 5070 Centennial Blvd., Colorado Springs, CO 80919, (800) 338-3232, www.chefscatalog.com

Good, all-purpose catalog. Keep an eye out for sales and specials.

The Gluten-Free Pantry, PO Box 840, Glastonbury, CT 06033, (800) 291-8386 www.glutenfree.com

Beth Hillson has developed a number of products for people who have gluten sensitivities. Get on her mailing list and she'll keep you informed as she develops new products that you can order through the mail.

Ovencrafters, 5600 Marshall-Petaluma Rd., Petaluma, CA 94952, (415) 663-9010 www.ovencrafters.net

Alan Scott's customized wood-fired brick ovens have become legendary. Contact him for either standard designs (from $100 up) or customized models. Ask about participating in an "oven raising," similiar to Amish barn raisings, to really get a sense of the mystique of the world of wood-fired ovens.

Sassafras Enterprises, 1622 West Carroll Ave., Chicago, IL 60612, (800) 537-4941 www.sassafrasenterprises.com

Makers of La Cloche, and other stoneware and baking tools.

Sourdoughs International, PO Box 670, Cascade, ID 83611, (208) 382-4828 www.sourdo.com

Ed Wood, the yeast master and author of *World Sourdoughs from Antiquity*, also cultivates and sells a number of sourdough cultures. He has strains from Russia, Egypt, San Francisco, Finland, Saudi Arabia, Bahrain, and Austria. Each one has particular characteristics, so choose accordingly.

Sur La Table, 5601 Sixth Ave. South, Seattle, WA 98108, (800) 243-0852 www.surlatable.com

> It began as a kitchenware shop and bookstore in Seattle, replicated itself in other cities, and then evolved into an excellent mail-order catalog of hard-to-find cooking products.

Williams-Sonoma catalog and stores, PO Box 7456, San Francisco, CA 94120, (800) 541-1262 www.williams-sonoma.com

> The mother of all kitchenware catalogs, this often has close-out bargains, sales, and unusual ingredients or mixes.

GRAIN

Most flour available in the United States and Canada is excellent. The large mills, like ConAgra, Archer Daniels Midland, and General Mills all produce high-quality flour, and it is available in most supermarkets. You can feel free to use it for the formulas in this book. However, a number of regional mills grind in small batches, with an emphasis on minimal starch damage to the grain (usually by milling with stones or hammer mills, as they grind cooler than the high-speed rollers used by large mills). The following companies offer many varieties of grain, some "organically grown," without pesticides or chemical fertilizers, some "commercially grown." Call, visit, or write each for details. Most will ship small quantities; some can supply both home bread makers as well as artisan bakeries.

Bob's Red Mill, 5209 SE International Way, Milwaukie, OR 97222, (800) 349-2173 www.bobsredmill.com

Food Distributors of America, 2701 Hereford St., St. Louis, MO 63110, (314) 781-1211

Certified Foods, Inc. (Joseph Vanderliet), 1055 Montague Ave., San Leandro, CA 94577, (510) 483-1177 www.certifiedfoods.com

Cook Natural Products, 2109 Frederick St., Oakland, CA 94606, (800) 537-7589

The Fowler's Milling Company, 12500 Fowlers Mill Rd., Chardon, OH 44024, (800) 321-2024 www.fowlersmilling.com

Giusto's Specialty Foods, 344 Littlefield Ave., South San Francisco, CA 94080, (650) 873-6566 www.giustos.com

Gray's Grist Mill, 638 Adamsville Rd., Westport, MA 02790 www.graysgristmill.com

Great Grains Milling Co., PO Box 427, Scobey, MT 59263, (406) 783-5588 www.greatgrainsmilling.com

Great Valley Mills, RD 3, County Line Road, Box 1111, Barto, PA 19504, (800) 688-6455 www.greatvalleymills.com

King Arthur Flour Company, PO Box 1010, Norwich, VT 05055-0876, (800) 827-6836 www.kingarthurflour.com

Morgan's Mills, 168 Payson Rd., Union, ME 04862, (207) 785-4663

Rocky Mountain Flour Milling, 400 Platte St., Platteville, CO 80651, (888) 785-7636

War Eagle Mill, 11045 War Eagle Rd., Rogers, AR 72756, (501) 789-5343 www.wareaglemill.com

Weisenberger Flour Mills, Box 215, Midway, KY 40347, (859) 254-5282 www.weisenberger.com

White Lily Flour, PO Box 871, Knoxville, TN 37901, (800) 264-5459 www.whitelily.com

SCHOOLS AND TRAINING PROGRAMS

New programs appear regularly. For an updated list and descriptions,
contact the Bread Baker's Guild of America

American Institute of Baking,
1213 Bakers Way, Manhattan, KS 66502,
(800) 633-5137 www.aibonline.org

A tremendous technical resource for
professional bakers. Programs are offered in
Manhattan, Kansas, throughout the year
and road-show programs circulate throughout
the country.

California Culinary Academy (CCA),
625 Polk St., San Francisco, CA 94102,
(800) 229-2433 www.ccahospitality.com

In addition to the longer eighteen-month chef
program, the CCA offers an excellent thirty-week
baking and pastry program, which includes a
five-week bread intensive course developed,
and currently taught by, well, me. The CCA is
now part of the Cordon Bleu Culinary School
system, with many campuses located across
the United States.

Culinary Institute of America (CIA),
Hyde Park Campus: 1946 Campus Dr.,
Hyde Park, NY 12538, (845) 452-9430

Greystone Campus: 2555 Main St.,
St. Helena, CA 94574, (707) 967-1100

The Hyde Park campus is world famous and
has both a chef and baking/pastry program.
The Greystone campus in St. Helena offers a
variety of customized baking options, intensive
courses, and bread programs. A first-rate
faculty and facility.

The French Culinary Institute,
462 Broadway, New York, NY 10013-2618,
(212) 219-8890 www.frenchculinary.com

Offers a six-week artisan bread intensive course
called "The Art of International Bread Making,"
designed by Daniel Leader. The course can also
be taken in three two-week installments.

Johnson and Wales University, campuses
in Denver, Miami, Charlotte, NC, and at
8 Abbott Park Place, Providence, RI 02903,
(800) 342-5598, www.jwu.edu

All campuses offer associate degrees in baking
and pastry, and the Providence campus also
offers a bachelors degree in baking and pastry
arts. Johnson and Wales is the largest culinary
school in the world, and its faculty have won
numerous awards in worldwide competitions.

**Kansas State University, Dept. of Grain
Science and Industry,** 201 Shellenberger
Hall, Manhattan, KS 66506, (800) 355-5531

Acclaimed programs for undergraduate and
graduate-level studies in cereal chemistry and
baking science.

**King Arthur Flour Baking Education
Center,** 135 Route 5 South, Norwich, VT
05055, (802) 649-3361
www.kingarthurflour.com

Under the direction of baker extraordinaire
Jeffrey Hamelman, the educational programs
at King Arthur are top-notch. The program is
always changing so call or log on for details.

Institute of Culinary Education (ICE),
50 West 23rd St., New York, NY 10010,
(212) 847-0700 www.iceculinary.com

Under the direction of master baker Nick Malgieri, the baking program is excellent for both
general and specialty courses.

The San Francisco Baking Institute (SFBI),
480 Grandview Dr., South San Francisco, CA
94080, (650) 589-5784 www.sfbi.com

An outgrowth of Michel Suas's bakery equipment
business, the institute offers excellent theme programs throughout the year taught by Michel's
head baker, Lionel Vatinet, and guest instructors.

BAKERIES AND FRANCHISES

It is virtually impossible to keep up with them, but great bakeries continue to emerge almost daily. Rather than attempt to give a comprehensive list, which would soon be out of date and bound to offend someone who was left off, let me list a few seminal bakeries. This does not mean that there aren't many others of similiar caliber, each specializing in products of uncommon quality, but that there are just too many to list them all. These few represent aspects of bread quality discussed throughout this book and would be worth a visit if you happen to be in the neighborhood. Some of those listed make their products available through outlets or markets as well as their own stores. Some do not have stores of their own but have made such an impact on local culture that I feel obliged to include them in this list. Enjoy!

Acme Bread Company, 1601 San Pablo Ave., Berkeley, CA 94702, (510) 524-1021

Alvarado Street Bakery, 500 Martin Ave., Rohnert Park, CA 94928, (707) 585-3293 www.alvaradostreetbakery.com

Amy's Bread, 672 Ninth Ave., New York, NY 10036, (212) 977-2670 www.amysbread.com

Artisan Bakers, 750 West Napa St., Sonoma, CA 95476, (707) 939-1765 www.artisanbakers.com

Bay Bread, 241 East Harris Ave., South San Francisco, CA 94080, (650) 866-4262

Big Wood Breads, 270 Northwood Way #102, Ketchum, ID 83340, (208) 726-2034

Borealis Breads, 1860 Atlantic Hwy., Waldoboro, ME 04572, (207) 832-0655

Bouley Bakery, 130 W. Broadway, New York, NY 10013, (212) 608-5829

Bracken Mountain Bakery, 34 South Broad St., Brevard, NC 28712, (828) 883-4034

Bread Alone, Route 28, Boiceville, NY 12412, (800) 769-3328, (845) 657-3328 www.breadalone.com

Bread and Cie, 350 University Ave., San Diego, CA 92103, (619) 683-9322

BreadCrafters, 12635 North Tatum Blvd., Phoenix, AZ 85020, (602) 494-4442

The Bread Line, 1751 Pennsylvania Ave., Washington, D.C. 20006, (202) 822-8900

Breadsmith (franchise, multiple locations), office: 409 East Silver Spring Dr., White Fish Bay, WI 53217, (414) 962-1965 www.breadsmith.com

The Breadworks, 2110 Brighton Rd., Pittsburgh, PA 15212, (412) 231-7555

Bruno Bakery, 602 Lorimer St., Brooklyn, NY 11211, (718) 349-6524

The Clear Flour Bakery, 178 Thorndike St., Brookline, MA 02146, (617) 739-0060

Companion Baking Company, 4555 Gustine Ave., St. Louis, MO 63116, (314) 352-4770

The Corner Bakery (multiple locations), headquarters: 5920 Pasture Ct., Carlsbad, CA 92008, (760) 444-9800

Daily Bread Bakery, 188 Broadway or 198 Wayland, Providence, RI 02903, (401) 331-4200 or (401) 331-1800

Delphina's Neighborhood Baking Co.,
4200 NE Wygant St., Portland, OR 97218,
(503) 221-1829

Ecce Panis, 3rd Ave. at 65th or Madison Ave.
at 90th, New York, NY 10021,
(212) 535-2099 or (212) 348-0040

Eli's Bread, 1064 Madison Ave., New York,
NY 10028, (212) 772-2011 (store) and
403 E. 91st St., New York, NY 10128,
(212) 831-4800 (bakery)

The Firehook Bakery (various locations in
the Washington, D.C. area), main bakery:
14701 Flint Lee Rd., Chantilly, VA 20151
(703) 263-2253

Gayle's Bakery and Rosticceria,
504 Bay Ave., Capitola, CA 95010,
(408) 476-7016

Grace Baking, 3200 G Regatta Blvd., Rich-
mond, CA 94804 (510) 231-7210

Grand Central Bakery, 214 First Ave. South,
Seattle, WA 98134, (206) 622-3644

Great Harvest Bread Company (multiple
locations), headquarters: 28 S. Montana St.,
Dillon, MT 59725-2434, (800) 442-0424

Hi-Rise Bread Company, 208 Concord Ave.,
Cambridge, MA 02138, (617) 876-8766

Iggy's Breads, 130 Fawcett St., Cambridge,
MA 02138, (617) 924-0949

Il Fornaio (multiple locations), headquarters:
770 Tamalpais Dr., Ste. 400, Corte Madera,
CA 94925, (800) 291-1505

King Arthur Flour, The Baker's Store, 135
Route 5 South, Norwich, VT 05055, (802)
649-3361

Kirchhoff's Bakery, 118 Market House Sq.,
Paducah, KY 42001, (270) 442-7117

La Brea Bakery, 15963 Strathern St., Van
Nuys, CA 91406, (818) 742-4242

Le Bus (various locations), main bakery:
220 Krams Ave., Manayunk, PA 19127,
(215) 930-0255

Le Quotidian Pain Bakery Cafe,
1131 Madison Ave., New York, NY 10028,
(212) 327-4900

Macrina Bakery, 2408 First Ave., Seattle,
WA 98121, (206) 448-4032

Metropolitan Bakery (multiple locations),
headquarters: 2625 19th St., Philadelphia,
PA 19103, (215) 545-6655

The Model Bakery, 1357 Main St.,
St. Helena, CA 94574, (707) 963-8192

Noe Valley Bakery and Bread Company,
4073 24th St., San Francisco, CA 94114,
(415) 550-1405 www.noevalleybakery.com

Olga's Cup and Saucer, 103 Point St., Providence, RI 02903, (401) 831-6666

Panera Bread Company (multiple
locations), headquarters: 6170 Clayton Rd.,
St. Louis, MO 63117, (314) 633-7100

Pan-O-Rama, 1209 N. McDowell Blvd.,
Petaluma, CA 94954, (800) 808-7077
www.panoramabaking.com

The Pearl Bakery, 102 NW 9th Ave.,
Portland, OR 97209, (503) 827-0910
www.pearlbakery.com

Semifreddi's (multiple locations),
headquarters: 4242 Hollis St., Emeryville,
CA 94608, (510) 596-9930

Seven Stars Bakery, 820 Hope St.,
Providence, RI 02906, (401) 521-2200

Sweetish Hill Bakery, 1120 West Sixth,
Austin, TX 78703, (512) 472-1347
www.sweetishhill.com

Tom Cat Bakery, 43-05 Tenth St., Long Island City, NY 11101, (718) 786-4224

Vermont Bread Company, 80 Cotton Mill Hill, Brattleboro, VT 05301, (802) 254-4600

The Village Bakehouse, 7882 North Oracle Rd., Tucson, AZ 85704, (520) 531-0977 www.villagebakehouse.com

The Village Bakery, 7225 Healdsburg Ave., Sebastopol, CA 95472, (707) 829-8101

Weaver Street Market, 101 East Weaver St., Carrboro, NC 27510, (919) 929-0010

WheatFields Bakery Cafe, 904 Vermont St., Lawrence, KS 66044, (785) 841-5553 www.wheatfieldsbakery.com

Whole Foods Bakehouse, 4201 South Congress Ave., #108, Austin, TX 78745, (512) 442-2171

Zingerman's Bakehouse, 3711 Plaza Dr., Ann Arbor, MI 48108, (734) 761-2095 www.zingermansbakehouse.com

More Baking Books from Ten Speed Press

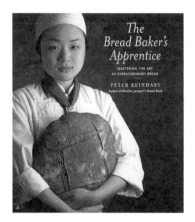

The Bread Baker's Apprentice
Mastering the Art of Extraordinary Bread
by Peter Reinhart
9 x 10 inches, 320 pages, full color
ISBN-13: 978-1-58008-268-6
ISBN-10: 1-58008-268-8
2002 James Beard Cookbook of the Year
2002 IACP Cookbook of the Year

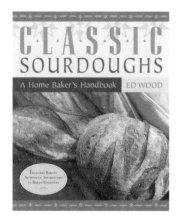

Classic Sourdoughs
A Home Baker's Handbook
by Ed Wood
7³⁄₈ x 9¹⁄₈ inches, 224 pages, two color
ISBN-13: 978-1-58008-344-7
ISBN-10: 1-58008-344-7

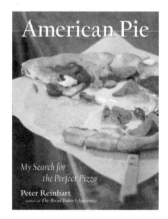

American Pie
My Search for the Perfect Pizza
by Peter Reinhart
7 x 9 inches, 272 pages, two color
ISBN-13: 978-1-58008-422-2
ISBN-10: 1-58008-422-2

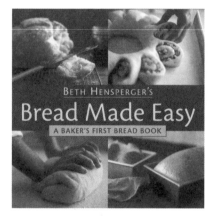

Beth Hensperger's Bread Made Easy
A Baker's First Bread Book
by Beth Hensperger
9 x 9 inches, 128 pages, full color
ISBN-13: 978-1-58008-112-2
ISBN-10: 1-58008-112-6

Available from your local bookstore, or order direct from the publisher:
www.tenspeed.com • order@tenspeed.com • (800) 841-2665